Ultimate
TRAIN

Ultimate
TRAIN

PETER HERRING

A Dorling Kindersley Book

Dorling Kindersley

LONDON, NEW YORK, AUCKLAND, DELHI,
JOHANNESBURG, MUNICH, PARIS, AND SYDNEY

DK www.dk.com

Project Art Editor Philip Ormerod
Project Editor Peter Adams
Designer Amir Reuveni
Editor Nichola Thomasson
DTP Designer Jason Little
US Editors Jill Hamilton, Alrica Goldstein
US Consultant Joseph J. Cunningham

Senior Managing Art Editor Bryn Walls
Senior Managing Editor Jonathan Metcalf
Production Silvia La Greca
Picture Research Sean Hunter

First published in 2000 by Dorling Kindersley Publishing, Inc.
95 Madison Avenue, New York, New York 10016

2 4 6 8 10 9 7 5 3 1

Library of Congress catalog card number 99-055256

ISBN 0-7894-4610-3

Color reproduction by GRB Editrice, Verona, Italy
Printed and bound in Hong Kong

CONTENTS

PART THREE

RAILROAD INNOVATORS 142–161

PART ONE

THE HISTORY OF TRAINS

Until locomotives were invented, the top speed a person could travel on land was restricted to the pace of the fastest horse. First employed in Britain at the start of the nineteenth century, steam trains transformed the world, enabling materials and people to be transported *en masse* at unprecedented speeds. This freedom of movement not only boosted commerce, it also hastened the settlement of continents, allowed cities to expand rapidly, and extended people's leisure options. This chapter explores the impact trains have had over the last 200 years and reveals the developments that have let them keep pace in a changing world.

The HISTORY of TRAINS

The first steam-powered engines to run on rails were built for industrial use at the start of the nineteenth century. Within 50 years, a global railroad network that facilitated a worldwide growth in trade and revolutionized social mobility had developed. The subsequent development of diesel and electric traction has maintained a vital transportation role for trains right up to the present day.

The Babylonians used stone tracks to control the movement of wheeled vehicles as long ago as 2,200 BC. In due course the Greeks, and then the Romans, developed their own stone wagonways. In medieval times, wooden tracks along which trucks were pulled either by horses or by miners were laid in mines in northern England and Central Europe. Around 1790, iron started to be used in place of wood, first in the manufacture of wheels and then in the construction of the track. Within a decade, plans were put forward to build a railroad on which horses would pull freight wagons between London and Portsmouth on the south coast of England. However, until steam-powered locomotives were developed, canals were the principal transport arteries for the movement of freight and bulky raw materials, such as coal.

RAISING STEAM

The first significant use of steam power was not for locomotion at all, but to drive static engines that pumped water out of flooded mineshafts. These pump engines were developed in the early eighteenth century by French engineer Denis Papin and by two English inventors, Thomas Savery and Thomas Newcomen. Newcomen's design was the most successful, but it used large amounts of fuel. During the 1760s, the fuel efficiency of the Newcomen engine was greatly improved through modifications made by Scottish engineer James Watt. Watt went on to demonstrate how, by fitting a system of gears, the up-and-down movement of a steam engine could be transformed into a rotary movement that was able to turn the wheels of a vehicle. However, Watt left it to others to develop a mobile steam engine.

In 1770, Nicholas-Joseph Cugnot, an artillery officer in the French army, built a steam-powered wagon that was designed to haul field guns. He demonstrated the

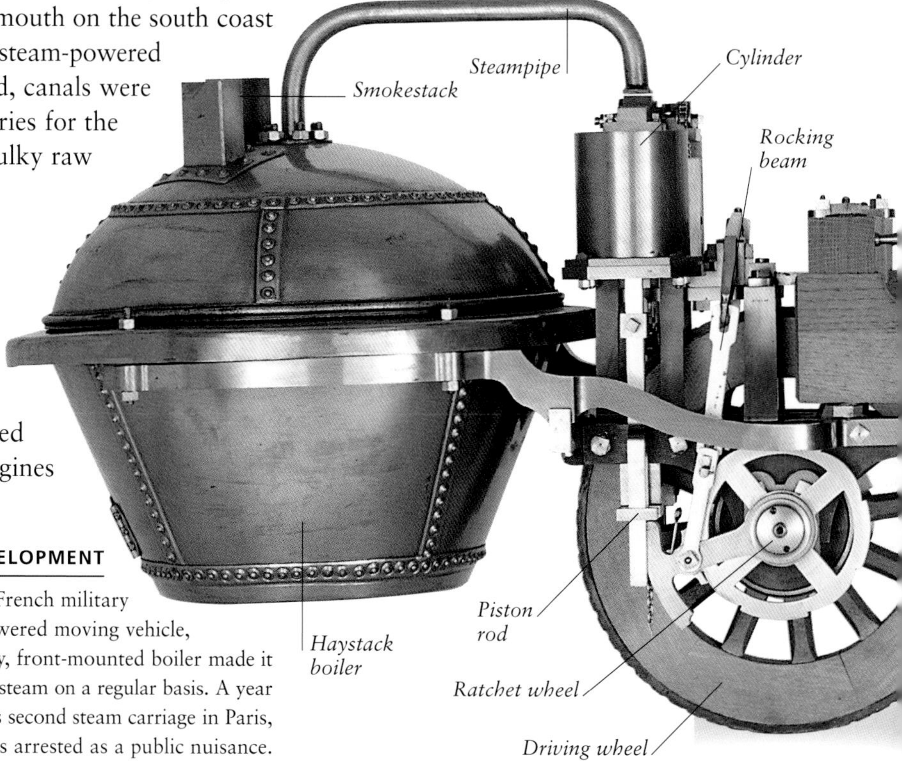

WATT'S STATIC ENGINE

Built in 1769 by Scottish engineer James Watt, this beam engine was used to drive pumps that drew water from flooded mineshafts. It was the first engine to have a separate condenser, an invention that greatly enhanced the efficiency and power of steam engines.

ARRESTED DEVELOPMENT

In 1769, Nicholas Cugnot, a French military engineer, built the first steam-powered moving vehicle, which is pictured here. The heavy, front-mounted boiler made it difficult to steer, and it ran out of steam on a regular basis. A year later, while Cugnot was driving his second steam carriage in Paris, it overturned and he was arrested as a public nuisance.

Smokestack
Steampipe
Cylinder
Rocking beam
Piston rod
Haystack boiler
Ratchet wheel
Driving wheel

device in Paris by using it as a passenger-carrying engine, but it ran short of steam too often to be of practical use. In the latter half of the eighteenth century, an assortment of steam-driven coaches appeared on the roads of France and Britain, but all of them were hampered by insufficient power because they used steam at low pressure. Despite the limitations of these vehicles, they did demonstrate the potential of steam power.

THE FIRST STEAM LOCOMOTIVES

For sustained power, a boiler capable of producing high-pressure steam and of withstanding that pressure was necessary. The challenge of building such a boiler was met by Cornish inventor Richard Trevithick. On Christmas Eve 1801, Trevithick drove his first high-pressure, steam-powered carriage around Camborne, in Cornwall, England. In 1803, Trevithick began building a steam locomotive that was designed to run on rails for the Coalbrookdale iron foundry in Shropshire, England. It is uncertain if this machine ever ran.

Trevithick's next locomotive did run, however. In 1804, at the Penydarran Ironworks near Merthyr Tydfil in South Wales, a steam-powered locomotive hauled a train of wagons on rails for the first time. Although the journey was not completely successful, because the weight of the train broke the rails, this experiment did not go unnoticed. Several engineers working for mining companies in the north of England, including George Stephenson,

COALS TO NEWCASTLE

Wooden wagons, called chaldrons, were used by collieries in England to carry coal. Originally, they were drawn by horses to the River Tyne, where the coal was discharged into the holds of barges bound for Newcastle.

were quick to see the significance of Trevithick's achievement and set out to produce reliable steam locomotives based upon his concepts. The colliery managers, however, were only persuaded to replace horses with these untried and unpredictable machines because of the impact of the Napoleonic Wars, waged between 1800 and 1815, which caused the price of horse fodder to rise to unprecedented levels.

While colliery managers saw an advantage in converting to steam power, since they owned the fuel that powered these engines, steam locomotion was not adopted outside these private industries. The first public railroad, the Surrey Iron Railway, which opened in the southeast of England in 1803, used horse-drawn wagons on its line. The role of this railroad, and the other horse-drawn lines that opened before 1820, was freight transport. Passenger conveyance was an afterthought. Even by 1824, the advantage of steam traction over horse power was still hotly disputed.

This argument was resolved in 1825, with the opening of the Stockton & Darlington Railway. An association of the Society of Friends (Quakers) in County Durham contracted George Stephenson, a local engineer with prior

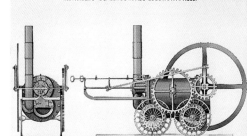

TREVITHICK'S COALBROOKDALE LOCOMOTIVE (1803)

TREVITHICK EXPERIMENTS

The above illustrations show what the world's first railroad locomotive looked like from the front and the side. It was built in 1803 by Cornish pioneer Richard Trevithick, at Coalbrookdale in England. It had flangeless wheels, and a single horizontal cylinder mounted inside the boiler. There is no evidence that it was ever operated.

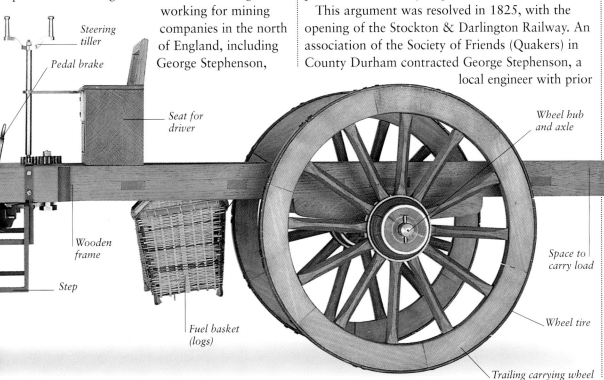

Steering tiller

Pedal brake

Seat for driver

Wooden frame

Step

Fuel basket (logs)

Wheel hub and axle

Space to carry load

Wheel tire

Trailing carrying wheel

experience on colliery railroads, to construct the line. Stephenson, who had built his first locomotive in 1814, persuaded them to utilize steam power on this 25-mile (40-km) route. When it opened on September 25, 1825, Stephenson drove one of his own engines, *Locomotion No.1*, at the head of a train of six

COUPLED MOTION

In 1825, *Locomotion No.1* pulled 28 coal-filled wagons at the head of the first train to operate on the Stockton & Darlington Railway. Designed by George Stephenson, this locomotive was both the first steam engine to operate on a public railroad and the first locomotive to have its wheels linked by coupling rods, which enabled them to turn together.

loaded wagons that are reported to have contained 450 passengers, at speeds of up to 8 mph (13 kph). Such was the interest generated by *Locomotion*'s inaugural journey on the world's first public steam railroad that within nine months plans were being drawn up to build the first "intercity" railroad between Manchester and Liverpool.

THE FIRST "INTERCITY" RAILROAD

The main motive for building the Manchester to Liverpool railroad was that cotton mill owners in Manchester and neighboring towns were being charged extortionate rates to ship goods to the seaport of Liverpool by barge owners on the Bridgwater Canal. George Stephenson was again chosen to

survey and build the 64-km (40-mile) long line. He was not, however, given the automatic right to supply the locomotives, which may have been because his earlier engine, *Locomotion No.1*, ceased to haul passenger trains shortly after its inaugural journey on the Stockton & Darlington. It had failed to prove itself powerful enough for the job and, as a result, the passenger service on this line reverted to horse-drawn coaches until 1828. Trials to identify the right type of steam locomotive for use on the Liverpool & Manchester were held on a test track at Rainhill, near Liverpool, in October 1829. At the trials, five locomotives competed against each other for a winner's prize of £500. Of the five entries, *Rocket*, a locomotive built by George Stephenson and his son Robert, was the victor. In addition to collecting the prize money, the Stephensons also won an order to supply eight further locomotives, and *Rocket* was selected to head the first train to operate on the Liverpool & Manchester when the line opened on September 15, 1830.

Rocket was a much more advanced locomotive than *Locomotion No.1*. The improvements in its design are largely attributable to the engineering prowess of Robert Stephenson who, in developing *Rocket*, created a blueprint for the fundamental working principles of a steam locomotive, which have remained unaltered to the present day. *Rocket* and the other engines supplied by the Stephensons proved capable of moving people as well as goods at speeds that had previously been unimaginable. In the first ten years of operations, five million people traveled on the Liverpool & Manchester.

RAILROAD MANIA

The first public steam-hauled train to operate in southern England made its debut on the Canterbury and Whitstable Railway in Kent, on May 3, 1830. Soon every town in Britain wanted access to a railroad. The money to finance the construction of these lines was provided by a multitude of eager investors, who saw the railroads as offering a golden opportunity to make a quick profit. As a result, 1830 marked the start of a 20-year period of frantic line building in Britain, which was dubbed "Railroad Mania." By 1842, over 2,080 km (1,300 miles) of track had been laid in Britain. London was connected with all the major industrial cities in the Midlands and the north-west of England. It was also linked to Southampton, on the south coast, and to the west coast port of Bristol. From 1840 to 1850, a total of 7,200 km (4,500 miles) of track were added to Britain's railroad network, including the completion of the east coast and west coast mainlines that still run between London and Scotland.

A FLAWED SYSTEM

By 1870, Britain had laid 13,500 miles (21,600 km) of track. The expansion of the rail network was largely uncontrolled, however, since there had been no agreed strategy for its development at government level. Instead, entrepreneurs such as George Hudson tried to integrate scores of private railroads into a

BRITAIN'S RAILROAD KING

Born in Yorkshire in 1800, George Hudson financed the construction of many of Britain's railroads. During the "Railroad Mania" of the 1830s and 1840s, he tried to establish a national strategy for railroad building, but his financial misdeeds led to his downfall.

national network in a bid to avoid duplication of service on long-distance routes. These plans failed as competing lines continued to be be built and investors soon began to suffer the financial consequences. The long-term effect of Britain's failure to regulate its railroad network continued to be felt in the twentieth century, as even the largest railroad companies struggled for profitability. Despite this, very few line closures occurred until all of Britain's main-line railroads were nationalized in 1948.

PARALLEL LINES

In tandem with the expansion of Britain's railroads came improved locomotive designs. The vertical cylinders used on early engines, which often broke the rails, were replaced by nearly horizontal ones. After 1825, the chains that linked the axles were replaced by sturdy coupling rods. In 1827, the first six-wheeled locomotive was developed by Timothy Hackworth. Its extended wheelbase allowed the use of a larger boiler and offered greater adhesion. Extended fireboxes were built that burned coal rather than coke, which generated more heat and produced more steam.

INTERCITY EXPRESS

Rocket became the world's first intercity express in September 1830 when it headed the first train to run between Liverpool and Manchester. The full-sized replica of this train, pictured below, displays the original yellow livery of this service.

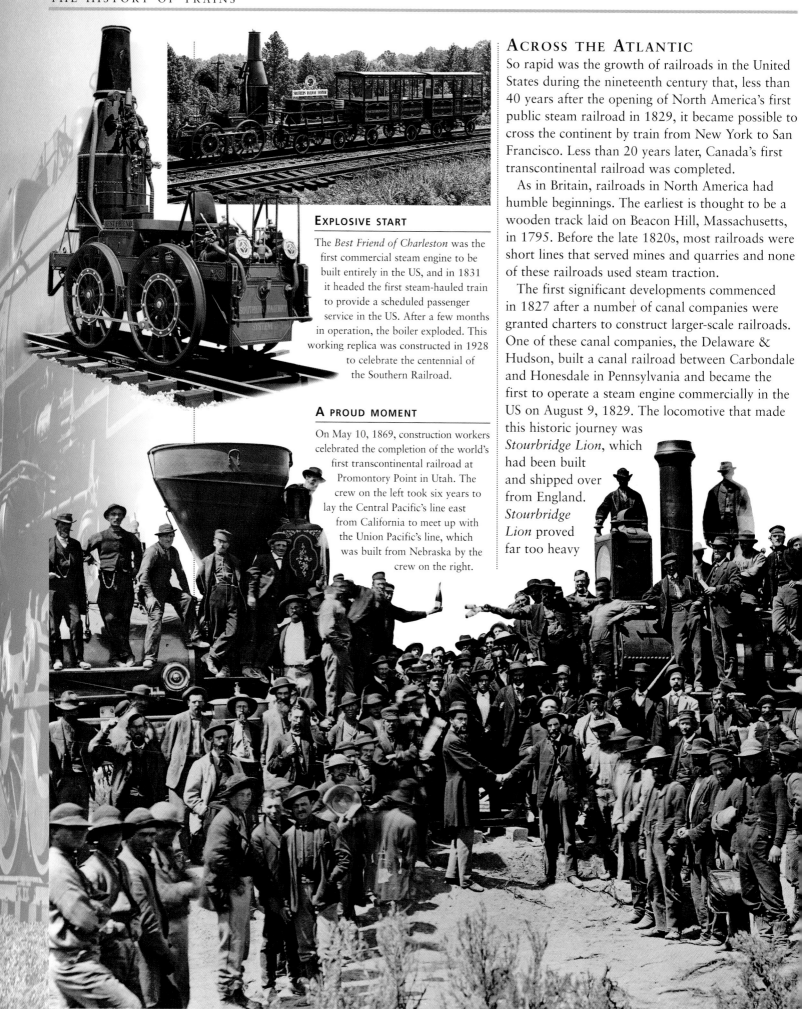

EXPLOSIVE START

The *Best Friend of Charleston* was the first commercial steam engine to be built entirely in the US, and in 1831 it headed the first steam-hauled train to provide a scheduled passenger service in the US. After a few months in operation, the boiler exploded. This working replica was constructed in 1928 to celebrate the centennial of the Southern Railroad.

A PROUD MOMENT

On May 10, 1869, construction workers celebrated the completion of the world's first transcontinental railroad at Promontory Point in Utah. The crew on the left took six years to lay the Central Pacific's line east from California to meet up with the Union Pacific's line, which was built from Nebraska by the crew on the right.

ACROSS THE ATLANTIC

So rapid was the growth of railroads in the United States during the nineteenth century that, less than 40 years after the opening of North America's first public steam railroad in 1829, it became possible to cross the continent by train from New York to San Francisco. Less than 20 years later, Canada's first transcontinental railroad was completed.

As in Britain, railroads in North America had humble beginnings. The earliest is thought to be a wooden track laid on Beacon Hill, Massachusetts, in 1795. Before the late 1820s, most railroads were short lines that served mines and quarries and none of these railroads used steam traction.

The first significant developments commenced in 1827 after a number of canal companies were granted charters to construct larger-scale railroads. One of these canal companies, the Delaware & Hudson, built a canal railroad between Carbondale and Honesdale in Pennsylvania and became the first to operate a steam engine commercially in the US on August 9, 1829. The locomotive that made this historic journey was *Stourbridge Lion*, which had been built and shipped over from England. *Stourbridge Lion* proved far too heavy for the track, and was taken out of service almost immediately. The frequent derailments of engines imported from Britain led engineers in the US, such as Matthias Baldwin, Thomas Rogers, and William Norris, to design and build locomotives that were tailored to US railroad conditions.

NORTH AMERICAN ENTERPRISE

The first scheduled steam-hauled service to run on a North American railroad was inaugurated by the South Carolina company on January 15, 1831, when the first full-sized locomotive to be built in the US, *Best Friend of Charleston*, ran a combined passenger and freight service out of Charleston. By 1833, the railroad it ran on had been extended to Hamburg, 136 miles (218 km) in distance, making it the longest railroad in the world at that time.

Railroad building in the US was rapid during the 1830s, but all of it was concentrated in the states east of the Mississippi and Missouri rivers, where the majority of the US's 13 million residents lived. By 1840, 2,800 miles (4,480 km) of track had been laid. By 1860, the railroad network had extended westward beyond Chicago, in Illinois, and the total length of railroad had multiplied more than tenfold to 30,635 miles (49,016 km). Railroad building in Canada followed the same pattern, beginning on the eastern seaboard and then expanding westward. The first public railroad in Canada, the Champlain & St. Lawrence, opened between La Prairie in

POSTER FOR THE NEW
TRANSCONTINENTAL LINE

Quebec, and Saint John in New Brunswick, on July 24, 1836. Twenty years later, in 1856, through services began running on the Grand Trunk Railway between Montreal and Toronto.

CROSSING THE CONTINENT

The outbreak of the Civil War in 1861 brought mixed fortunes for the railroads. Some prospered from the increased wartime traffic, but in the Confederate states many lines were blown up. The war was the principal motive for President Abraham Lincoln signing an enabling act in 1862, which authorized the creation of a transcontinental railroad, because he was desperate to cement the Union's ties with California and the other western states and territories. In this act, the Union Pacific railroad was empowered to build to the western boundary of the Nevada territory, while the Central Pacific railroad was appointed to build eastward from California. The demands of the Civil War delayed the laying of any track until July 1865, but rapid progress was made from then on. On May 10, 1869, at a ceremony held at Promontory Point, Utah, the Union Pacific and Central Pacific railroads were joined together and the world's first transcontinental railroad was complete, at a cost of $115,214,587 (and 70 cents). Railroad construction continued after the Civil War, reaching a peak in the 1880s when 112,000 km (70,000 miles) of track were laid within the US.

The arrival of steam traction in North America had a profound impact on the development of the continent, which would not have been settled nearly as quickly without it. Entire communities grew up

LEGENDARY LOCOMOTIVE

Of the 25,000 4-4-0s built for US railroads, none was more famous than *General*. During the Civil War of 1861–65, this engine was hijacked by Union soldiers who planned to use it to help them blow up a bridge. Confederate troops on board another 4-4-0 pursued them and eventually, after an eight-hour, 139-km (87-mile) chase, caught up with *General* and recaptured it.

along railroads. Trains also became the US's first "big business," making fortunes for "railroad barons" such as the Vanderbilts, who financed the construction of lines in exchange for control of them. The assembling of US-designed steam engines also provided the US with a manufacturing industry that, within a decade of its inception, was able to produce locomotives that could compete with those of Britain and the other industrialized nations of Europe. The most famous was the 4-4-0, which was so popular in North America that it came to be known as "The American."

EUROPE TAKES THE TRAIN

As in North America, no steam locomotives ran in continental Europe until 1829. The first engine to run there was an experimental locomotive built by Marc Séguin, a French engineer, which was tested on November 7, 1829, on a line built for horse-drawn freight carts between St. Etienne and Andrézieux. The locomotive utilized a multitubular boiler, an invention patented by Séguin two years earlier. By 1840, Germany, Belgium, the Netherlands, Russia, the Austro-Hungarian Empire, and Italy had all joined France in developing the foundations of a railroad network. Unlike in Britain and the US, however, the pace of development on the European mainland during the 1830s was fairly orderly. In France, for instance, only 350 miles (550 km) of track had been laid for the use of steam traction by 1838. Germany's first steam-operated railroad was the Ludwigsbahn, built between Nuremberg

AMERICAN INFLUENCED

Built in Germany in 1847, *Limatt* was one of a quartet of locomotives to launch the first train service in Switzerland on the Schweizerische Nordbahn. Although the Swiss engineer Nikolaus Riggenbach took the credit for its design, *Limatt* is in fact a modified version of the 4-2-0s then being exported to Europe by US engine-builder William Norris.

ITALY WELCOMES THE TRAIN

This painting captures the excitement of the large crowd that gathered on October 3, 1839, to witness the passage of the first train to operate in Italy. It ran from Naples to Portici, and was headed by *Bayard*, a British-built 2-2-2.

and Fürth. The locomotive that hauled the first train to run on this line, which opened in 1835, was a standard 2-2-2 named *Der Adler* (The Eagle), supplied by Robert Stephenson & Co. of England. Four years later, the first long-distance line opened between Leipzig and Dresden, a distance of 75 miles (120 km). Belgium also opened its first steam railroad in 1835. In 1837, a line was constructed in Russia linking St. Petersburg with Tsarskoye, a resort used by the Romanov royal family, but subsequent rail building was slow. By 1850, only 370 miles (590 km) of track had been laid in the whole vastness of Russia. The year 1837 also saw Austria operate its first steam engine on the Kaiser Ferdinand Nordbahn railroad out of Vienna. Two years later, the first train to run in Italy drew large crowds when it steamed between Naples and Portici. The first steam-hauled train to operate in the Netherlands also commenced service in 1839.

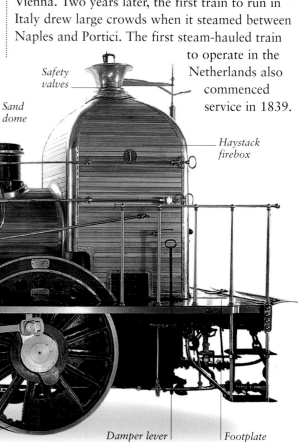

Smokestack

Riveted smokebox

Wooden boiler cladding

Regulator rod

Sand dome

Safety valves

Haystack firebox

LIMMAT

Cylinder

Counterweight

Damper lever

Footplate

FULL STEAM AHEAD IN EUROPE

The pace of development accelerated considerably during the 1840s, when France, Germany, and Switzerland, (which operated its first steam-hauled train in 1844), all developed their own locomotive-construction facilities. Railroads reached Denmark in 1847, Spain in 1848, Sweden in 1850, and the first transalpine railroad, the Semmering, was opened in 1851, providing a link between Vienna and the Italian Adriatic seaport of Trieste.

During this period, the US also began to make significant inroads into Britain's dominance of the European railroad market. Austria first imported a US locomotive in 1837, and such was its success that its designer, William Norris of Philadelphia, set up a locomotive-building factory in Vienna. By 1850, a growing number of European countries believed that US-designed locomotives displayed significant advantages over British ones, since they were more powerful and robust, and often proved to be much more adaptable. When Russia began to expand its railroad network in the 1850s, the US influence proved decisive. A North American engineer, George Washington Whistler, was hired to survey and oversee the construction of Russia's first main-line route, which ran between Moscow and St Petersburg. He opted to use a wide, 5-ft (152-cm) gauge, which became the standard for over 85,000 miles (136,000 km) of railroad built in Russia during the next 100 years. The gauge was also used on the Trans-Siberian Railway, which opened in 1903, providing a link between Moscow and the Pacific-coast port of Vladivostok. The Russian-manufactured engines that ran on these lines after 1850 emulated the design of US-built steam engines.

The rest of continental Europe developed a more independent approach to locomotive design, and by the end of the nineteenth century was providing innovations that were to transform the future development of rail travel. In 1879, the German engineer Ernst von Siemens successfully operated a small, electric-powered locomotive on an electrified track for the first time. Another German engineer, Rudolf Diesel, pioneered the first working diesel engine, which he demonstrated in 1893. Steam power also benefited from European ideas. Injectors, compounding, and superheating were all developed in Europe.

EUROPEAN INNOVATION

When, in 1908, Nord Railway in France built this 4-6-0, they had the advantage of being able to fit several innovative new features that had been developed in Europe.

The most significant of these were four-cylinder compounding, injectors, steam-powered sanders, Walschaerts valve gear, and superheating.

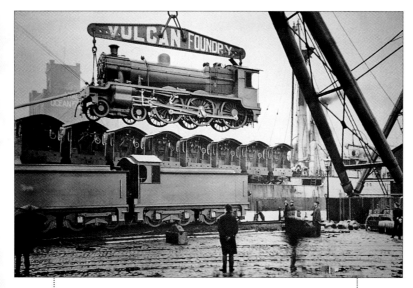

BRITAIN'S EXPORT ADVANTAGE
This Vulcan Foundry-built 4-6-0 being loaded onto a ship at Liverpool docks was sent to India to haul passenger and mail trains. Britain's overseas empire ensured a ready market for its locomotive industry.

RULE BRITANNIA

Britain's most famous twentieth-century statesman, Winston Churchill, described railroads as one of the great civilizing influences on mankind. It would, however, be misleading to believe that the earliest railroads built by Britain in its empire were designed to provide social benefits for the indigenous people in the countries where they were constructed. Commercial considerations were clearly the primary concern, as is demonstrated by the establishment of the first railroad to be constructed outside of Europe and North America. This 12-mile (19-km) line was built in 1845 between Kingston and Spanish Town in Jamaica to transport the sugarcane grown in this British colony. The first line built in South America, in 1848, also served a totally functional purpose. Running between Georgetown and Mahiba in British Guiana (now Guyana), it was used to transport bauxite.

As in the development of the railroads in Britain itself, there was no coordinated strategy in the construction of the railroads in Britain's empire. This was to create long-term problems in Australia, after the first steam-hauled train operated there in 1854, because states adopted different gauges. This meant that both passengers and freight had to be transferred from one train to another wherever a gauge change occurred. As a result, railroads played a much smaller role in opening up the heartland of this country than they did in the US and Canada, where a standard gauge was adopted. Individual enterprise, however, did play

AMERICAN EXPORT
Although the Mallet type was a French invention, US builders made the greatest use of these articulated engines, both for domestic and export use. This 2-6-6-2 Mallet was built at the Baldwin works in the US in the 1940s and ran on the Doña Teresa Cristina Railway in Brazil for many years.

a crucial role in the development of the railroad network in southern Africa, much of which was pioneered by Cecil Rhodes, the maverick British administrator. His original impetus for building railroads was to transport diamonds mined at Kimberley to the port of Cape Town. When gold was discovered in the Transvaal, he built an extension to Johannesburg, which was completed in 1892. Rhodes' ambitions did not end there. He conceived a plan to build a railroad running the length of Africa, from Cape Town to Cairo, as he was convinced that the cost of this line would be offset by trade picked up along the route. By the time of his death in 1902, the line had extended to the town of Bukama in the Belgian Congo (now the Democratic Republic of the Congo), 2,600 miles (4,160 km) north of Cape Town.

The political need for a more coherent railroad-building policy was most clearly demonstrated in India. The first steam train operated there in 1853, but the railroad network stayed small until the outbreak of India's war of independence, known in Britain as the Indian Mutiny, in 1857. This brief but bloody conflict impressed on the British administration the need to develop better transportation links to maintain control of this vast domain. By 1910, more than 32,000 miles (51,200 km) of railroad crisscrossed the Indian subcontinent.

RIVAL INTERESTS

Like Britain, the other European industrial nations regarded the railroads as offering an opportunity to both gain a profitable locomotive-building export industry at home and to set up a transport network that enabled the mineral and agricultural wealth of their overseas empires to be easily accessed. This meant that the pattern of railroad development around the world was, to a large extent, governed by who owned what territory. France, for instance, which controlled much of North Africa, constructed a line across the Sahara and also set up the railroads in Algeria. Germany built a number of railroads in East Africa. Belgium reinforced its control of West Africa by constructing railroads in the Belgian Congo, and the Netherlands established railroads on Java, in East Asia, where they had a controlling interest. In these controlled territories, the ruling colonial power had a virtual monopoly on the locomotives used, which were usually adaptations of engines used at home. In the nineteenth century, Britain exported standard designs, such as the 0-6-0, which were not always suited to local conditions. In order to win export orders, the US took more trouble to design engines that met the requirements of the local conditions.

One of the first US engines designed specifically for export was the Mogul, built for use in Peru. This 2-6-0, which had a flangeless middle set of driving wheels, was well adapted to the tight curves on Peru's mountainous railroads, and Moguls soon replaced the British-built engines operating there.

MIKADOS AND MANDARINS

By the end of the nineteenth century, the US was supplying the vast majority of the locomotives used in South America. It also displaced Britain's dominance in Japan by providing that nation with the world's first 2-8-2, or Mikado, in 1897. Such was the success of US exports that they were used in some British colonies, notably New Zealand, where the Pacific design was employed for the first time in 1901. The same pattern occurred in China, which, until it nationalized its railroads in 1908, had been supplied locomotives by several countries. After 1908, Chinese-built engines closely emulated US-designs.

DUTCH PULLING POWER

Britain was not the only European power to obtain a market for its locomotives in its overseas colonies. A factory in Holland built this 2-6-6-0 Mallet for the PNKA railroad of Java, which remained a territory of the Dutch East Indies (now Indonesia) until 1949. This engine was pictured in 1979, still hard at work in Java.

MADE IN INDIA

Due to the vast expansion in the size of India's railroad network, Britain was unable to meet all the locomotive needs of this dominion. In 1895, this outside-cylinder F class 0-6-0 made history, becoming the first locomotive to be built entirely in India.

GERMAN SUCCESS

No.38.1182 was one of over 3,400 P8 4-6-0s to be built, making this German design one of the most numerous classes ever. Introduced in 1906, P8s were widely used in both Europe and Africa.

URBAN EVOLUTION

The changing face of late nineteenth-century public transportation is reflected in this German cityscape. Horse-drawn carriages still share the road with modern electric tramcars, while barges ply their trade along the river. On the far bank of the river, a station that serves the new overhead electrified railroad has been erected.

THE URBAN REVOLUTION

Rising urban populations in both Europe and North America during the nineteenth century spurred the development of complex public transportation networks. The first railroad to venture through the heart of a city, the Metropolitan, opened in London in 1863. The trains used on this, the first underground line, were steam-hauled, and traveling conditions were often unpleasant, despite efforts to reduce the level of smoke emission and provide ventilation in the stations and tunnels. As an alternative to traveling underground, a number of

cities in the US built elevated railroads. The first and most famous of these was New York City's elevated railroad, opened in 1867, which used cable-hauled cars until 1871. The steam engines that replaced them also created pollution problems as they spewed out cinder-laden exhaust onto the streets below.

The key to developing urban railroads was to find an alternative to steam traction, and this was achieved by German engineer Ernst von Siemens, who built the world's first electrically powered urban line at Lichterfelde, near Berlin, in 1881. To utilize this new motive power underground, a hydraulic tunneling shield was developed that was capable of digging deep tunnels. It had cutting edges fixed around a circular cast-iron plate. The first deep-level, electrically powered "tube," as it became known, was opened in London in 1890. Its success led to a massive expansion of London's underground network, as well as the development of underground railroads in scores of other cities. The first underground in continental Europe opened in Budapest, Hungary, in 1896, and two years later the first subway in the US opened in Boston, Massachusetts. The inaugural line of the Paris Metro opened in 1900, while the first stretch of the New York Subway

STEAM UNDER LONDON

London's first underground railroads were powered by steam locomotives like this Metropolitan Railway 4-4-0 tank built in 1866. Although efforts were made to reduce the exhaust emissions by condensing steam back to water, fumes and smoke in the tunnels and stations still caused problems.

Coal bunker

Driving wheel

Cab spectacle plate

Condensing pipe from cylinder

Steam dome

METROPOLITAN 23 RAILWAY.

opened in 1904. With the exception of the Boston subway, all of these new undergrounds were built with electric lines, which increasingly came to be employed on surface routes as well. In the US, the steam trains introduced on Chicago's elevated line were replaced by electric trains in 1895. In July of that year, the Baltimore & Ohio Railroad began using electric locomotives on its Belt line, making it the first main-line operator to employ electric traction. Innovative uses for electric traction were also developed in Germany, where a number of suspended railroads were constructed by Ernst Von Siemens. The best known of these was the Wuppertal Schwebebahn, which opened in 1901.

The expansion of urban railroads had a profound social impact, as they allowed people to live at a distance from their place of work and also gave them far more mobility during their leisure hours. Urban railroads also had a dramatic effect on the layout of cities as suburbs were developed along the main commuter routes.

MAIN LINES ADAPT

The early railroad companies saw themselves as freight carriers. However, the public had other ideas, and from 1830 onward passenger transportation became big business. People of all classes not only took trains to and from work, they also used them during their leisure time to get away from the polluted industrial cities. During the nineteenth century, seaside resorts and spa towns grew prosperous through this trade. Holiday express and excursion trains quickly became a popular

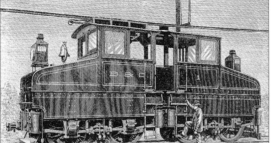

Route indicator board

A CURE FOR SMOKING

In 1895, pollution from steam locomotives had made conditions in Baltimore's railroad tunnels intolerable, so the Baltimore & Ohio Railroad brought in three of these 1,080-hp B-B electric locomotives to pilot trains in the tunneled city section. They were the first main-line electric engines to work in the world.

feature of every timetable, since the journey itself was seen as an important and pleasurable part of the holiday. The passenger transport revolution owes a large debt to an American carpenter, George Pullman, who in 1864 built the largest and most luxurious sleeping car seen on any railroad. Four years later, he introduced the first purpose-built restaurant car. Such was the demand for these cars that in 1880 the town of Pullman was founded to build luxury railroad cars. Pullman also built coaches for use in Britain and inspired Georges Nagelmackers to set up Compagnie Internationale des Wagons Lits in Belgium. This firm supplied luxury sleeping carriages and dining cars to numerous European railroads. In 1883, Nagelmackers went on to establish his own luxury train service, the Orient Express, which remained synonymous with luxury European rail travel well into the twentieth century.

As the numbers of passengers increased, freight haulage was divided off as a separate service. From the 1860s onward, US engineers began designing locomotives that were fitted with extra driving wheels for added pulling power. The US continued to dominate the development of high-powered freight locomotives until Anatole Mallet, a French engineer, patented the first articulated design in 1884. The Mallet principle was increasingly used in the US in the twentieth century because the dual sets of driving wheels allowed larger locomotives to be built without compromising maneuverability. Another highly successful articulated locomotive type, the Beyer Garratt, was developed in Britain in 1909. It had an even lighter axle-loading than the Mallet type, and was exported in large numbers as it operated well on lightlylaid track.

A LASTING SUCCESS

This Garratt-type articulated engine was developed for freight work and for use on overseas railroads. From its introduction in 1909, the type established itself as the major export success of Britain's locomotive industry. Some 2,000 Garratts were built, a few of which remain at work in southern Africa, mainly in coal-rich Zimbabwe.

SPEED FOR SPEED'S SAKE

Before World War I, few regular scheduled services anywhere in the world, including the US, averaged more than 50 mph (80 kph). There were exceptions, but these usually occurred on routes where two or more railroad companies were in competition. In Britain, intense rivalry on the London to Scotland route existed between the East and West Coast Main Line companies. In the summer of 1895, this rivalry reached a peak in what became known as the "Races to the North." The climax of the races came in August 1895, when a night train on the East Coast line completed the 524-mile (840-km) journey between London and Aberdeen in 8 hours 40 minutes at an average speed of 63 mph (100 kph). The following evening, the West Coast service bettered that time by eight minutes, a record that was not improved upon until new high-speed electric trains were introduced in 1978.

Improvements in locomotive design, as well as better signaling systems, enabled steam trains to reach a top speed of almost 100 mph (160 kph) by the end of the nineteenth century. One of the earliest and most publicized claims that this speed had been exceeded was made by the New York Central & Hudson River Railroad for *No.999*, a 4-4-0 locomotive that is alleged to have reached 112 mph (180 kph) at the head of the Empire State Express on May 10, 1893. This claim is contested, as is the 102-mph (163-kph) run *City of Truro* is said to have made hauling the Ocean Mails Express on the Great Western Railway in Britain on May 9, 1904. As most steam locomotives were not fitted with speedometers, it was not until 1934 that the first authenticated 100-mph (160-kph) run by a steam engine was recorded for *No.4472 Flying Scotsman* on England's London & North Eastern Railway. It is generally agreed, however, that many locomotives, including *City of Truro*, achieved this speed.

Speed records for electric traction were also set in Germany at the beginning of the twentieth century. The German army built a test track called the Zossen Military

AMERICAN EXPRESS

The New York Central & Hudson River Railroad built *No.999* in 1893 to speed up its prestigious Empire State Express service between New York and Chicago. At this time, average speeds were low and *No.999's* achievement of completing the 960-mile (1,536-km) journey in 20 hours at an average speed of 48 mph (77 kph) was outstanding.

A BRITISH FLIER

On November 30, 1934, *No.4472 Flying Scotsman* became the first steam engine to achieve an authenticated running speed of 100 mph (160 kph) on Britain's London & North Eastern Railway. This record-breaking run sparked off four years of intense speed competition between Britain, Germany, and the US.

Railway, on which they ran their new, experimental electric trains. In 1901, an eight-wheel electric locomotive built by Siemens & Halske reached a maximum speed of 101 mph (162 kph) between Zossen and Marienfeld. More amazing feats followed. In October 1903, a 12-wheel electric railcar attained the unprecedented speed of 126 mph (202 kph), and later that month a second railcar of the same design bettered this speed, reaching 131 mph (209 kph).

Although these performances illustrated the potential of electric traction, Germany did not pursue electrification because the railcars damaged the track and the power cables, and were unstable at these speeds. Furthermore, the side-mounted current delivery system was impractical for a public railroad and, as there was no discernible need at this time to provide a 100-mph (160-kph) rail service, the Zossen experiment was not pursued.

NEW COMPETITION

Passenger traffic reached a peak on the US railroads in the 1920s. However, by the end of this decade a massive escalation in the level of car ownership and improvements in the road network meant that the automobile posed a threat that could not be ignored. Freight traffic was also affected by road transport. To make matters worse, during the Great Depression that followed the Wall Street Crash of 1929 the average income of the citizens of North America was halved. This pattern was repeated around the world and railroad operators everywhere were forced to look for a motive power that was cheaper to run than steam power, as well as being glamorous enough to persuade more people to travel by train. Oil fuel-powered engines were seen to offer the best solution and the frontrunner in their development was Germany. The fastest machine of all was a propeller-driven, gasoline-powered railcar named *Schienenzepplin*, which reached 143 mph (229 kph) between Ludwigslust and Wittenberge on June 21, 1931. However, the propeller system was deemed to be too hazardous, so more attention was paid to the *VT877* diesel railcar, constructed by Deutsche Reichsbahn, which attained a top speed of 103 mph (163 kph) in December 1932. This achievement led to the introduction of the Flying Hamburger diesel service between Berlin and Hamburg in 1933.

When it was launched, the trains on this route offered the fastest scheduled railroad service in the world, averaging 77 mph (124 kph), and provided Adolf Hitler, who was appointed Chancellor that year, a valuable propaganda coup.

National and political prestige was a governing factor in the improvement of Italy's railroads during the 1930s. The Italian dictator Benito Mussolini saw efficient railroads as clear evidence of strong government, and his greatest achievement remains making Italy's trains run on time. As a consequence of not having a domestic coal supply, Italy began developing an electrified rail network at the start of the twentieth century. Mussolini was determined to develop high-speed electric trains that could match

GERMAN RECORD-BREAKER

The Nazi Party in Germany was well aware of the propaganda value of technological achievements. A large crowd witnessed the departure of the first streamlined Flying Hamburger diesel-express between Berlin and Hamburg in 1933. In trials, one of them set an unofficial diesel speed record of 124 mph (198 kph).

AHEAD OF ITS TIME

This electric railcar was one of two experimental engines built in Germany that achieved unprecedented speeds on the Zossen Military Railway. The 131 mph (209 kph) clocked made them far and away the fastest railroad engines in the world. This world speed record remained unbroken until after World War II.

OFFERING ALTERNATIVES

In the mid-1930s, the Chicago, Burlington & Quincy Railroad ran a high-speed diesel service headed by streamlined diesel Zephyrs, like the one seen on the right below. To be on the safe side, they built a streamlined 4-6-4 steam engine, shown on the left, to give substitute motive power if these untested diesels broke down.

the new generation of diesel trains for pace and efficiency. His efforts were rewarded in July 1939, six weeks before the outbreak of World War II, when an Elettrotreno Rapido 200 set a scheduled electric-traction speed record of 126 mph (203 kph).

On the other side of the Atlantic, several railroads introduced express diesel services in the mid-1930s. In May 1934 a streamlined diesel train, the *Pioneer Zephyr*, set an official diesel speed record of 112 mph (180 kph) and greatly reduced the journey time between Denver and Chicago. This success initiated a period of fierce competition among three railroad companies: the Chicago, Burlington & Quincy; the

Chicago, Milwaukee, St. Paul & Pacific; and the Chicago & North Western. All three competed for passengers between Chicago and the twin cities of Minneapolis/St. Paul, and in late 1934 each railroad reduced its ten-hour schedule for the run by an astonishing 3 hours 30 minutes. To achieve this, the Burlington line had the Budd company build twin-car diesel-electric units based on the *Pioneer Zephyr* and inaugurated the Burlington Zephyr service. The Burlington's rivals kept faith with steam traction: The Chicago & North Western retained their conventional locomotives; while the Chicago, Milwaukee, St. Paul & Pacific introduced the new Hiawatha service, which was steam-hauled by streamlined 4-4-2s. One of these locomotives set a new world steam-traction speed record of 112 mph (180 kph) in May 1935.

INTERNATIONAL RIVALRY

In the late 1930s intense rivalry to set new speed records developed between Britain, Germany, and the US. The world steam speed record established by the US-built Hiawatha was equalled in September 1935 when the first of Nigel Gresley's A4 Pacifics, *No.2509 Silver Link*, ran at over 112 mph (180 kph) in Britain. Germany then gained the record in 1936 when *No.05001*, a streamlined 4-6-4, hit a top speed of 124 mph (199 kph). The culmination of these record-breaking steam runs came in July 1938, when another of Gresley's A4 Pacifics, *No.4468 Mallard*, set the record of 126 mph (202 kph) which stands to this day. Germany officially regained the world record for diesel traction in 1939 when an aluminum-bodied diesel train, the *Flying Silver Fish*, recorded a top speed of 134 mph (214 kph) on a run from Hamburg to Berlin.

Although speed records captured the headlines during the 1930s, the legacy of accelerated rail services was of wider importance. However, these improvements were shortlived. The outbreak of World War II in September 1939 made passenger services a low priority and delayed the widespread adoption of diesel- and electric-hauled trains.

WORLD WAR II

During World War II, railroad networks across much of Europe were devastated by artillery shells, aerial bombing, and sabotage attacks. As fuel supplies dwindled during the the course of the war, trains played an increasingly large role in transporting ammunition

and vital supplies to the troops on both sides, so a large number of railroads were hastily rebuilt. To cope with the poor state of quickly laid track, both sides designed and built rugged steam engines that had eight or more driving wheels and consequently had a light axle-loading. The most famous German design was the Kriegslok (War Locomotive), which had ten driving wheels.

After the war, reconstruction rather than record-breaking preoccupied Europe's railroad operators. France and Germany, who received Marshall Aid to repair their damaged railroad networks, used the money to modernize them. Germany invested in both diesel and electric traction, while the French national railroad authority, the SNCF, opted to concentrate on electrification. Other countries that undertook major electrification schemes included Russia and Japan. In contrast, Britain continued to build steam locomotives for domestic main-line use up until 1960. This failure to modernize and upgrade was largely a result of underfunding.

THE DIESEL AGE

Unlike the railroads in Europe, the railroads in North America emerged unscathed from World War II and remained in private ownership. To improve the efficiency of their service and to lower operating costs, all mainline railroads quickly replaced their steam locomotives with diesel-electrics for both passenger and freight service. The most successful diesel-electric series in the 1940s and 1950s were the E and F series built by the Electro-Motive Division of General Motors. These snub-nosed locomotives were widely used across North America, and were also exported abroad in large numbers. Successors of the F series still haul the prestigious Indian Pacific service in Australia.

DESIGNED FOR WAR

Wartime railroad conditions demanded simple, robust machines and Germany's Kriegslok (War Locomotive) was an ideal design. Over 6,000 of these 2-10-0s were built between 1942 and 1945 and they continued to be built up until 1952. This Kriegslok remained in service on Turkish Railways into the 1970s.

However, North American prosperity after the war led to increased car ownership in the US, which had a detrimental effect on passenger traffic. This threat was compounded by the development of an affordable internal airline service. After the first domestic jet airliner took to the skies in 1959, many long-haul railroads found that they could not compete with these airplanes and were forced to abandon their passenger services altogether. Despite the introduction of luxury dome car services railroads were forced to drastically curtail passenger services in the 1960s.

A NEW HIGH-SPEED ERA

In Europe, the postwar era saw the development of faster trains, culminating in a number of record-breaking runs. In 1954, *No.CC7121*, an electric engine built in France, set a world speed record for all forms of rail traction of 151 mph (242 kph). The following year, *No.BB9004* became the

ALLEZ FRANCE

In March 1955, this French-built, 4,000-hp electric engine, *No.BB904*, broke all previous rail-speed records when it attained 206 mph (329 kph) on a test run. Its performance assured France's status as Europe's leading developer of high-speed trains.

third French-built electric locomotive to smash this record when it attained a top speed of 206 mph (329 kph). The foundation for these impressive results was laid in 1950, when French Railways (SNCF) introduced the electrically hauled Mistral express between Paris, Lyons, and Marseilles. It symbolized the regeneration of France's war-battered

A BRIGHT NEW DAWN

A new era of European high-speed train travel was initiated by France's TGV (Train à Grand Vitesse). The inaugural TGV Sud-Est service between Paris and Lyons commenced in 1982 using these orange-liveried, ten-car, articulated trains on a purpose-built high-speed line.

railroad system, and demonstrated a commitment to offer significantly higher scheduled speeds to compete with road and air transport. France's achievements inspired Europe's most ambitious early high-speed service, the Trans-Europ Express (TEE), which began as a cross-border diesel service in 1957. By the early 1960s, most of the routes had been electrified and ran trains that could cope with the different electric currents employed in France, Germany, Italy, Switzerland, and the Netherlands. In 1967, TEE trains that could run on different gauges were built, so that they could travel from France into Spain, which had a wider gauge. The problem with these services was that they operated on track used by slower passenger and freight trains, and the speed the high-speed trains ran at was well below their potential ceiling. This meant that the TEE eventually lost most of its passengers on long-haul routes to the airlines.

A HIGH-SPEED SOLUTION

Japan experienced the same speed restrictions on its electrified lines, so in 1958 permission was given to build from

JAPAN'S HIGH-VELOCITY BULLET

Japan's "Bullet Trains" have been undergoing constant redevelopment since they pioneered high-speed rail travel in 1964. This Nozomi 500 16-car train set entered service in 1998 and has a top speed in service of 188 mph (300 kph).

scratch a passenger-only, high-speed line linking Tokyo and Osaka. The opening of the Tokaido Shinkansen (New Railway) on October 1, 1964 coincided with the Tokyo Olympic Games and marked the beginning of Japan's post-war rebirth as a modern industrial society. Within a year, the "Bullet Trains" on the Shinkansen were offering the world's first regular 100-mph (160-kph) service. Since then, Japan has remained a leading force in high-speed rail travel. One of the newly developed "Bullet Trains," *300X*, can reach a top speed of 275 mph (443 kph).

Within a year of the Shinkansen opening, French Railways produced a draft plan for a network of purpose-built, high-speed lines, on which would would run the Train à Grand Vitesse (TGV). The first gas-turbine TGVs were tested in 1972, but these were discarded in favor of electric-powered TGVs, the first of which entered service in 1982 on the high-speed Paris to Lyons line. These TGVs slashed the record time of the Mistral from 3 hours 47 minutes to 2 hours 40 minutes.

The success of France's TGVs overshadowed the achievements of the British diesel-powered High-Speed Train (HST), or InterCity 125, which entered service in 1973. Although this set a 1987 world speed record for diesel traction of 148 mph (237 kph), which has yet to be beaten, it was no match for the new generation of high-speed electric trains.

Most European railroad operators have followed the French lead and records for electric traction continue to be broken, both by the

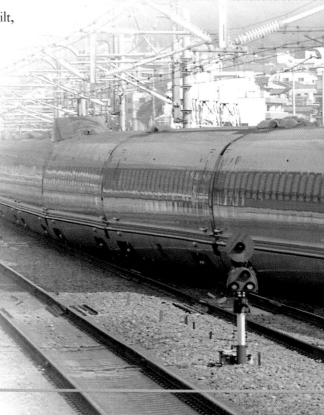

TGV and its German equivalent, the Inter-City Express (ICE). Between April 1988 and May 1990, the world record climbed from 240 mph (385 kph), set in Germany, to an astonishing 322 mph (515 kph), set in France by a TGV Atlantique – a record that remains unbeaten for conventional rail traction.

In addition to individual high-speed feats, there has been a rapid expansion of high-speed networks – in France, Germany, Italy, Spain, Belgium, and Sweden. In Britain, only the East Coast Main Line, which was electrified between London and Edinburgh in 1991, offers a comparable service to these European lines. Until the high-speed link between London and the Channel Tunnel opens, Eurostars traveling to Paris will only be able to reach their top speed of 186 mph (298 kph) on French soil.

Until recently, the North American contribution to high-speed rail travel had been minimal. However, Amtrak, which took over the majority of passenger services in the US in the 1970s, and improved the speed of Metroliner trains on the electrified line between Washington DC and New York in 1983; these have a top operational speed of 125 mph (200 kph). Amtrak has also introduced high-speed Acela trains on the same route, which can attain 150 mph (240 kph). Further electrification projects here include the Florida Overland Express, which may use French TGV expertise to maximize the speed of its service. High-speed services are also being set up in Russia, between Moscow and St. Petersburg, and are hoped to operate at a top

speed of 220 mph (352 kph). In Asia, Taiwan and Korea are both constructing high-speed lines and it is possible that China will soon follow suit.

SPEED WITHOUT WHEELS

From the beginning of their history, trains have relied on wheels running on rails, but the next century may bring a faster alternative. Experiments with high-speed magnetic levitation (maglev) trains, which float on a magnetic field above a guideway and are propelled by linear induction motors, have been underway for some time in Japan. A test vehicle, the *MLX01*, reached 343 mph (549 kph). Maglevs are also being developed in Japan for urban use. However, the first long-distance application of maglev trains is likely to occur in Germany, where a guideway connecting Berlin with Hamburg is scheduled for completion in 2005. Trials for the Transrapid maglevs that will run on this 181-mile (290-km) route are well underway, and it is hoped that they will be able to complete the journey in one hour or less.

Whether the future for trains is with or without wheels, improved designs and better organization have ensured that both passenger and freight trains will continue to play a vital role in transportation in the twenty-first century.

FUTURE PLANS

Seen on its elevated concrete guideway at the Emsland test center in Germany, *TR07* is one of a fleet of Transrapid test vehicles paving the way for the world's first inter-city maglev (magnetic levitation) service. Transrapid trains are scheduled to be propelled by electromagnetic force between Berlin and Hamburg in 2005.

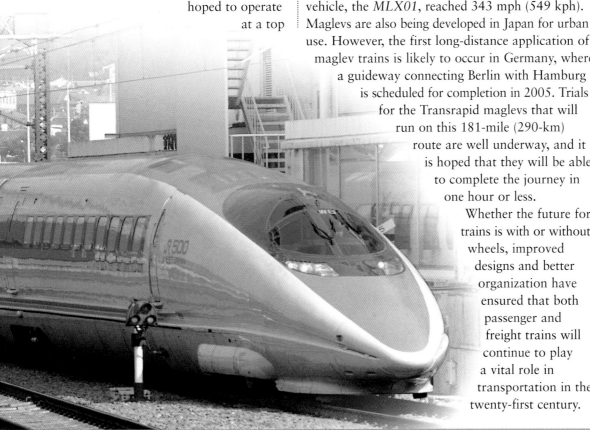

PART TWO

ULTIMATE TRAINS

The trains in this section have earned the title "ultimate" for many different reasons. There are locomotives, like *Rocket*, that set the standard for the rest to follow. There are trains that set new standards of service or luxury; those that have made traveling around cities faster; and those that have ushered in a new era, such as the pioneering diesel and electric engines. Some designs display supreme engineering excellence and beauty of line; others, like the articulated giant, Big Boy, impress with size and power. Exciting modern developments, such as Germany's *TRO7* maglev train, point the way to the future. Whether they are the largest, fastest, most luxurious, most powerful, or most innovative, they all deserve a place in this collection.

BRITAIN LEADS AND THE WORLD FOLLOWS

I N THE EARLY 1800s, it was accepted that freight could be carried in wagons formed into trains that ran on rails. Few people believed that anything other than horses could pull these trains. The first attempts to power a steam locomotive along rails occurred in 1803 in Britain, where these engines continued to be developed almost exclusively for industrial use until 1825, when the world's first public steam-hauled train service opened. It was not until 1829, when Robert Stephenson produced *Rocket* for use on the Liverpool and Manchester Railway, that steam traction won universal approval. The year 1829 also saw the first steam trains operating outside of Britain – in Continental Europe and North America. The next ten years witnessed a massive expansion of the railroad networks, particularly in Britain and the US, which was matched by a correspondingly rapid advance in the design and performance of locomotives.

BUILT IN 1835, *DER ADLER* WAS THE FIRST
LOCOMOTIVE TO RUN IN GERMANY

1800–1840 THE FIRST LOCOMOTIVES

THE FIRST STEAM ENGINES to run on rails were built in Britain at the start of the nineteenth century. The Cornish-born inventor Richard Trevithick built the first working one in 1804. His use of high-pressure steam was taken up by engineers working in northern England, where steam engines revealed their potential on the colliery wagonways. However, until iron rails came to replace traditional wooden tracks, they proved far too heavy for effective use. After 1810, rising fodder costs and rapid advances in locomotive design led many industrialists in England to abandon horses for haulage and to adopt steam traction instead.

RICHARD TREVITHICK

Cross beam

Piston rod

Driving cab was not part of the original design

Cylinder mounted within boiler

Wooden buffers

Vertical rod drives wheels

Coupling rod

Sandbox

STEPHENSON'S HETTON COLLIERY LOCOMOTIVE

Beginning in 1822, George Stephenson supplied five locomotives to Hetton Colliery in County Durham. These engines enjoyed remarkably long lives and the one seen here was still at work in 1908.

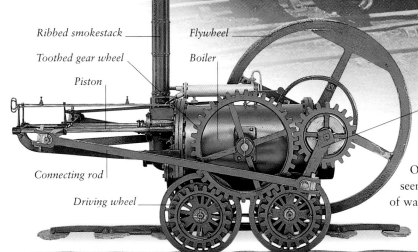

Ribbed smokestack

Toothed gear wheel

Piston

Connecting rod

Driving wheel

Flywheel

Boiler

Driving crank

THE FIRST WORKING LOCOMOTIVE

On February 13, 1804, a locomotive built by Richard Trevithick, seen here in model form, became the first steam engine to pull a train of wagons. It was loaded with ten tons of iron and 70 men, and ran on the Pen-y-Darren ironworks tramway in South Wales. The engine weighed five tons and traveled at up to 5 mph (8 kph).

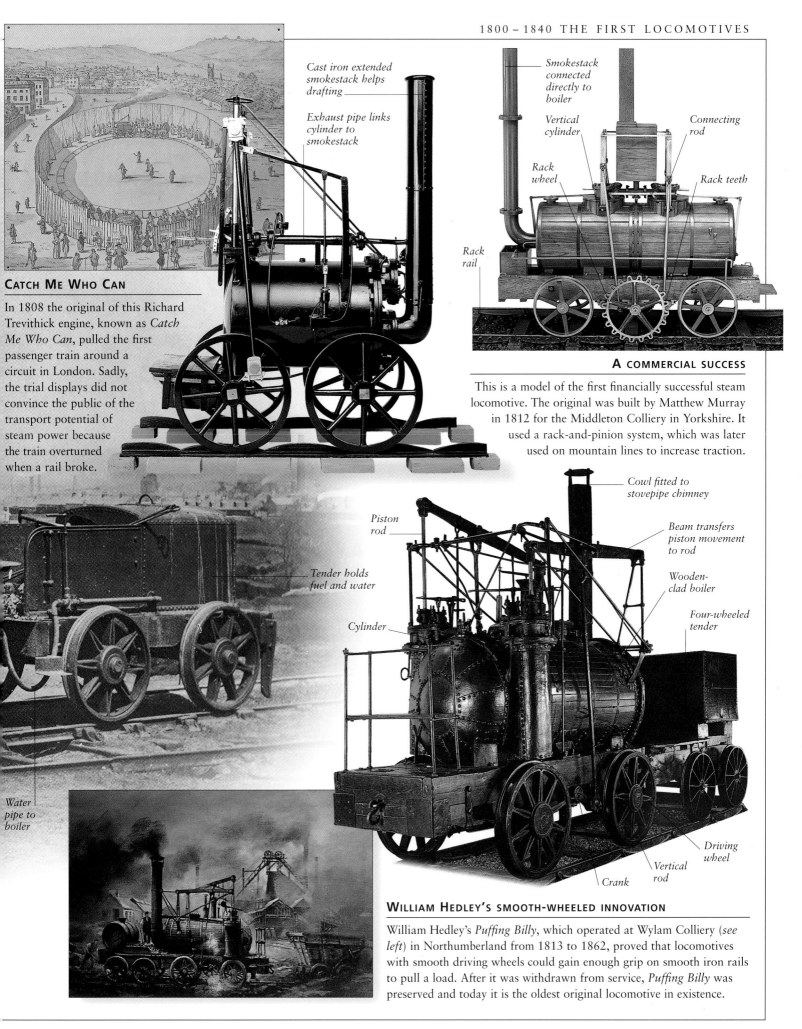

Cast iron extended
smokestack helps
drafting

Exhaust pipe links
cylinder to
smokestack

Smokestack
connected
directly to
boiler

Vertical
cylinder

Connecting
rod

Rack
wheel

Rack teeth

Rack
rail

CATCH ME WHO CAN

In 1808 the original of this Richard
Trevithick engine, known as *Catch
Me Who Can*, pulled the first
passenger train around a
circuit in London. Sadly,
the trial displays did not
convince the public of the
transport potential of
steam power because
the train overturned
when a rail broke.

A COMMERCIAL SUCCESS

This is a model of the first financially successful steam
locomotive. The original was built by Matthew Murray
in 1812 for the Middleton Colliery in Yorkshire. It
used a rack-and-pinion system, which was later
used on mountain lines to increase traction.

Cowl fitted to
stovepipe chimney

Piston
rod

Beam transfers
piston movement
to rod

Tender holds
fuel and water

Wooden-
clad boiler

Cylinder

Four-wheeled
tender

Water
pipe to
boiler

Driving
wheel

Vertical
rod

Crank

WILLIAM HEDLEY'S SMOOTH-WHEELED INNOVATION

William Hedley's *Puffing Billy*, which operated at Wylam Colliery (*see
left*) in Northumberland from 1813 to 1862, proved that locomotives
with smooth driving wheels could gain enough grip on smooth iron rails
to pull a load. After it was withdrawn from service, *Puffing Billy* was
preserved and today it is the oldest original locomotive in existence.

1800–1840 ROCKET

ROCKET.

BUILT BY Robert Stephenson and his father George, *Rocket* was entered into trials held at Rainhill, Lancashire in 1829 to select the best type of locomotive to run on the Liverpool & Manchester Railway (L&MR). Through its flawless performance, *Rocket* proved that steam locomotives could operate reliably over long distances, and it was awarded the first prize of £500. It was also chosen to haul the first train on the L&MR when it opened in 1830, making it the world's first successful passenger express locomotive. *Rocket* was a much more advanced machine than the cumbersome, slow-moving engines that had operated in Britain up until then. Many of the improvements it introduced embodied core design principles that were incorporated into the engineering of every steam locomotive built after 1830.

Control regulates flow of water into boiler

Boiler sectioned for display

Cylinder

Regulator admits steam to cylinders

Firebox backhead

Steampipe from boiler to cylinde

Firebox encased by an external water jacket

Exhaust steam pipe

Firehole door

Funnel

AN EXPOSED ATTRACTION

George Stephenson enjoyed driving *Rocket* and won the admiration of Fanny Kemble, a famous actress whom he took for windswept rides on the exposed footplate of this engine. At the Rainhill trials, *Rocket* hit a top-speed of 29 mph (47 kph) as it shuttled to and fro for 75 miles (120 km) along the test track.

Water barrel

Fuel space

BLUEPRINT FOR THE FUTURE

Some of the innovations that ensured *Rocket's* success are seen in this cross-sectioned replica which was built in 1980. The unprecedented speeds it reached were made possible by fitting, on either side of the firebox, inclined cylinders that were both connected to single driving wheels by short connecting rods. This provided more direct thrust than the beam arrangement on earlier locomotives. Other key features were the multiple tube boiler and the smokestack blastpipe, both of which significantly improved the production of steam.

Tender

SPECIFICATION	
Manufacturer	Robert Stephenson & Co, Newcastle-upon-Tyne, England
Classification	*Rocket* class 0-2-2
Date built	1829
Number built	7
Fuel	Coke
Top speed	29 mph (47 kph)
Length	24 ft (7.3 m)
Height	16 ft (4.9 m)
Total weight	3½ tons
Tractive effort	Unrecorded

Leaf spring

Axlebox

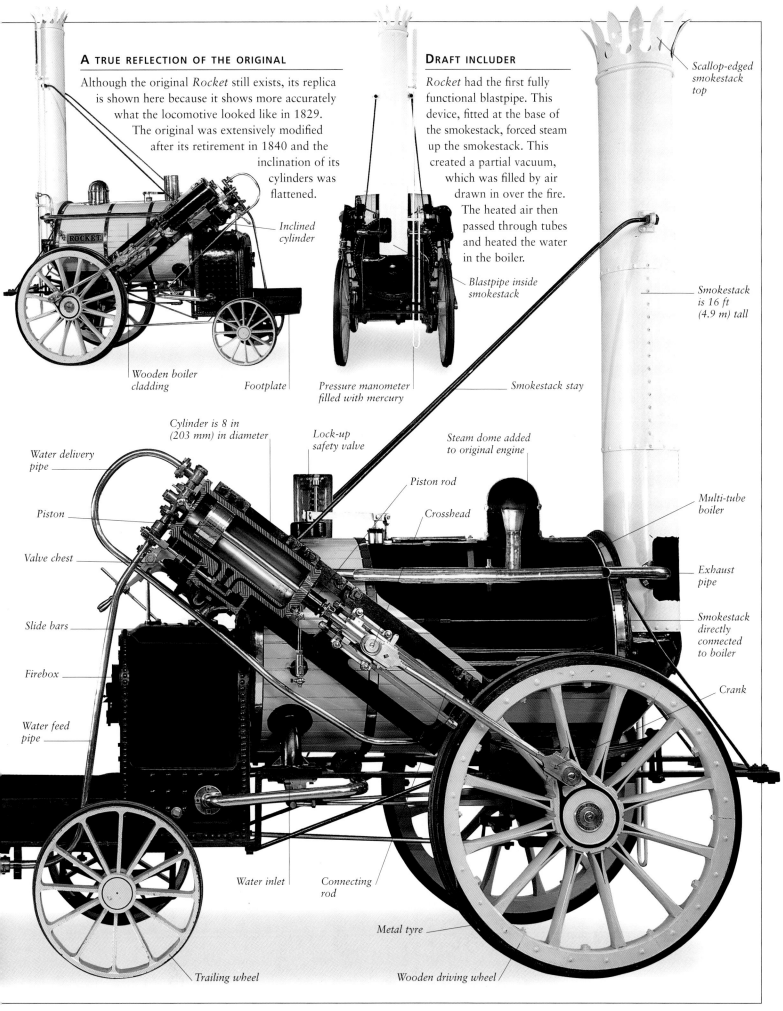

A TRUE REFLECTION OF THE ORIGINAL

Although the original *Rocket* still exists, its replica is shown here because it shows more accurately what the locomotive looked like in 1829. The original was extensively modified after its retirement in 1840 and the inclination of its cylinders was flattened.

Inclined cylinder

Wooden boiler cladding

Footplate

DRAFT INCLUDER

Rocket had the first fully functional blastpipe. This device, fitted at the base of the smokestack, forced steam up the smokestack. This created a partial vacuum, which was filled by air drawn in over the fire. The heated air then passed through tubes and heated the water in the boiler.

Blastpipe inside smokestack

Pressure manometer filled with mercury

Smokestack stay

Scallop-edged smokestack top

Smokestack is 16 ft (4.9 m) tall

Cylinder is 8 in (203 mm) in diameter

Lock-up safety valve

Steam dome added to original engine

Piston rod

Crosshead

Multi-tube boiler

Water delivery pipe

Piston

Valve chest

Slide bars

Firebox

Water feed pipe

Exhaust pipe

Smokestack directly connected to boiler

Crank

Water inlet

Connecting rod

Metal tyre

Trailing wheel

Wooden driving wheel

1800-1840 EUROPE

THE OPENING OF the first public steam railroad, the Stockton & Darlington, in 1825 prompted a huge demand for steam traction across Europe. Much of this demand was met by British engineers, such as Robert Stephenson, who strove to improve the efficiency and reliability of their engines during this period. Among the major developments were the introduction of horizontal cylinders, coupled wheels, steam brakes, and multi-tube boilers that greatly increased the amount of steam generated.

Smokestack made from riveted iron plates

Horizontal beam links piston with connecting rod

Vertical cylinder

THE FIRST RUSSIAN LOCOMOTIVE

Russia's first ever locomotive, a 2-2-0 designed by M. Cherepanov, was built as early as 1833. It ran on a short-haul industrial line laid at Nizhni-Tagil in the Ural Mountains region.

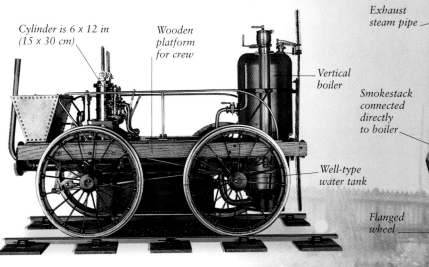

Cylinder is 6 x 12 in (15 x 30 cm)

Wooden platform for crew

Vertical boiler

Exhaust steam pipe

Smokestack connected directly to boiler

Well-type water tank

Flanged wheel

A NOVEL DESIGN

Built by John Braithwaite in 1829, the vertically-boilered 0-4-0 *Novelty* was the first locomotive to have its cylinders inside the frames. During the Rainhill Trials that year, *Novelty* attained the top speed of 24 mph (38 kph), but broke down in the trials after its bellows failed.

Multi-tube boiler

Covered tender

Rotary fan

A FIRST FOR FRANCE

French engineer Marc Séguin patented the multi-tube boiler in 1827 and first employed it on a locomotive of his own design in 1829. This locomotive was the first to be built in France. It reached a speed of 4½ mph (7 kph) on its trial run from St. Etienne to Lyons in November 1829.

Single driving wheel

Firebox

Flared tender to prevent coal spillage

Buffer beam

Brake shoe

THE GERMAN EAGLE

The first successful steam engine in Germany was another of Robert Stephenson's single-wheeler 2-2-2s. It was bought for the Nuremburg-Fürth Railway in 1835 at a cost of $2,887. Named *Adler* (Eagle), it remained in service until 1857. This replica of it was constructed in 1935 to mark the centennial of German railroads.

BRITISH EXPORT IN ITALY

Railroads came to Italy in 1839 and one of the first engines to run there was *Bayard*. This 2-2-2 was built to a single-wheeler design patented by Robert Stephenson in 1833.

Water barrel

Boiler containing 62 copper tubes

Vertical connecting rod

Early car design resembled a road stagecoach

Water tank

54-in (137-cm) driving wheels

Cast-iron riveted smokebox

THE FIRST PASSENGER ENGINE

George Stephenson's *Locomotion No.1* made history on September 27, 1825, when it hauled the first public steam service train in the world on the Stockton & Darlington Railway. The train consisted of 21 passenger wagons and a further six laden with coal. *Locomotion No.1* was the first engine to employ coupled wheels.

Four-wheel tender

Coupled wheel

Crank

Open-sided wooden car

Outside frame

Wooden buffer

PATTERN FOR THE FUTURE

Robert Stephenson's 2-2-0 *Planet*, constructed in 1830 for the Liverpool & Manchester Railway, had cylinders placed horizontally at the front. The design, which offered more even weight distribution and a consequent improvement in stability, set a pattern that was followed for over 150 years.

1800–1840 GREAT WESTERN RAILWAY

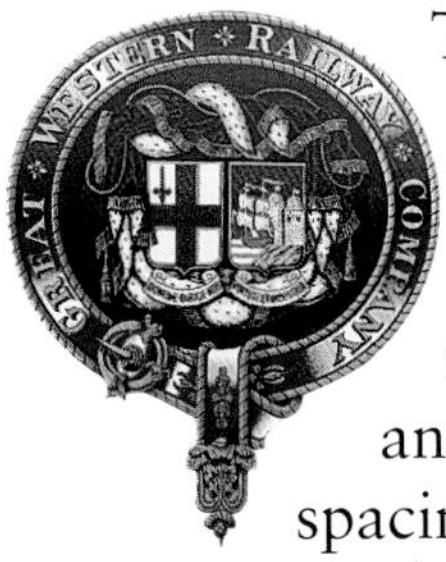

THE BUILDING OF the Great Western Railway (GWR) was the inspiration of Isambard Kingdom Brunel, the British-born engineering genius. After the network was approved in 1835, Brunel resolved to lay broad-gauge tracks along the key routes to the southwest of England and Wales because he argued that a broad 7-ft (2-m) spacing provided more stability and would allow his trains to travel faster. His vision proved correct, and for many years the GWR offered the world's best and fastest rail service. Although the entire network had converted to standard gauge by 1892, the GWR retained its reputation for innovation and excellence.

DUAL TRACKING

Pressure to link the GWR with other rail networks in Britain forced it to lay standard-gauge track inside its broad-gauge lines. Two sets of tracks are evident in this 1880s photograph.

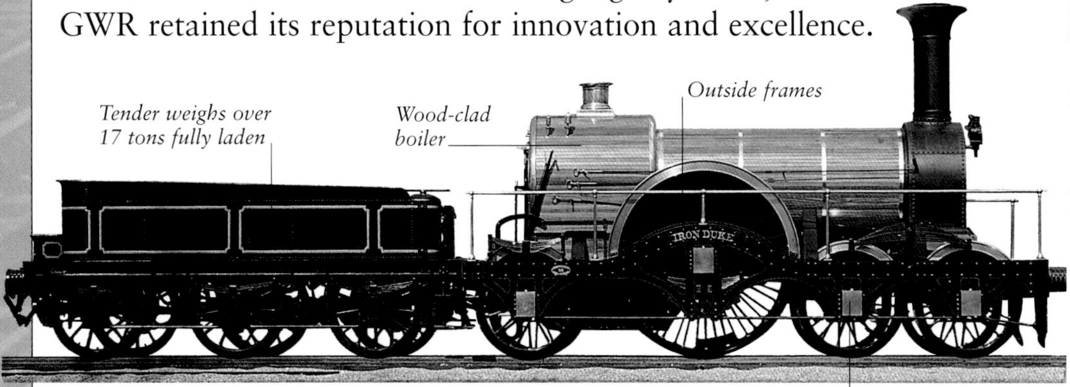

Tender weighs over 17 tons fully laden

Wood-clad boiler

Outside frames

Axlebox

GOOCH'S GREATEST

The GWR's broad-gauge system allowed engineers such as Daniel Gooch to design larger and more powerful locomotives. Arguably the best were his Iron Duke 4-2-2s; 29 were built between 1847 and 1855 to haul passenger trains. This replica was built in 1985.

Belpaire firebox

Smokebox saddle

Double "sandwich" frames

RECORD-BREAKER

A maximum speed of 102 mph (163 kph) was recorded by *City of Truro* on a GWR track from Plymouth to London in May 1904. It is widely believed to be the first time that a steam locomotive traveled at more than 100 mph (160 kph).

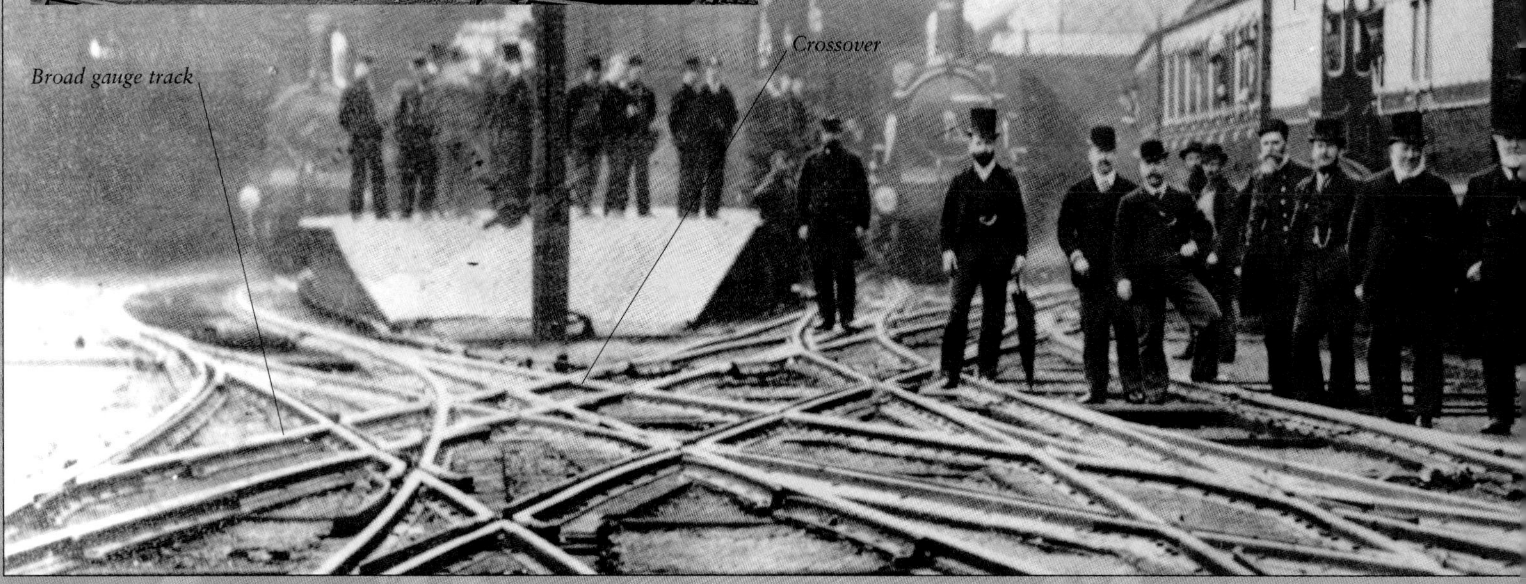

Guard's windshield

Guard's van

Clerestory roof

Crossover

Broad gauge track

FAMOUS CASTLES

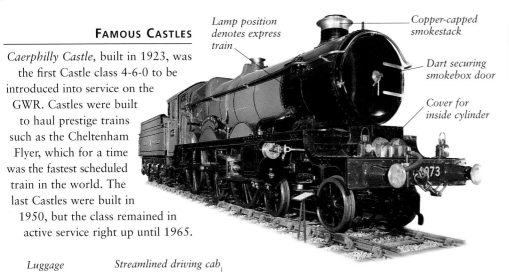

Lamp position denotes express train

Copper-capped smokestack

Dart securing smokebox door

Cover for inside cylinder

Caerphilly Castle, built in 1923, was the first Castle class 4-6-0 to be introduced into service on the GWR. Castles were built to haul prestige trains such as the Cheltenham Flyer, which for a time was the fastest scheduled train in the world. The last Castles were built in 1950, but the class remained in active service right up until 1965.

THE GREAT WESTERN RAILWAY

ENGLAND
WALES

Milford Haven
Swansea
Cardiff
Bristol
Hereford
LONDON Paddington
Reading
Bristol Channel
Plymouth
Penzance
English Channel

The first GWR train ran between London and Maidenhead in 1838. By 1841, track had been laid to Bristol, and by March 1867 GWR's broad-gauge track connected London with Plymouth, Penzance, and Swansea. This map shows only these key routes. The entire GWR network, much of which used standard-gauge track, extended up into north Wales and the West Midlands.

STREAMLINED PRACTICALITY

Luggage compartment

Streamlined driving cab

Engine housing

"Chocolate-and-cream" livery unique to GWR

GWR was the first British railroad to make extensive use of diesel-powered railcars. The first of them entered service in 1934. The preserved railcar shown here, *No. W22*, was built in 1940 and has a maximum speed of 40 mph (64 kph).

FAREWELL TO BROAD GAUGE

On May 20, 1892, a crowd gathered to witness the last westbound departure of a GWR broad-gauge train from London Paddington. The 10:15 express was headed by *Bulkeley*, a Rover class 4-2-2. Within three days, the entire GWR network had been converted to standard gauge.

Single driving wheel

Leaf spring

Safety valve bonnet

Regulator rod

Cylinder cover

1800-1840 NORTH AMERICA

DURING THE EARLY 1800s, North America lacked both the facilities and the expertise to develop its own locomotives. Consequently, the first engines to run in the United States were British-built. The majority of British designs did not suit the lightly laid North American tracks, however, as they were far too heavy. This prompted US railroad visionaries, such as Peter Cooper and Isaac Dripps, to experiment with novel locomotive designs in the 1830s. By 1840, North American steam locomotives were significantly different from the British originals. The alterations made had a lasting effect on the design of US-built locomotives.

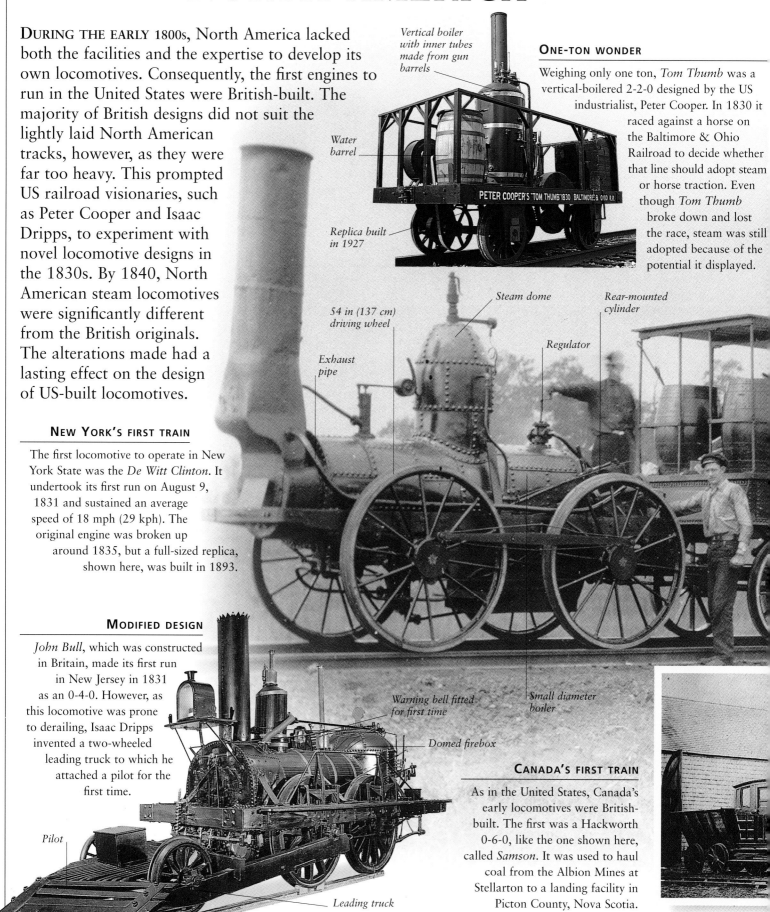

Vertical boiler with inner tubes made from gun barrels

Water barrel

Replica built in 1927

ONE-TON WONDER

Weighing only one ton, *Tom Thumb* was a vertical-boilered 2-2-0 designed by the US industrialist, Peter Cooper. In 1830 it raced against a horse on the Baltimore & Ohio Railroad to decide whether that line should adopt steam or horse traction. Even though *Tom Thumb* broke down and lost the race, steam was still adopted because of the potential it displayed.

Steam dome

Rear-mounted cylinder

54 in (137 cm) driving wheel

Regulator

Exhaust pipe

NEW YORK'S FIRST TRAIN

The first locomotive to operate in New York State was the *De Witt Clinton*. It undertook its first run on August 9, 1831 and sustained an average speed of 18 mph (29 kph). The original engine was broken up around 1835, but a full-sized replica, shown here, was built in 1893.

MODIFIED DESIGN

John Bull, which was constructed in Britain, made its first run in New Jersey in 1831 as an 0-4-0. However, as this locomotive was prone to derailing, Isaac Dripps invented a two-wheeled leading truck to which he attached a pilot for the first time.

Warning bell fitted for first time

Small diameter boiler

Domed firebox

Pilot

Leading truck

CANADA'S FIRST TRAIN

As in the United States, Canada's early locomotives were British-built. The first was a Hackworth 0-6-0, like the one shown here, called *Samson*. It was used to haul coal from the Albion Mines at Stellarton to a landing facility in Picton County, Nova Scotia.

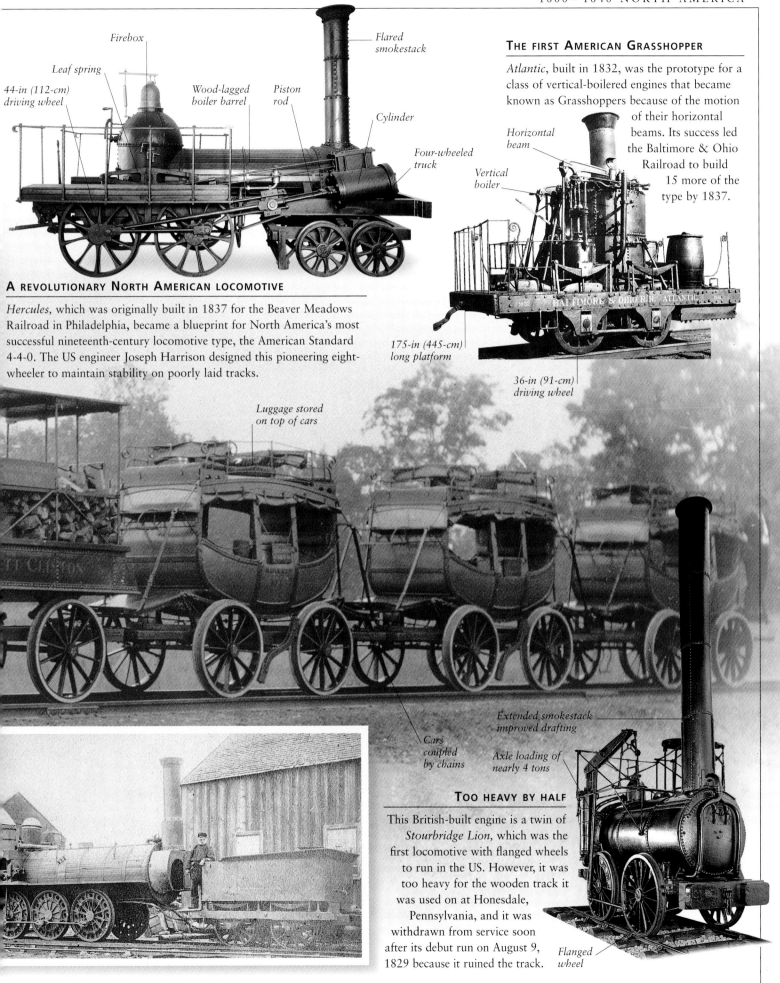

Firebox

Leaf spring

44-in (112-cm)
driving wheel

Wood-lagged
boiler barrel

Piston
rod

Flared
smokestack

Cylinder

Four-wheeled
truck

A REVOLUTIONARY NORTH AMERICAN LOCOMOTIVE

Hercules, which was originally built in 1837 for the Beaver Meadows
Railroad in Philadelphia, became a blueprint for North America's most
successful nineteenth-century locomotive type, the American Standard
4-4-0. The US engineer Joseph Harrison designed this pioneering eight-
wheeler to maintain stability on poorly laid tracks.

THE FIRST AMERICAN GRASSHOPPER

Atlantic, built in 1832, was the prototype for a
class of vertical-boilered engines that became
known as Grasshoppers because of the motion
of their horizontal
beams. Its success led
the Baltimore & Ohio
Railroad to build
15 more of the
type by 1837.

Horizontal
beam

Vertical
boiler

175-in (445-cm)
long platform

36-in (91-cm)
driving wheel

Luggage stored
on top of cars

Cars
coupled
by chains

Extended smokestack
improved drafting

Axle loading of
nearly 4 tons

TOO HEAVY BY HALF

This British-built engine is a twin of
Stourbridge Lion, which was the
first locomotive with flanged wheels
to run in the US. However, it was
too heavy for the wooden track it
was used on at Honesdale,
Pennsylvania, and it was
withdrawn from service soon
after its debut run on August 9,
1829 because it ruined the track.

Flanged
wheel

1840-1870
NORTH AMERICA COMES TO THE FORE

U NTIL 1840, the vast majority of locomotives were designed and built in Britain, then imported by the user country. This pattern began to change in the 1840s, when both France and Germany developed their own locomotive-building facilities. Initially, the majority of the designs were British-inspired, but this predominance became less significant from the 1850s onward. It was in the US, however, where the greatest changes occurred, because British designs had proved too heavy for North American railroads. This inspired US engineers to develop a range of locomotives that were lighter, more resilient, and more flexible, qualities that were embodied in the the classic American 4-4-0. This not only became the standard general-purpose locomotive in the US and Canada, but it was also exported to Europe. The expansion of the US railroad network, which culminated in the completion of the world's first transcontinental railway link in 1869, prompted the development of larger and more powerful engines.

IN 1847, *LIMATT* BECAME THE FIRST
LOCOMOTIVE TO RUN IN SWITZERLAND

1840–1870 EUROPE

COUNTRIES IN CONTINENTAL EUROPE swiftly recognized the significance of the railroads and by the mid-1840s trains were operating throughout most of the continent. Initially, most of the engines were imported from Britain and followed tried and tested designs. In the 1840s, most passenger engines had a single driving axle, while freight engines normally had six-coupled wheels. By the 1850s, heavier trains were running and engines with two driven coupled-axles were either imported from the US, or built locally.

Bulb-shaped smokestack

Boiler band

SIX-WHEELED STANDARD

In Britain, the 2-cylinder 0-6-0 was the preeminent freight engine until the turn of the century. *No.25 Derwent*, built in 1845 to a Timothy Hackworth design, served for a long time on the Stockton & Darlington Railway in northeast England. It was secured for preservation in 1898.

GERMAN MIGHT

Wesel, this imposing outside-cylinder 2-4-0, was built in Germany by Borsig of Berlin in 1851, for use on the Cologne to Minden railroad. Borsig, one of Germany's first locomotive builders, delivered their first engine in 1841. Over the next decade they built 66 more engines.

A FRENCH VETERAN

No.33 St. Pierre was built for the Paris-Rouen Railway in 1844 and is the oldest surviving locomotive built in France. This 2-2-2 was designed by the English engineer William Buddicom, who manufactured most of his engines for railroads in continental Europe.

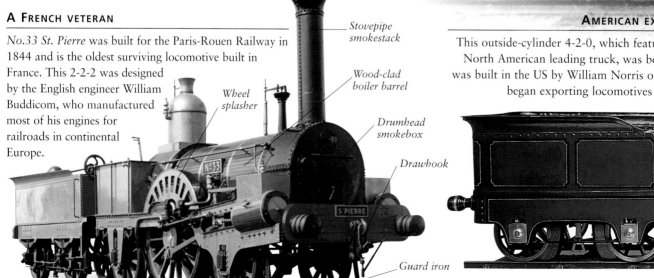

Stovepipe smokestack

Wheel splasher

Wood-clad boiler barrel

Drumhead smokebox

Drawhook

Guard iron

AMERICAN EXPORT IN AUSTRIA

This outside-cylinder 4-2-0, which features a characteristic North American leading truck, was bought by Austria. It was built in the US by William Norris of Philadelphia, who began exporting locomotives to Europe in 1837.

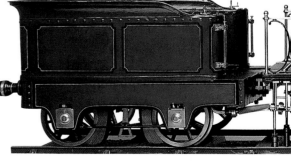

NATIONAL PRIDE

Dressed in their finest clothes, Austrian railroad workers display conspicuous pride in the latest addition to their locomotive fleet. This 2-4-0 steam engine named *Brugg*, constructed in 1856 by the German firm of Maffei in Munich, was used in the service of the Austro-Hungarian Empire.

Single pair of driving wheels

SPAIN'S FIRST MAINLINE ENGINE

Spain's first railroad opened between Barcelona and Mataro in 1848, but it was not until the 1850s that the first mainlines were laid there. At this time, the British engine builders Beyer Peacock supplied Spain with this 2-2-2 locomotive, which was built to a design first patented by Robert Stephenson in the 1830s.

Steam dome

Safety valve bonnet

Handrail

Running board

Open footplate

Numberplate on smokestack

Saddletank

Wheel spring

C.P.M.D. 2049

PORTUGUESE SADDLETANK

This 2-2-2 was constructed in England in 1862 by Beyer Peacock for use on Portugal's South Eastern Railway. *No.02049*, which carries its water supply in a saddletank mounted on top of the boiler, stayed in service for over 70 years.

SWISS SHOWMANSHIP

Limatt, this long-boilered outside-cylinder 4-2-0, was built by Emil Kesslerin in Germany. It headed the first train on a railroad built between Zurich and Baden, which opened in August 1847. Its ornate livery is typical of the period, and shows the excitement that trains generated.

Spring balance pressure gauge

Tall smokestack improves draft for fire

Haycock firebox

Valve chests

AUSTRIA

Inclined cylinder

Conical smokestack

Firebox cladding

Wheel splasher

Cylinder

1840–1870 CRAMPTON

IN 1843, BRITISH-BORN ENGINEER Thomas Russell Crampton patented a "single-wheeler" engine that combined a low center of gravity with large driving wheels. This design allowed the engine to retain stability at high speed. The locomotive also housed a large boiler that generated ample steam. The first batch of three Cramptons was built in 1845 and the type became popular in France, Belgium, and Germany. A total of about 320 of these engines were built and some of them remained in service for 75 years, including the *No.80 Le Continent,* built for the Paris-Strasbourg Railway in 1852.

Hinged cap

Smokebox door

PARIS A STRASBOURG

SPECIFICATION	
Manufacturer	J.F. Cail & Co, Paris, France
Classification	Crampton 4-2-0
Date built	1852
Number built	320
Fuel	Coal
Top speed	90 mph (144 kph)
Length	43 ft (13.1 m)
Height	13 ft (4 m)
Total weight	47½ tons
Tractive effort	5045½ lb (2,288 kg)

TAKING THE CRAMPTON

The sight of a Crampton approaching became so familiar in France that the phrase *prendre le Crampton* became a colloquialism for catching a train.

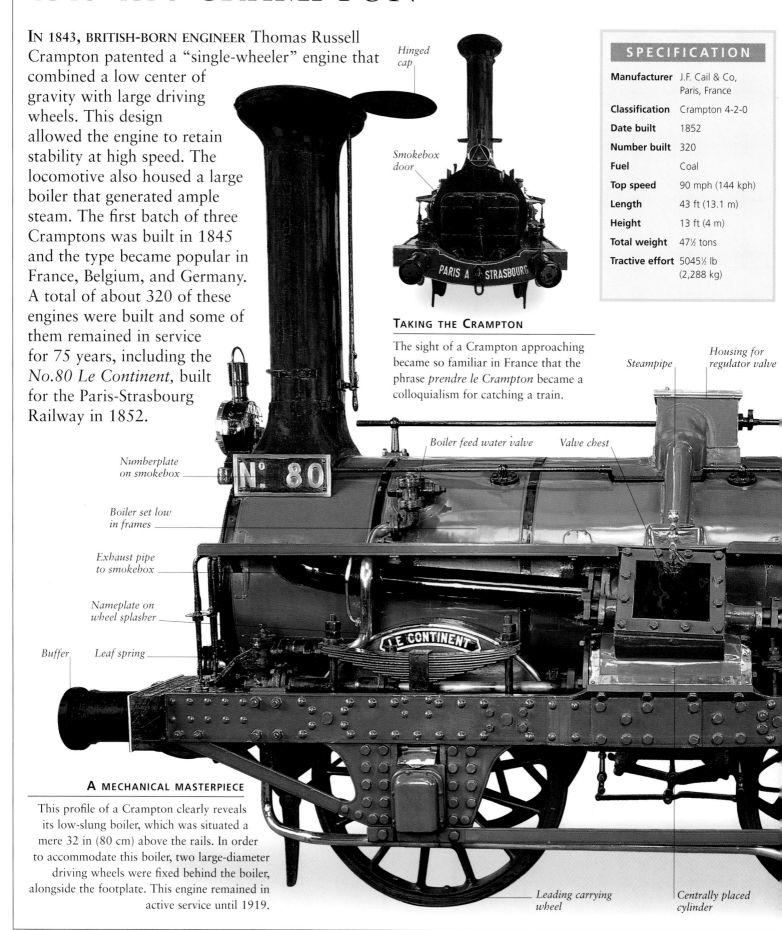

Steampipe

Housing for regulator valve

Boiler feed water valve

Valve chest

Numberplate on smokebox

No 80

Boiler set low in frames

Exhaust pipe to smokebox

Nameplate on wheel splasher

LE CONTINENT

Buffer   *Leaf spring*

A MECHANICAL MASTERPIECE

This profile of a Crampton clearly reveals its low-slung boiler, which was situated a mere 32 in (80 cm) above the rails. In order to accommodate this boiler, two large-diameter driving wheels were fixed behind the boiler, alongside the footplate. This engine remained in active service until 1919.

Leading carrying wheel

Centrally placed cylinder

Tender holds 7 tons of coal and 1,848 gallons (7,000 liters) of water

Stovepipe chimney

Capuchon

Oil-fired headlight

N°80

Bar frame

RECORD BREAKER

A Crampton's low adhesive weight meant that it was best-suited to hauling light trains at fast speeds. On June 20, 1890, a Crampton set a new world speed record of 90 mph (144 kph) at the head of a 157-ton train during trials on the Paris Lyon-Mediteranée railroad.

Curved bufferbeam

Boiler pressure gauge

Water-gauge glass

Regulator handle

Handrail

Reversing lever

Splasher enclosing driving wheel

Brake handle

Firehole door

Footplate for crew

SPARTAN CONDITIONS

Cramptons have an open footplate that provides no protection for its crew, apart from the enormous wheel splashers fitted to the driving wheels on either side. The locomotive controls are also minimal, but they include Thomas Crampton's patented regulator, which controls the passage of steam to the cylinders.

Safety valve bonnet

Spring control for safety valve

Maker's plate

Crank incorporating drive axle

Regulator rod

Connecting rod

Handbrake

Handrail

J.F. CAIL & Cᵉ
1852. PARIS. N° 189.
SYSᵐᵉ CRAMPTON.

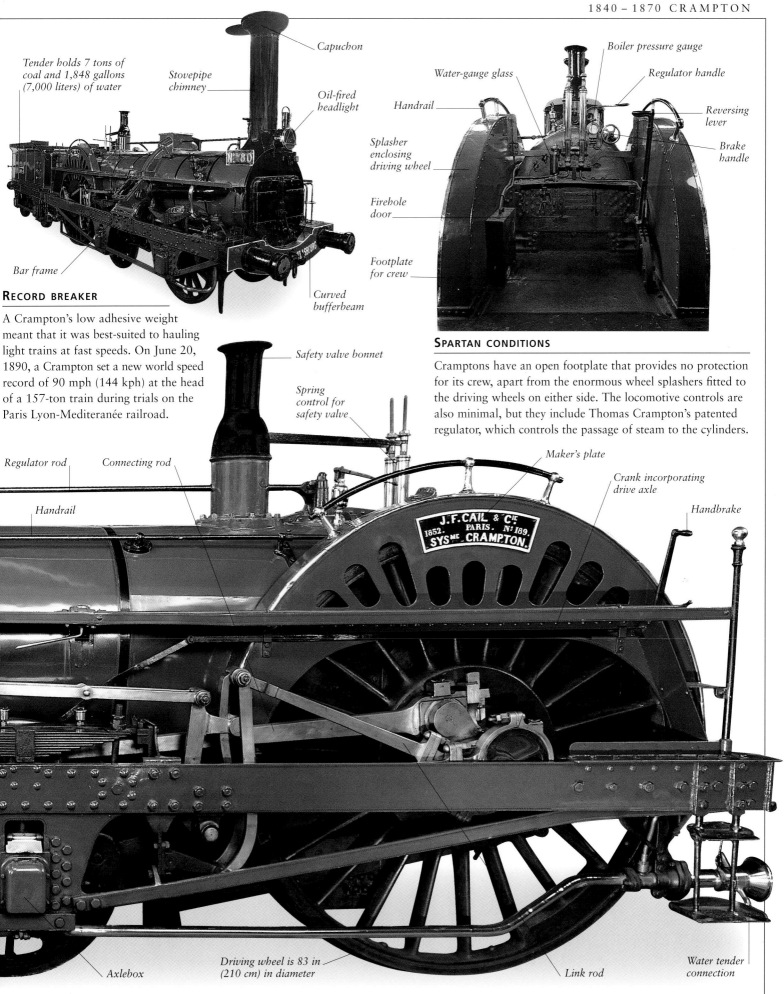

Axlebox

Driving wheel is 83 in (210 cm) in diameter

Link rod

Water tender connection

1840–1870 NORTH AMERICA

By 1840, TRAINS HAD BECOME a popular form of transportation in North America. The next 30 years saw the railroads expand rapidly westward, culminating in the completion of a transcontinental railroad in 1869. It also saw the production of locomotives treble, and by 1860, 11 companies in the eastern US were engaged in their construction. Throughout this time the 4-4-0 type was the leading general-purpose engine but, as the haulage demands on the railroads grew, a range of bigger and more powerful locomotive types began to evolve.

Fuel bunker

Steam whistle

Single driving axle

THE PURSUIT OF POWER

Alexander Mitchell designed this, the first 2-8-0, to pull 300-ton coal trains up the 1-in-40 grade of the Lehigh Valley in Pennsylvania. Built by the Baldwin company in 1866, *Consolidation* became the first of tens of thousands of 2-8-0s to be deployed around the world.

A LIGHTWEIGHT SPRINTER

Pioneer was built in 1851 for the the Cumberland Valley Railroad in Pennsylvania. Despite its fragile appearance, this locomotive remained in full-time service until 1880 and covered 255,673 miles (409,077 km). It also attained a remarkably fast top speed of 70 mph (112 kph).

Flared coalguard

Truck tender

Fireman's platform

Firebox

Driving cab mounted above boiler

RIDING HIGH

To increase visibility, Ross Winans built an engine with the driving cab mounted on top of the boiler for the Baltimore & Ohio Railroad in 1848. The type became known as Camels. Around 120 were built up to 1875 and some lasted 40 years.

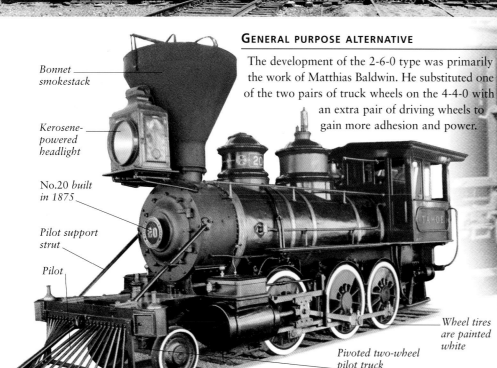

GENERAL PURPOSE ALTERNATIVE

The development of the 2-6-0 type was primarily the work of Matthias Baldwin. He substituted one of the two pairs of truck wheels on the 4-4-0 with an extra pair of driving wheels to gain more adhesion and power.

Bonnet smokestack

Kerosene-powered headlight

No.20 *built in 1875*

Pilot support strut

Pilot

Pivoted two-wheel pilot truck

Wheel tires are painted white

Pioneer *was a wood burner*

Tender rides on two four-wheel trucks

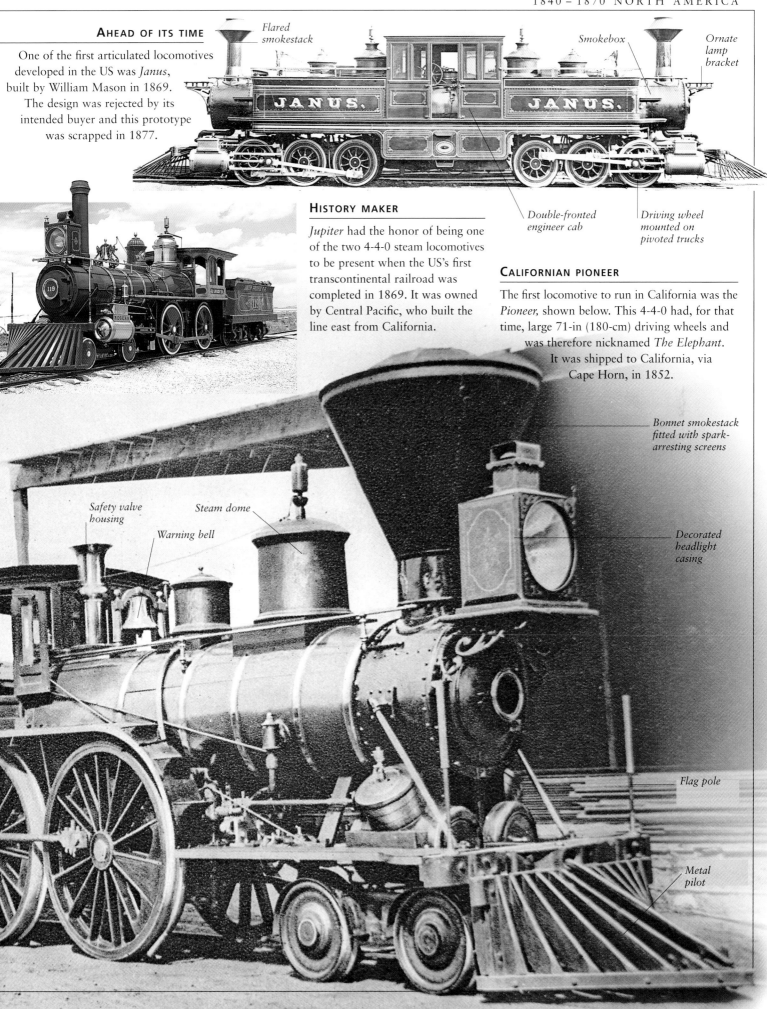

AHEAD OF ITS TIME

One of the first articulated locomotives developed in the US was *Janus*, built by William Mason in 1869. The design was rejected by its intended buyer and this prototype was scrapped in 1877.

Flared smokestack

Smokebox

Ornate lamp bracket

Double-fronted engineer cab

Driving wheel mounted on pivoted trucks

HISTORY MAKER

Jupiter had the honor of being one of the two 4-4-0 steam locomotives to be present when the US's first transcontinental railroad was completed in 1869. It was owned by Central Pacific, who built the line east from California.

CALIFORNIAN PIONEER

The first locomotive to run in California was the *Pioneer*, shown below. This 4-4-0 had, for that time, large 71-in (180-cm) driving wheels and was therefore nicknamed *The Elephant*. It was shipped to California, via Cape Horn, in 1852.

Bonnet smokestack fitted with spark-arresting screens

Safety valve housing

Steam dome

Warning bell

Decorated headlight casing

Flag pole

Metal pilot

1840–1870 THATCHER PERKINS

NO.117 *THATCHER PERKINS*, which was built in 1863 by the Baltimore and Ohio Railroad, was one of around 16,500 4-6-0s built in the US before 1910. The world's first 4-6-0, also known as a "Ten-Wheeler," was constructed in 1847 for the Philadelphia & Reading Railroad and was primarily used for freight duties. By 1870, the 4-6-0 was replacing the less powerful 4-4-0 as North America's leading general-purpose locomotive type. The 4-6-0's extra set of driving wheels improved adhesion, and its longer chassis was able to support a larger firebox, allowing more power output. This enabled 4-6-0 locomotives to haul heavier loads at higher speeds than 4-4-0s.

SPECIFICATION	
Manufacturer	Baltimore & Ohio Railroad Mount Clare Workshops
Classification	B class 4-6-0
Date built	1863
Number built	11
Fuel	Wood
Top speed	60 mph (96 kph)
Length	53 ft (16 m)
Height	14 ft (4.3 m)
Total weight	45.tons
Tractive effort	10,350 lb (4,699 kg)

Headlight lit by kerosene

Number plate

Pilot

Bonnet smokestack has a spark-arresting screen

Sand box

Boiler is made of Russian iron plates covered by insulation under external cladding

Locomotive number

Handrail

THE AMERICAN APPROACH

From the front, *Thatcher Perkins'* most distinctive features are its bulbous bonnet smokestack, the ornate kerosene headlight, and a grilled pilot (or cowcatcher). All these are distinguishing features of a classic post-1850 US-built wood-burning steam locomotive.

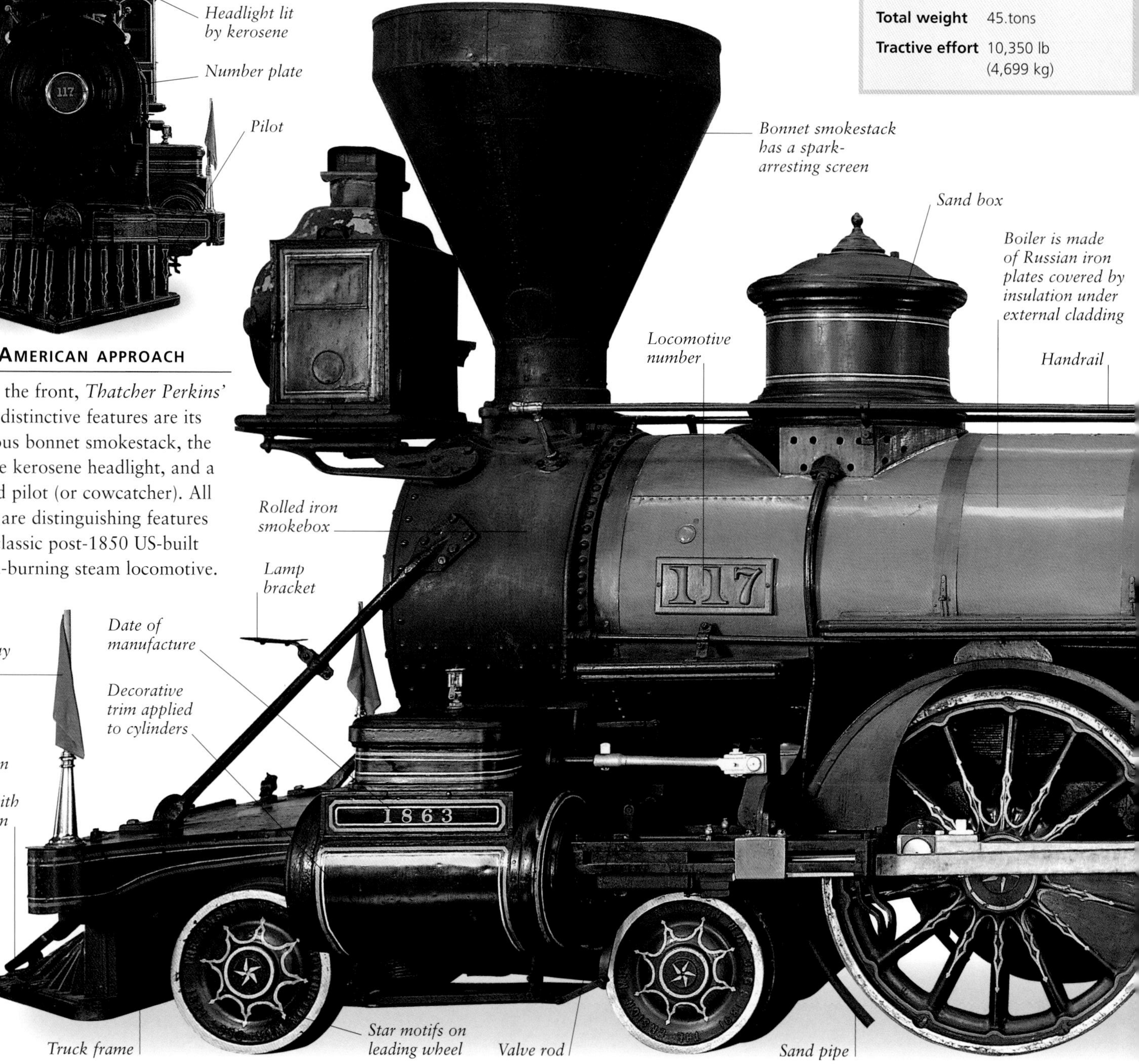

Rolled iron smokebox

Lamp bracket

Display flag

Date of manufacture

Decorative trim applied to cylinders

Wooden slated pilot with iron rim

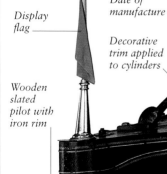

Truck frame

Star motifs on leading wheel

Valve rod

Sand pipe

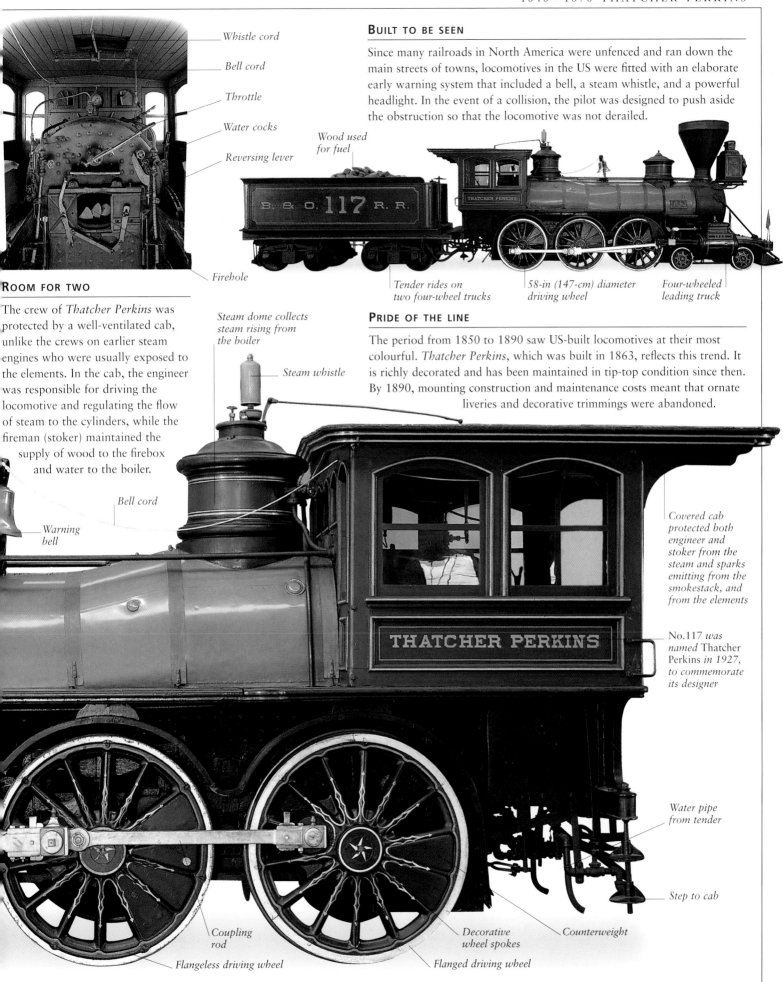

Whistle cord

Bell cord

Throttle

Water cocks

Reversing lever

Firehole

BUILT TO BE SEEN

Since many railroads in North America were unfenced and ran down the main streets of towns, locomotives in the US were fitted with an elaborate early warning system that included a bell, a steam whistle, and a powerful headlight. In the event of a collision, the pilot was designed to push aside the obstruction so that the locomotive was not derailed.

Wood used for fuel

B. & O. 117 R. R.

Tender rides on two four-wheel trucks

58-in (147-cm) diameter driving wheel

Four-wheeled leading truck

ROOM FOR TWO

The crew of *Thatcher Perkins* was protected by a well-ventilated cab, unlike the crews on earlier steam engines who were usually exposed to the elements. In the cab, the engineer was responsible for driving the locomotive and regulating the flow of steam to the cylinders, while the fireman (stoker) maintained the supply of wood to the firebox and water to the boiler.

Steam dome collects steam rising from the boiler

Steam whistle

Bell cord

Warning bell

PRIDE OF THE LINE

The period from 1850 to 1890 saw US-built locomotives at their most colourful. *Thatcher Perkins*, which was built in 1863, reflects this trend. It is richly decorated and has been maintained in tip-top condition since then. By 1890, mounting construction and maintenance costs meant that ornate liveries and decorative trimmings were abandoned.

Covered cab protected both engineer and stoker from the steam and sparks emitting from the smokestack, and from the elements

THATCHER PERKINS

No.117 *was named* Thatcher Perkins *in 1927, to commemorate its designer*

Water pipe from tender

Step to cab

Coupling rod

Flangeless driving wheel

Decorative wheel spokes

Flanged driving wheel

Counterweight

1840-1870 UNION PACIFIC

"DONE, DONE, DONE," was the telegraph message sent from Promontory Point, Utah, on May 10, 1869, alerting the United States that the world's first transcontinental railroad was complete. Union Pacific was organized in July 1862, during the Civil War, to construct the line westward from Omaha, Nebraska, to link up with a line being constructed eastward by Central Pacific. As operators, Union Pacific went on to play a vital role in transporting people across the western United States until the 1960s. Today, Union Pacific runs more than 125 transcontinental freight trains every day, some of which can exceed 1 mile (1.5 km) in length.

HISTORY IN THE MAKING

Between November 1865 and May 1869, a workforce of 12,000 laborers laid 1,086 miles (1,738 km) of track across Nebraska, Wyoming, and Utah in spite of freezing winters, scorching summers, and attacks by Native Americans.

Wood stored in tender   *Clerestory roof*

945

FRONTIER TRAIN

With a wood-burning 4-4-0 at its head, this Union Pacific passenger train is a classic example of the type that served the new frontier communities in the western US from 1869 up to the 1890s. The wooden cars had clerestory roofs to aid ventilation.

KINGS OF THE RAILROAD

An increase in the volume of freight traffic in the western United States after 1935 prompted Union Pacific to adopt a fleet of Challengers in 1936 and of Big Boys in 1941. Seen below double-heading a long freight train up the 1-in-66 grade of Sherman Hill in Wyoming is Challenger *No.3999* followed by Big Boy *No.4011*.

Tender holds 25½ tons of coal

UP Big Boy

Articulated chassis

68 in (173 cm) driving wheel

UP Challenger No.3999

UNION PACIFIC'S ORIGINAL ROUTE

The map above shows the route of the first railroad to be built between Chicago and San Francisco, which was completed in May 1869. Track already connected Omaha, Nebraska, to Chicago when work began in 1865. The Union Pacific laid the track from Omaha to Promontory Point in Utah. Central Pacific built the western section of line from Sacramento, California to Promontory Point.

HIGH-SPEED PIONEER

In 1932, Union Pacific tested the M-10000, an early streamlined oil-driven train. It reached a top speed of 120 mph (192 kph) and later went into service as the *City of Salina*.

Smoke deflector

STEAM SURVIVOR

Regular steam operation on the Union Pacific ended in 1958, but a few of its steam engines survived. The FEF-2 class 4-8-4 heading this commemorative train was one of them. It was the last passenger steam engine to be built for Union Pacific, in 1944.

DIESEL SUPERPOWER

In 1969, Union Pacific celebrated a century of operations by introducing the Centennial. These 6,600-hp freight units were the world's most powerful and, at 98 ft (30 m), also the longest single-unit diesel locomotives. The Centennial has a top speed of 71 mph (114 kph).

Fan to cool 6,600-hp engine

Eight-axle D-D trucks

Air horn

1870-1900
TRAINS DIVERSIFY AND LINK THE WORLD

DURING THE FINAL DECADES OF the nineteenth century, trains became the world's principal form of land transportation, as railroad networks were established on every inhabited continent. To cope with the differing track conditions and terrain, a new range of locomotives were developed in this period. The major advances, however, were prompted by the demand for faster, safer, and more luxurious passenger trains and ever more powerful freight engines. The introduction of better braking systems in the US allowed manufacturers to build larger locomotives specifically for passenger or freight use, which led to the phasing out of general-purpose engines such as the 4-4-0. European engineers sought to increase power through greater efficiency. Two inventions were crucial in this respect: superheating and compounding. This period also saw a rapid development in the design of specialized mountain trains capable of ascending steep gradients, and of urban trains, which were the first to successfully employ electric traction.

IN 1895, THIS F CLASS 0-6-0 BECAME THE
FIRST LOCOMOTIVE TO BE BUILT IN INDIA

1870–1900 EUROPE

THE RAPID GROWTH of railroads throughout Europe presented a challenge to engineers and designers to meet the demand for faster passenger services and more powerful freight engines. Small, general-purpose engines were no longer adequate for either purpose. During this period, four-coupled locomotives, such as 4-4-0s, 2-4-2s, and 4-4-2s, were the passenger express engines of choice and the 0-6-0 became the dominant freight type. In France, however, the articulated freight engine was developed, while in Germany an increase in power was generated by superheating and compounding the steam.

STEAMING UP ON THE CÔTE D'AZUR

In the late 1870s at Cannes, on France's Côte d'Azur, a 121 class 2-cylinder 2-4-2 prepares to depart for Toulon. In all, 400 of these state-of-the-art 2-4-2s were built after 1876, featuring the latest innovations, such as air-braking.

FRENCH ARTICULATION

This 0-6-0+0-6-0, seen on the Vivarias railroad at Tournon in France, uses the articulated principle patented in 1884 by the French engineer Anatole Mallet. In Mallet's design, two sets of cylinders drive separate trucks, or engine units, that are directly linked by an articulated joint or hinge.

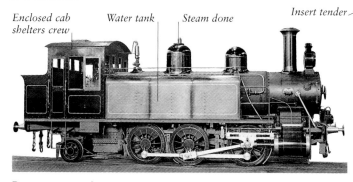

Enclosed cab shelters crew *Water tank* *Steam done* *Insert tender*

RUSSIA BUYS AMERICAN

By the 1860s, the growth of railroads in Russia had outstripped the capacity of its engine builders. Large numbers of locomotives were imported from the US, including this 0-6-2 tank engine, which was built at Baldwin's workshops in Philadelphia in 1898. The enclosed cab is typically Russian.

A FASHIONABLE ITALIAN

This 1899 4-4-0, *Giovanna d'Arco* (Joan of Arc), was built by Cesare Frescot in Turin for passenger express duty on Italy's Mediterraneo Railway. It was capable of hauling 160-ton trains at an average speed of 50 mph (80 kph).

A LONG STORY

This British 1001 class 0-6-0 was built for the North Eastern Railway in 1874. The engine was the final development of Robert Stephenson's "long boiler" principle, which was designed to optimize the heat transference of gases in the boiler.

Steam dome *Boiler barrel is 14 ft (4.25 m) long* *Six-wheel tender* *Six-wheeled tender*

Toolbox

Wheel splasher

Scallop-edged buffer beam *Sandbox*

AUSTRIAN INNOVATION

This 2-8-0, which remained in working order until 1974, was designed by one of Europe's best engineers, Karl Gölsdorf of Austria. The outstanding performance of the 2-8-0 type in the US led him to design and build more than 900 similar engines for Austrian State Railways.

Cap covers smokestack when engine is out of use

Leading steam dome

Smokebox door handle

Brake compressor

Cab spectacle glass

Air-brake reservoir

56 3297

Valve chest

Coupling hook

BRIGHTON'S BELLE

Built in 1882, *Gladstone* is the only surviving B1 0-4-2 to be designed by Britain's William Stroudley. All of his engines were renowned for their elegance, but the B1 class was also fast. It ran the 50-mile (80-km) route between London and Brighton in one hour.

Piston tail rod

Whistle

Brake pump

Royal train insignia

Capuchon (or lip) to stack

Cast-iron smokebox

214

GLADSTONE

1870-1900 NORTH AMERICA

TOTAL TRACK LENGTH in the US increased from 53,000 miles (85,000 km) in 1870 up to 222,000 miles (355,000 km) in 1906. This expansion coincided with numerous advances in locomotive technology. The most marked of these stemmed from coal replacing wood as the principal fuel; because coal generates more steam, more powerful engines could be developed. This led to a threefold increase in the average size of locomotives in the US.

Main crank

Main rod

Cylinder steam chest

Leading truck wheel

ATLANTIC COAST LINE.

MASON'S INNOVATIVE TANK ENGINE

William Mason's 0-6-6 Mason Bogie tank engine of 1874 was one of his most innovative designs. The use of driving wheels attached to a pivoting truck helped it to negotiate sharp curves.

A NEW BREED OF PASSENGER LOCOMOTIVE

No.153 was one of a batch of 4-4-2s built by Baldwin between 1894 and 1895 for the Atlantic Coast Line, and thereafter the type became known as Atlantics. The first 4-4-2 was built in 1888 and for the next ten years they were the most popular express passenger locomotive in the US.

Logging wagon

SUBURBAN SOLUTION

Bonnet smokestack

Smaller locomotives, such as this Illinois Central 2-4-4 tank built in the 1880s, were designed for use on the tight curves of Chicago's urban lines. Since it only made short runs, it did not need a large tender to carry water and fuel.

Two-wheel leading truck

Bunker

Four-wheel rear truck

GEARED FOR ROUGH TERRAIN

No.91 was one of around 600 geared Heisler engines, built by the Heisler Locomotive Works of Erie, Pennsylvania between 1891 and 1941. Heisler engines remained in service on the steeply graded and twisting logging lines of North America up until 1955.

A CLAIM TO FAME

The New York Central & Hudson River Railroad built 4-4-0 No.999 to haul its *Empire State Express*. Running on large 86-in (218-cm) diameter driving wheels, No.999 was designed for speed. In May 1893 it was claimed to have reached 112 mph (179 kph). This claim is now disputed.

Cylinder steam chest

Cylinder valve chest

Tapered boiler

Air-brake compressors

Exhaust pipe to smokebox

Running board

Gear shaft driven by cylinders

Swiveling four-wheel truck

Smokebox door

Passenger car

Spark arrestor

Steam dome

Handrail

Cylinder head

FIRST MADE FOR JAPAN

No. X45 was one of the 9,000 2-8-2s built in the US for domestic use from 1897 onward. These trucks were popularly known as Mikados because the first 2-8-2s were exported to Japan. Mikados went on to replace 2-8-0s as the standard freight type in the US.

AT HOME ON THE PRAIRIES

Introduced in 1885, the 2-6-2 type proved most popular with railroads in the midwestern states, earning it the nickname Prairie. This ex-Reading Railroad Prairie was used successfully for both freight and passenger duties.

1870–1900 EARLY URBAN TRAINS

CITIES THROUGHOUT WESTERN EUROPE and North America grew rapidly during the nineteenth century. As people began to live farther from their places of work, they demanded fast and reliable public transport. They also wanted mobility to enjoy all that cities had to offer. The most effective systems for conveying large numbers of people quickly and cheaply were overground and underground trains. However, the first inner-city trains, those in London, New York, and Chicago, were hauled by steam engines that produced unacceptable levels of pollution. It was not until electric traction was developed in the 1880s that the problem was finally solved.

Wooden coach body *Four-wheel truck*

EUROPE'S FIRST ELECTRIC UNDERGROUND

This eight-wheel car, which drew current from overhead electric power cables, was built in Germany by Ernst von Siemens' company. It was one of the original cars to run on an electrified underground railroad constructed in the Hungarian capital of Budapest. This railroad opened in 1896.

SPARKING A REVOLUTION

Compact electric cars like this one ran on the world's first public electrified railroad. The line, which was built by the electrical engineer Ernst von Siemens, opened in May 1881 at Lichterfelde, near Berlin, in Germany.

Rear boarding platform

RIDING HIGH

New York City's elevated railroad, the El, began operating along Ninth Avenue in 1867. Initially, trains were cable-hauled. Steam traction was introduced in 1871. Forney tank locomotives, like the one here, were the most widely used engines on the 280-mile (451-km) network, until electrification in 1902–03.

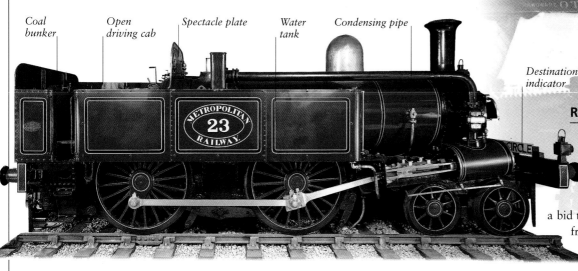

Coal bunker   *Open driving cab*   *Spectacle plate*   *Water tank*   *Condensing pipe*   *Destination indicator*

METROPOLITAN 23 RAILWAY

RECYCLING STEAM UNDER LONDON

This 4-4-0 condensing tank engine is a preserved example of the main type of passenger locomotive that ran on London's Metropolitan Railway between 1864 and 1870. In a bid to reduce pollution, exhaust steam from the cylinders was piped back into the side tanks where it condensed into water for reuse.

Car holds 35 passengers *Wooden coach body* *Entrance door*

Electric motor below car

Four-wheel chassis

RAILROAD IN THE SKY

Opened in 1901, the Wuppertal Schwebebahn in Germany is the most famous of the world's suspended railroads. This early scene shows how the cable-type cars were supported by an overhanging A-shaped steel frame while they were propelled along twin electrified tracks.

WIRED AND WOODEN

This four-wheel wooden-bodied car ran on the inaugural section of the Paris underground, known as Le Metro, which opened in 1900. The line ran northwest to southeast between Porte Maillot and Porte de Vincennes and still retains the title of Ligne 1 (Line One).

Wooden bodied car *Clerestory roof* *Track supported by steel girders* *Tank locomotive designed by Mathias Forney* *Short wheelbase could negotiate 64° curves* *Warning bell*

PRIDE OF CHICAGO

In 1893, this Forney 0-4-4 tank and passenger car posed for an official photograph at Oakley Boulevard on Chicago's newly opened Lake Street Elevated Railroad. Forney engines had a very tight turning circle, which enabled them to run efficiently on Chicago's looping overhead railroad.

1870–1900 CANADIAN PACIFIC

Streamlined smokestack

Cylinder is 22 in (56 cm) in diameter

THE FIRST TRANSCONTINENTAL RAILROAD in Canada was built after the governors of British Columbia demanded in 1871 the construction of a line linking their Pacific province to the Atlantic seaboard – a condition of joining the new Dominion of Canada. Canadian Pacific (CP) was formed in 1880 to do the work, but by 1885 it was facing bankruptcy with only half the line built. Fresh funds were granted after an uprising in western Canada and in 1886 a scheduled service ran the 2,920 miles (4,672 km) between Montreal and Port Moody in British Columbia. The line was extended to Vancouver in 1887. CP still operates freight trains and ran the passenger service until this was taken over by Via Rail in 1977.

DOUBLE CELEBRATION

No.374, the 4-4-0 engine that pulled Canada's first Ocean-to-Ocean train, is shown here on its arrival in Vancouver in British Columbia. The completion of this epic journey coincided with the Golden Jubilee of the coronation of Britain's Queen Victoria.

STRONG-ARMED CONSTRUCTORS

Workers are pictured here during the construction of the CP railroad. They are carrying crossties from a freight car that was hauled to the end of the line by a 4-4-0 engine named *The Countess of Dufferin*.

CONQUEROR OF THE ROCKIES

This semi-streamlined steam engine was one of the Canadian Pacific's 36 Selkirk 2-10-4s that were built between 1929 and 1938. Like the Selkirk shown below, they hauled 1,000-ton trains through the Rocky Mountains.

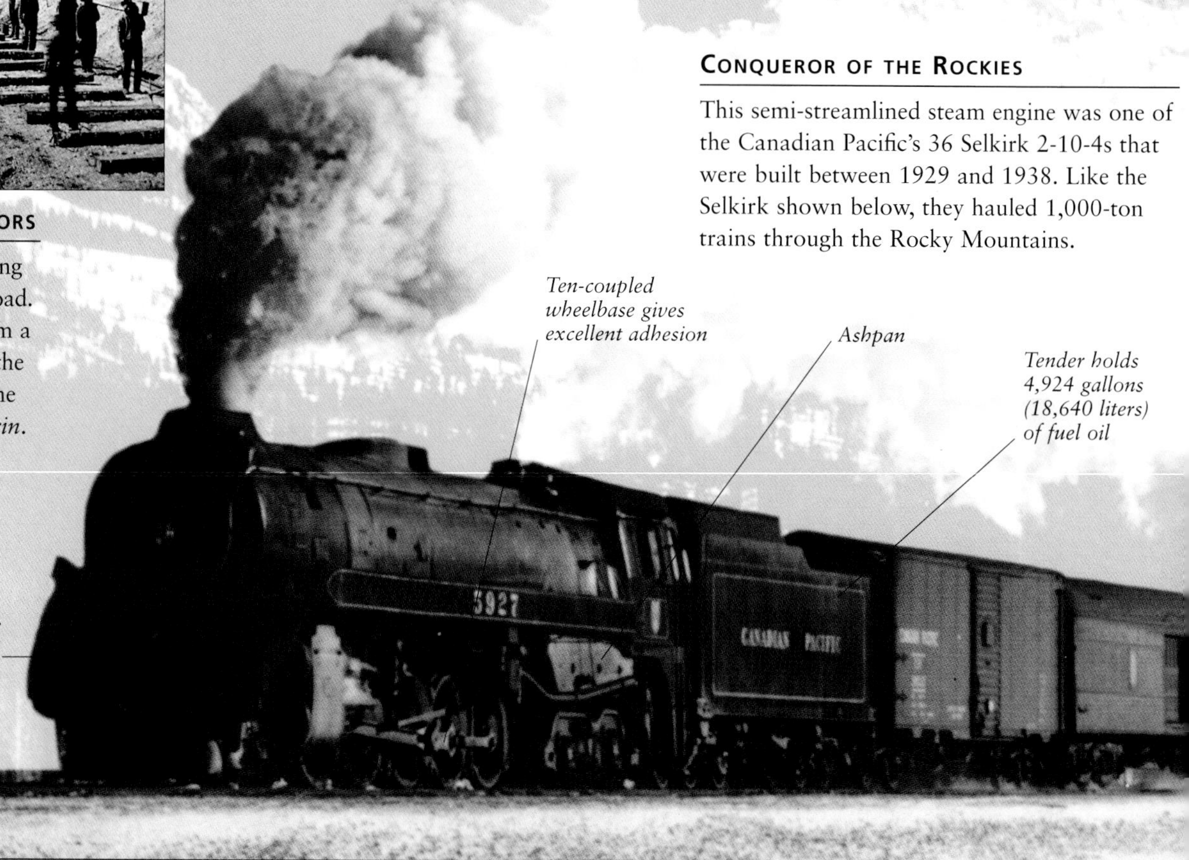

Ten-coupled wheelbase gives excellent adhesion

Ashpan

Tender holds 4,924 gallons (18,640 liters) of fuel oil

Locomotive with tender is 98 ft (30 m) in length

Oil-carrying tender

A ROYAL ENGINE

This 65 Class H1a-H1e 4-6-4 was one of the famous Royal Hudsons constructed between 1937 and 1940 for use on the Canadian Pacific railway. They acquired the title Royal Hudsons after one of the class pulled a train carrying Britain's King George VI and Queen Elizabeth in 1939.

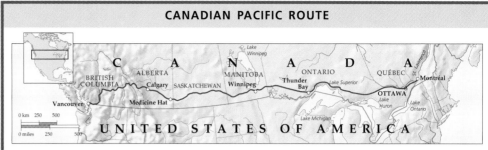

CANADIAN PACIFIC ROUTE

The governors of British Columbia allowed the constructors of the CP only ten years to build this railroad, which stretches right the way across Canada from Montreal in the east to Vancouver on the west coast. Despite early financial difficulties and the challenge of laying track across some of the most difficult terrain on Earth, the CP took just seven years to complete and was opened in 1887.

$200 MILLION REFURBISHMENT

Via Rail has just spent $200 million restoring its fleet of vintage stainless steel cars for use on the CP route. Seen here is the lower deck of a dome car with stairs leading up to the dome.

TRAIN WITH A VIEW

Two Canadian-built diesels, an FP7 and a GP9, stand at the head of a westbound Canadian train at Banff, Alberta. They are painted in the red livery of CP and the train they pull includes three vista-dome cars. Via Rail now run all passenger services on the CP route.

Dome car   *GP9 No.8521*   *FP7a No.4066*

Three lens indicator light

Ditch lights illuminate track

Radiator fan

Radiator air inlet

Fuel tank

READY FOR ACTION

These road-switcher diesels are now the principal type of freight engines on the CP route, conveying over 75 million tons each year. This pair was photographed in the 1970s; the front engine is painted in CP "Action Red."

Mail and baggage car

Clerestory roof

Saloon car

1870–1900 WORLD TRAINS

IN THE NINETEENTH CENTURY, railroads had a revolutionary impact on the settling of, and transportation of goods across, colonies and dependencies around the world. By 1860, trains were operating on every inhabited continent. The majority of the early railroads in Australasia, Asia, and South America were built by Britain and the United States, and these countries also supplied most locomotives and rolling stock. Germany and France became major exporters of trains to Africa, and by the 1890s, India was building a few of its own locomotives.

Canopy over engineer's cab

Wheel splasher

Drawhook

THE FIRST LOCOMOTIVE IN INDIA

Named *Fairy Queen*, this outside-cylinder 2-2-2 built by Kitson, Thompson & Hewitson in Britain began its career on the East Indian Railway in 1855. Restored in 1998, it is now the world's oldest working steam locomotive.

Cast-iron smokebox

Safety valve

Steam dome

Water tank

Brake rigging

SOUTH AFRICA'S FIRST LOCOMOTIVE

The first locomotive to work in South Africa was this 0-4-2 tank built by Hawthorn & Co. in Scotland, in 1859. It was used as a contractor's engine during the construction of the Cape Town to Wellington Railway, which opened in 1863.

Bonnet smokestack

Sandbox

Domed firebox

Nameplate

AN AMERICAN IN CHILE

This North American 4-4-0 was built by Norris Brothers of Philadelphia in 1850 and is the oldest surviving steam locomotive in South America. The US exported around 37,000 steam engines worldwide between 1830 and 1950.

EXPRESSLY FOR AUSTRALIA

Built in 1878 by Beyer Peacock of Manchester in England, *No.1210* was one of 68 4-4-0s that were the mainstay of express services on the New South Wales Government Railways of Australia for almost 20 years. Some remained on secondary services until 1957. *No.1210* hauled its first train into Canberra in 1914.

Headlight

Brake pump

Four-wheel leading truck

Belpaire firebox

PEACE TRAIN IN CHINA

The Chinese initially saw trains as an instrument of western imperialism and protested by hurling themselves in front of them. This 0-4-0 saddletank, built in 1886, was one of the first to be accepted. Aptly, it was named *Speedy Peace*.

Saddletank

Dübs & Co. diamond worksplate

APPEARANCES CAN BE DECEPTIVE

Although in every aspect of its design this is an American locomotive, this 4-4-0 that ran on the Mogiana Railway in Brazil was built by Sharp Stewart at its Atlas Works in Glasgow, Scotland. Delivered in 1892, it hauled trains of teak coaches along Brazil's Atlantic seaboard.

A TRAIN COMES TO TOWN

Photographed in the 1890s, this scene shows a passenger train arriving in the Algerian town of L'Arba. Both the small tank engine and the rolling stock were built in France. France opened the first railroad in Algeria in 1862.

Numberplate

Brake cylinder

Round-top firebox

Truck spring

Tender valance

JAPAN BUYS BRITISH

Japan's early railroads were almost entirely equipped with British-built locomotives and rolling stock. A British 4-4-0 similar to the preserved *No.5540* shown here inaugurated the first main line, between Tokyo and Yokohama, in 1872. After 1900, American designs were preferred.

1870-1900 F CLASS 0-6-0

THE MOST TYPICALLY BRITISH locomotive in this period was the inside-cylinder, six-wheeled freight engine. Almost every British mainline railroad had a quota of 0-6-0s and many thousands were employed overseas. In India, a total of 871 F class 0-6-0s worked on the country's 3-ft-3 in (meter-gauge) lines. The first of the class was built in Scotland in 1875. *No.F1-734*, shown here, has the honor of being the first locomotive to be entirely constructed in India. Completed in 1895, it was one of 23 F class 0-6-0s to be built by the Rajputana Malwa Railway. By 1958, *No.F1-734* and the majority of its class had been withdrawn from service. However, a few are still at work on industrial railroads in India.

SPECIFICATION

Manufacturer	Rajputana Malwa Railway, Ajmer, India
Classification	F class 0-6-0
Date built	1895
Number built	871
Fuel	Coal
Top speed	45 mph (72 kph)
Length	39 ft 11 in (12.2 m)
Height	10 ft 2 in (3 m)
Total weight	45 tons
Tractive effort	20,021 lb (9,080 kg)

Smokebox door

Sand box

Pilot

Silvered alloy smokestack cap

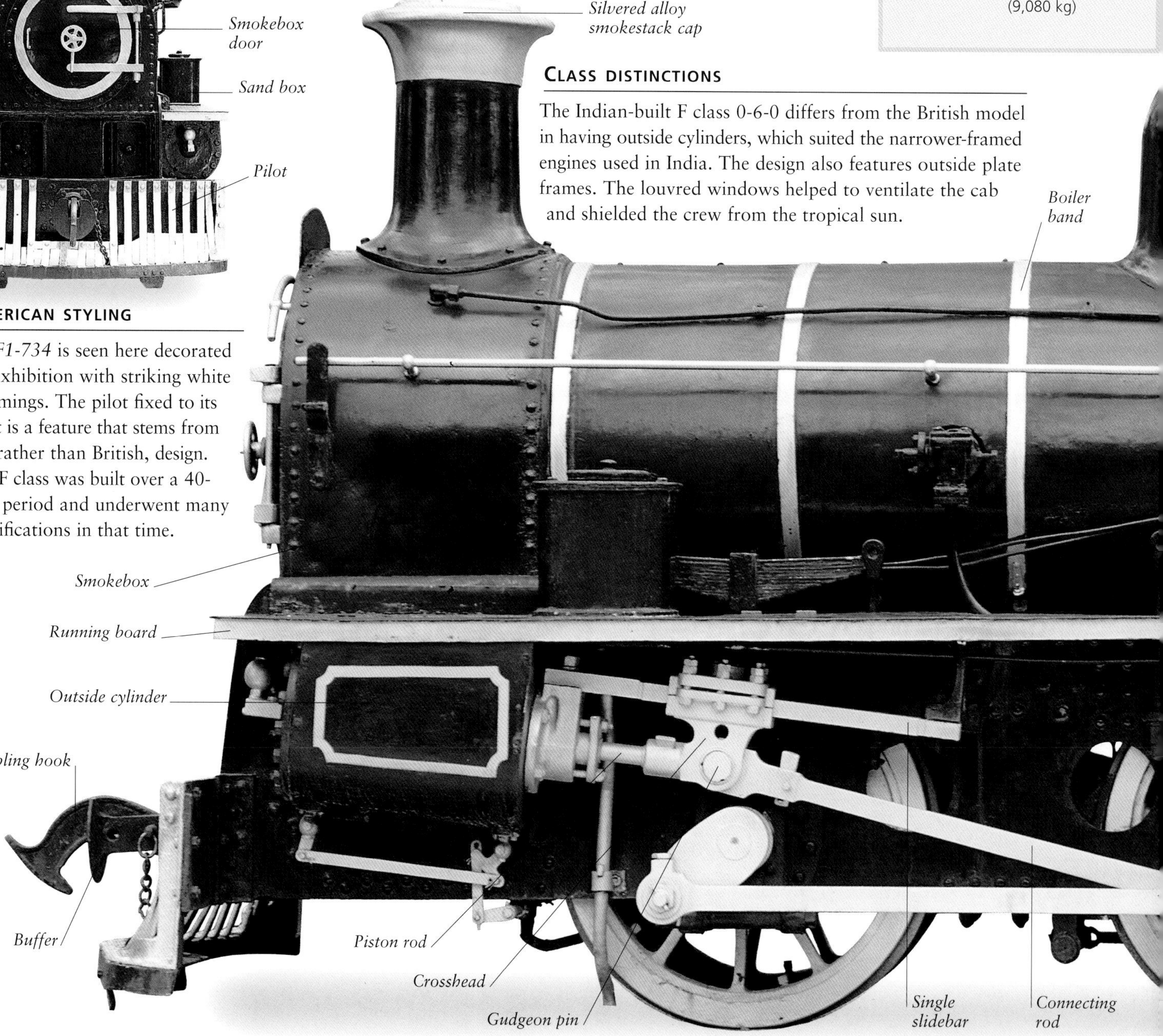

CLASS DISTINCTIONS

The Indian-built F class 0-6-0 differs from the British model in having outside cylinders, which suited the narrower-framed engines used in India. The design also features outside plate frames. The louvred windows helped to ventilate the cab and shielded the crew from the tropical sun.

Boiler band

AMERICAN STYLING

No.F1-734 is seen here decorated for exhibition with striking white trimmings. The pilot fixed to its front is a feature that stems from US, rather than British, design. The F class was built over a 40-year period and underwent many modifications in that time.

Smokebox

Running board

Outside cylinder

Coupling hook

Buffer

Piston rod

Crosshead

Gudgeon pin

Single slidebar

Connecting rod

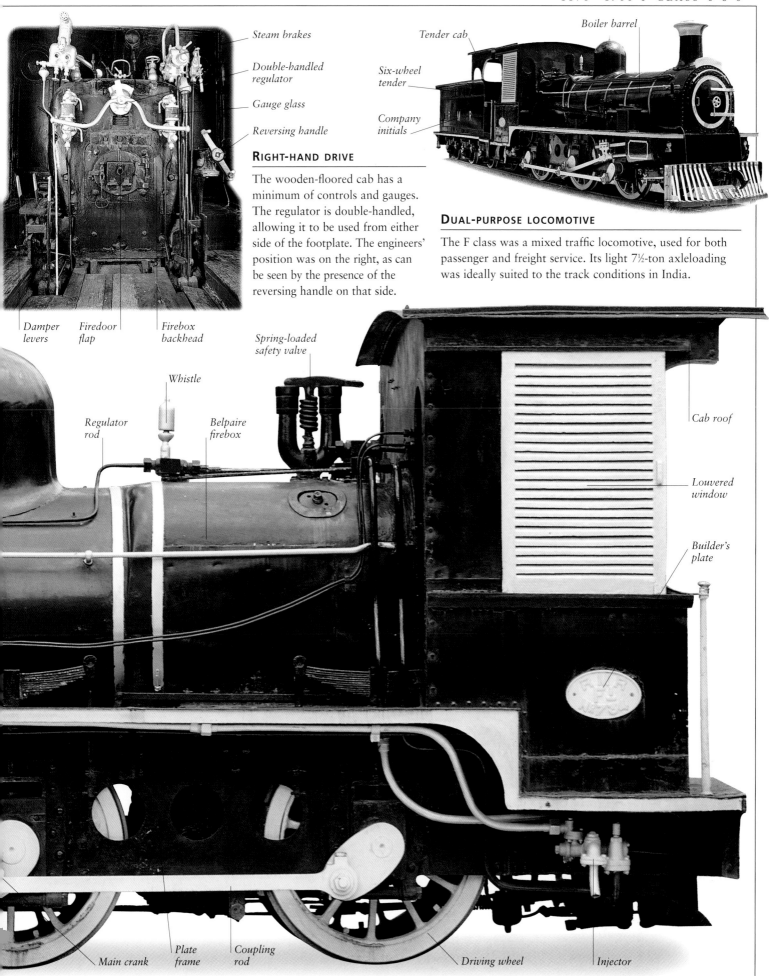

Steam brakes

Double-handled
regulator

Gauge glass

Reversing handle

Tender cab

Six-wheel
tender

Company
initials

Boiler barrel

RIGHT-HAND DRIVE

The wooden-floored cab has a
minimum of controls and gauges.
The regulator is double-handled,
allowing it to be used from either
side of the footplate. The engineers'
position was on the right, as can
be seen by the presence of the
reversing handle on that side.

DUAL-PURPOSE LOCOMOTIVE

The F class was a mixed traffic locomotive, used for both
passenger and freight service. Its light 7½-ton axleloading
was ideally suited to the track conditions in India.

Damper
levers

Firedoor
flap

Firebox
backhead

Spring-loaded
safety valve

Whistle

Regulator
rod

Belpaire
firebox

Cab roof

Louvered
window

Builder's
plate

Main crank

Plate
frame

Coupling
rod

Driving wheel

Injector

1870–1900 MOUNTAIN TRAINS

MANY EARLY MOUNTAIN RAILROADS, such as those in Switzerland, were built so that tourists could enjoy the breathtaking mountaintop views. Other railroads, such as those that crossed the Andes in South America, provided vital commercial and social links. Whatever their function, all mountain railroads had to solve the obstacle of providing their trains with sufficient adhesion to get up steeply graded slopes. The best solutions involved reducing the gradient the train had to climb, or using rack systems to increase the grip between locomotive and track.

UNDER THE VOLCANO

The only railroad to climb a volcano was built by the travel company Thomas Cook & Sons on Mount Vesuvius in Italy in 1880. This electrically powered funicular rail car has to cope with gradients steeper than 1-in-2.

Boiler pressure gauge

STILL STEAMED UP

This 0-6-2 rack engine, built by the Swiss Locomotive Works (SLM) at Winterthur in 1936, still operates on the Brienz-Rothorn Bahn (B-RB), which opened in 1892. B-RB, which is now Switzerland's only steam-worked mountain railroad, employs the rack system devised by Roman Abt.

Vertical boiler

Toothed rack wheel

Cylinder

CLIMBING THE HIMALAYAS

Pictured here, engine No.348 is seen on its approach to Ghoom curve on the Darjeeling railroad, which loops and zigzags its way up the Himalayas in India. No.348, which was built by Sharp Stewart of Scotland in 1888, is one of five 0-4-0 saddletank locomotives used on India's most celebrated mountain railroad.

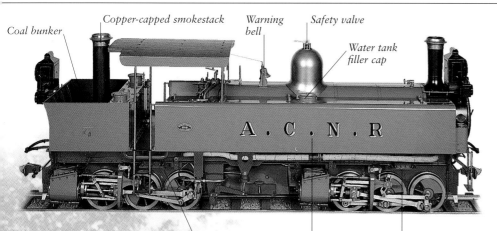

Coal bunker

Copper-capped smokestack

Warning bell

Safety valve

Water tank filler cap

A.C.N.R

Rear powered truck

Water tank

Front powered truck

TRANSANDINE ARTICULATED

This British-designed Kitson-Meyer 0-6-0+0-6-0 tank engine was used on the Transandine Railway in South America to haul minerals up the Andes. The engine, which was built by Kerr Stuart in Stoke-on-Trent in 1903, was a predecessor of the highly successful Garratt-type articulated locomotives.

Wood bunker

SPECTACULAR ASCENT

The cars that shuttle up and down the Niesen Railway in Switzerland's Bernese Oberland are rope-hauled through an average gradient of 1-in-1.5. During the 35-minute-long journey to the top, the cars ascend 5,479 ft (1,669 m) up the Niesen mountain from Lake Thun.

NEARING VERTICAL

An electric car climbs Mount Pilatus railroad in the Swiss Alps, the world's steepest rack line. It opened on June 4, 1889, using steam traction until it was electrified in 1937. This rack system has horizontal teeth on each side of the track to reduce the risk of slippage and derailment.

A DOUBLE FIRST FOR SWITZERLAND

No.7 was the first locomotive to be built for use on Europe's first rack-and-pinion railroad, the Vitznau-Rigi Bahn (V-RB), which opened in 1873. The V-RB was built to run from Lake Luzern up the 5,906-ft (1,779-m) high Rigi Mountain. After No.7 was retired from active duty it was preserved and later, in 1998, it was restored to working order.

Smokestack

Whistle

Vertical boiler

Cylinder

Luggage container

FIRST TO THE TOP

The first mountain rack railroad took its passengers to the top of 2,624-ft (800-m) Mount Washington, in New Hampshire. The line, which operated on an iron ladder-style rack and cog system, opened on July 3, 1869 and had a maximum gradient of over 1-in-3.

Wrought iron rack in center of track

Fuel and water bunker

Toothed central rack

Piston rod

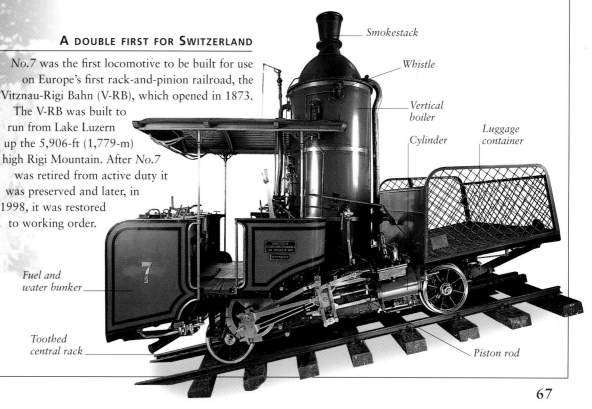

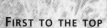

1900-1920
AN AGE OF LUXURY CUT SHORT BY WAR

MANY OF THE ADVANCES in steam traction pioneered at the close of the nineteenth century were implemented at the start of the twentieth century. The most successful steam locomotives developed at this time incorporated the longer-boilered designs developed in the US with European innovations, such as compounding and superheating. Along with speed came greater pulling power, which led to a proliferation of luxury passenger services in both Europe and North America. Freight engines also grew in stature and an increasing number of articulated designs were employed in this period. Advances were also made in electric traction, which for the first time was used on main-line railroads in Europe. Two years after the Siberian Railway was completed, linking Europe to the Pacific coast in Asia, this glittering era ended abruptly with the outbreak of World War I.

BUILT IN 1920, CROCODILE WAS ONE OF
SWITZERLAND'S FIRST ELECTRIC LOCOMOTIVES

1900-1920 PASSENGER TRAINS

THE INTRODUCTION OF steel-bodied passenger cars at the end of the nineteenth century meant that more powerful steam locomotives had to be developed to haul these heavier trains. Increasing the size of the engines had proved problematic, so in this period the main efforts were focused on improving the compounding and superheating efficiency of existing engine forms. This approach greatly improved the power and speed of earlier designs. Most successful of all the wheel formations was the 4-6-2, or Pacific, which by 1920 was the world's most popular passenger locomotive.

Belpaire firebox · *Riveted smokebox* · *Lamp iron* · *Engine number* · *Smokebox saddle*

LAST OF A FAST LINE

No.62660 Butler Henderson is the sole survivor of the 21 Director class 4-4-0s constructed for Britain's Great Central Railway between 1913 and 1920. Its efficient superheating provided it with pace and its small size made it economic.

US-styled block cylinder · *Windcutter*

GERMAN PACE-SETTING PACIFIC

The S3/6 Pacific boosted the pace of Germany's passenger services when the type was introduced onto the railroads of Baden and Bavaria in 1908. Built by Maffei, in Munich, the four-cylinder compound S3/6 averaged speeds of over 50 mph (80 kph). The last S3/6 retired in 1966.

TRANSFORMED BY SUPERHEATING

The early Prussian P8s were unreliable passenger engines until Wilhelm Schmidt used the type to test out his ideas on superheating. This later Class 38, was one of 4,000 highly successful superheated P8s built after 1906.

FRANCE'S STAR TURN

The pre-eminent European passenger engine between 1901 and 1910 was the 4-cylinder compound Atlantic designed by Alfred de Glehn and Gaston du Bousquet for France's *Chemin de Fer du Nord* (Northern Railway). This powerful locomotive could maintain speeds of up to 75 mph (121 kph).

Superheater header inside the smokebox · *Smoke deflector*

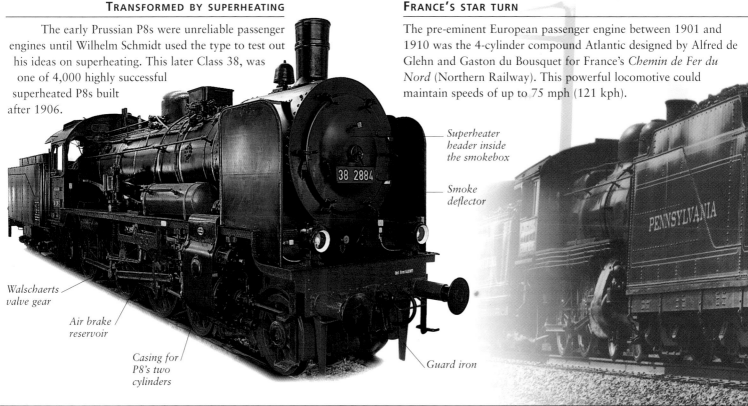

PENNSYLVANIA

Walschaerts valve gear · *Air brake reservoir* · *Casing for P8's two cylinders* · *Guard iron*

FRANCE STEPS UP THE PRESSURE

This 4-6-0 was one of 150 of its class built between 1907 and 1912 for France's *Chemin de Fer du Nord*. These four-cylinder compound locomotives were fitted with two high-pressure cylinders on the exterior and two low-pressure cylinders under the smokebox. Superheating was incorporated later.

Flared chimney

Chemin de Fer Nord monogram

Safety valve housing

High-pressure cylinder

Air brake compressor

Guard iron

Reversing rod

Enclosed cab

Wheel splasher

Decorated smokebox door

INDIA'S ROYAL SCOT

Built in 1907 by the North British Locomotive Company in Scotland, *No.EM922* was one of 19 E1 class Atlantics to be ordered by the Great Indian Peninsula Railway to haul mail trains and other prestigious passenger trains. This locomotive, which was superheated in 1922, also fronted royal trains.

AN AMERICAN ENLARGEMENT

Turn-of-the-century US passenger power is represented by this Class E2sd Atlantic, which pilots an 1885-built D16sb 4-4-0. The main design advance of the Atlantic, or 4-4-2, was its extra trailing axle, which supported a larger firebox.

Warning bell

Oil-fired headlight

Lugs secure smokebox door to keep the smokebox airtight

Running board

Coupler

1900-1920 PARIS-ORLÉANS PACIFIC

THE 4500 CLASS 4-CYLINDER compound 4-6-2s used by the Paris-Orléans (P-O) Railway were the first Pacific-type locomotives to run in Europe. The prototype, *No.4501*, came into service in July 1907. By 1910, 100 were operating in France, including *No.4546*, shown here, which was built by the American Locomotive Company (ALCO). Most of these engines operated between Paris and Toulouse, in southwest France, where they remained in service until this route was electrified in 1932. However, the story did not end there. Many of the sister engines (Class 3500) were rebuilt by André Chapelon to create the successful Nord Pacific type (*see pp.90–91*).

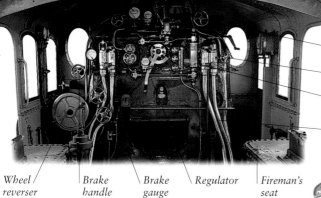

Water and steam pressure gauges

Wheel reverser — *Brake handle* — *Brake gauge* — *Regulator* — *Fireman's seat*

EVERYTHING TO HAND

The roomy cab of the P-O Pacific allowed the controls and gauges to be laid out in an ergonomically efficient manner. Two oval spectacle glasses at the front aided forward vision, and the inclusion of seats, which were a novelty at the time, provided the crew with a more comfortable ride.

Tender holds 6 tons of coal and 5,280 gallons (20,000 liters) of water

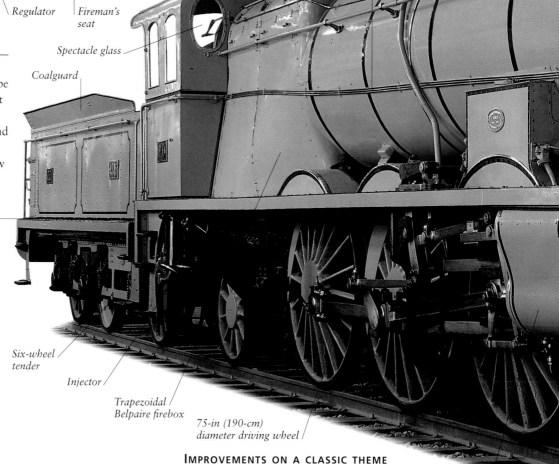

Injector handle
Water cock
Water gauge glass
Copper steampipe

Safety-valve bonnet
Washout plug
Sand dome
Lubricator pipe runs

Spectacle glass
Coalguard

Six-wheel tender
Injector
Trapezoidal Belpaire firebox
75-in (190-cm) diameter driving wheel
High-pressure cylinder
Cylinder cocks

SPECIFICATION

Manufacturer	American Locomotive Company (ALCO), Schenectady, New York
Classification	4500 class 4-6-2
Date built	1908
Number built	100
Fuel	Coal
Top speed	75 mph (120 kph)
Length	68 ft (20.8 m)
Height	14½ ft (4.35 m)
Total weight	136½ tons
Tractive effort	28,665 lb (13,000 kg)

IMPROVEMENTS ON A CLASSIC THEME

P-O's engineers adopted the 4-6-2 wheel arrangement of the Pacific type, which was developed in the US, and added a distinctive Belpaire firebox to the design in a bid to improve combustion and so increase the amount of steam generated. They also added the compounding system developed by Alfred de Glehn to maximize the power from each charge of steam.

ON A TRADITIONAL FRONT

With its squared-off smokebox saddle and curved fall plate, *No.4546* displays the traditional look of an original 4500 class. It was, however, rebuilt by Chapelon with an improved steam circuit, better drafting, and superheating, which together doubled its power output.

Hinged smokestack cap

Smokestack

Cylindrical smokebox

Steam dome

Air-brake compressor

Grab rail

Smokebox saddle

Fall plate

Oblong buffer

Truck frame

Screw coupling

Wheel opens smokebox door

Smokebox door

Engine number

Fallplate

Oil-fired headlight

Buffer beam

Oblong buffer

Coupling hook

Guard iron

Piston tail rod

Leading truck

1900-1920 WORLD FREIGHT

THE WORLDWIDE SPREAD of railroads diversified the role of trains and, by the beginning of the twentieth century, a marked contrast had developed between locomotives designed for freight service and those designed for passenger service. Huge freight engines such as the 2-10-0, which was developed in North America, were used on major freight routes around the world. Along with big engines, an array of small, lightweight locomotives were built to work on secondary lines.

Steam dome *Running plate*

History of engine recorded on side of tender

RUSSIAN WORKHORSE

Introduced in 1912, the outside-cylindered E class 0-10-0s went on to become the world's most numerous class. By 1947, 13,000 had been built and they played a major role in Russia's massive freight operations – at the peak, 250,000 loaded freight cars were moved each day.

Tapered boiler

Tender holds 4,200 gallons (15,900 liters) of water

NEW TO BRITAIN

In 1903, George Jackson Churchward designed the first British 2-8-0, the 2800 class, for Great Western Railway. The 2-8-0 replaced the widely utilized 0-6-0 type. Construction of the class continued until 1942 and some of the 164 2800s built remained in service until the mid-1960s.

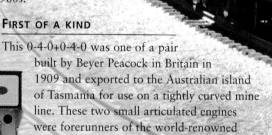

Engine unit *Safety valves*

FIRST OF A KIND

This 0-4-0+0-4-0 was one of a pair built by Beyer Peacock in Britain in 1909 and exported to the Australian island of Tasmania for use on a tightly curved mine line. These two small articulated engines were forerunners of the world-renowned Beyer-Garratt locomotives.

Wide firebox

SUCCESSFUL AROUND THE WORLD

Seen here in ex-works gray livery, this 4-6-2+2-6-4 was one of 2,000 Beyer-Garratts built between 1909 and 1968. These articulated engines, designed by Herbert Garratt, were the most successful British engines of the type, and worked on every continent other than North America.

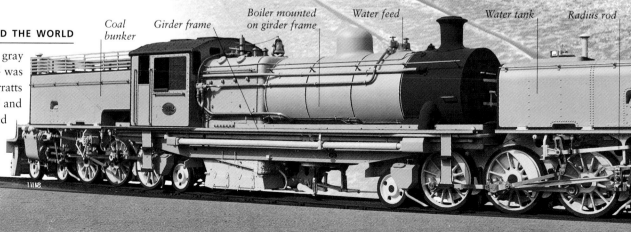

Coal bunker *Girder frame* *Boiler mounted on girder frame* *Water feed* *Water tank* *Radius rod*

Tender holds 10.8 tons of coal and 2,990 gallons (49,210 liters) of water

Largest boiler ever used – 118 in (3 m) in diameter

High-pressure cylinder

Air-brake reservoir

Single chimney

Walschaerts valve gear

Low-pressure cylinder

Four-wheeled tender truck

One of ten coupled rear driving wheels

A NORTH AMERICAN GIANT

This Mallet compound 2-10-10-2 was one of ten purchased by the Virginian Railroad in 1918 to haul coal trains on its steeply graded Clark's Gap line. The power of this articulated giant enabled it to pull 16,996-ton loads unaided.

BRITISH EXPORT TO INDIA

This HSM class 2-8-0 was built in Britain and exported to India for use on the South-Eastern Railway. Features such as its Belpaire firebox give the locomotive a typically British look.

Running board provides access to the smokebox

Air reservoir for brakes

Lubricator

Brake hose

PRIDE OF PENNSYLVANIA

No.4595, seen here in 1938 bringing a mixed freight train around Horseshoe Curve, was one of 598 I-1 class 2-10-0s built in the US. The I-1 class was the principal freight locomotive on the Pennsylvania Railroad for 20 years, up to the 1940s.

1900-1920 TRANS-SIBERIAN RAILWAY

LINKING MOSCOW with the Pacific coast, the 5,866-mile (9,440-km) Trans-Siberian Railway (T-SR) is the world's longest continuous line. Russia's tsarist rulers built the line to reinforce their control over Siberia, and to gain a link with the naval base of Vladivostok. Construction began in 1891 and within ten years it was possible to travel by train to the Pacific Ocean. By 1912, Wagons Lits were running a luxury service along the T-SR. A high level of comfort was kept during the Soviet era and the line was electrified after World War II.

OVERCOMING OBSTACLES

Until 1904 trains on the T-SR were loaded on to ferries and transported across Lake Baikal, the world's deepest lake. Since the lake freezes over from January to May, some of these ships were built with an ice-breaking capability.

Soviet star embosses smokebox door

Walschaerts valve gear

SURVIVING STEAM ENGINE

Seen on display at Ulan Ude, east of Irkutsk on the T-SR, this 2-6-2 is one of 2,500 Su class locomotives built between 1932 and 1951. These powerful passenger locomotives were widely employed across the former Soviet Union, including on the T-SR.

OUTSTANDING FREIGHT LOCOMOTIVE

This L class 2-10-0, photographed in the Ukraine in 1994, was one of 5,000 of this highly successful type built before the construction of steam engines was halted, by order of the Kremlin, in 1956. The class was used for freight duties.

Spark arrestor

Bonnet smokestack

Large headlamp (oil-burning)

Guard rail around running board

Steam dome

Spring-loaded safety valve

THE PRESENT ROUTE OF THE TRANS-SIBERIAN RAILWAY

Until 1914, passengers traveling from Moscow on the T-SR were obliged to transfer to trains owned by the Chinese Eastern Railway to complete the journey to Vladivostok. However the dangers of traveling across the northern Chinese province of Manchuria, which frequently involved these trains being attacked by bandits, prompted the Russians to construct an eastern extension to the T–SR that stayed within Russian territory. This map shows the revised route, which remains unchanged today.

DINING IN LUXURY

Dining cars on the prestigious T-SR services were like restaurants on wheels. In these lavishly decorated wood-paneled cars the standard of food, wine, and service matched the sumptuous decoration. Fresh fish, meat, and dairy products were taken on board each day during the eight-day-long journey.

VL classification stands for Vladimir Lenin

Current collector

PREPARED FOR THE COLD

Three examples of the VL80 class await their next duties as freight haulers on the T-SR. These B-B+B-B AC electric locomotives were designed in 1971 and can operate at a minimum temperature of -76°F (-60°C). They operate on a second T-SR line and transport minerals and oil from Siberia's Baikal-Amur area.

Current collector

Output is 5000 kw

HARD TRANSPORT

"Hard" and "Soft" have always been used as literal descriptions of the classes of accommodation on Russian trains. The rolling stock of this nineteenth-century T-SR train is all hard class. Heading the train is a wood-burning 2-4-0, which shows the influence that the US had on Russian engine design.

COMMEMORATIVE ELECTRIC LOCOMOTIVE

The crest on this VL65 class B-B-B electric, built in 1996, celebrates 60 years of locomotive construction at the NEVZ workshops. Pictured at Irkutsk, VL65-020 is one of a fleet of express passenger engines that operate on the T-SR at a maximum speed of 75 mph (120 kph).

Air intake

Crest

1900–1920 EARLY ELECTRICS

EXPERIMENTAL ELECTRIC RAILROADS were constructed in Britain, the Netherlands, and the United States as early as the 1830s but the first practical use of electric traction occurred in Germany in 1879. At first, electrification was used to overcome the smoke pollution problems caused by steam locomotives in the major cities. Subsequently, in around 1900, the first mainline electrifications were undertaken in the United States and Europe primarily to solve the problem of smoke in rail tunnels.

THE ELECTRIC LOCOMOTIVE COMES OF AGE IN BERLIN

The German engineer Ernst Werner von Siemens built the world's first successful electric locomotive for the Berlin Trades Exhibition in 1879. The 3-hp engine conveyed 30 passengers around a small oval track, carrying 150 volt direct current, at a speed of 4 mph (6.5 kph).

EARLY ITALIAN ELECTRIC

Since Italy had to import all its coal, its railroads were electrified early. This 1,200-hp, four-motor railcar was used on the Valtellina line, in the Lombardy region, which was electrified in 1902. It used a three-phase supply drawn from overhead wires.

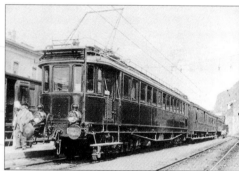

Side contact bows collect current

Wires carry current at 10 kvAC 50 Hz

Equipment in car transforms current to 435 v

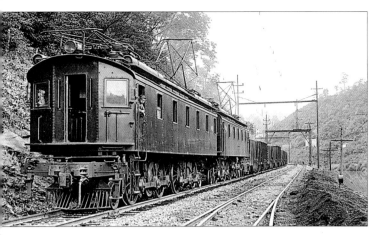

NORTH AMERICAN ELECTRIC FREIGHT TRAIN

This is one of the 36 1-B+B-1 electric freight locomotives built by the Baldwin company for use on the New York to New Haven and Hartford Railroad. Its line to Stamford, Connecticut was electrified in 1907.

FIT FOR A KING

In 1901, French railroads used this naturalistic art nouveau-style poster to promote the new electric rail link between central Paris and the suburb of Versailles, where Louis XIV built his palace. The poster emphasizes the environmental advantages that electric traction has over steam traction.

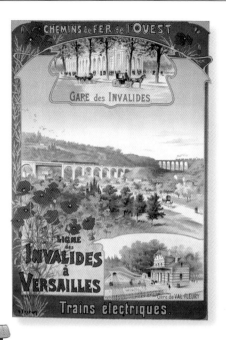

BRITISH NUMBER ONE

In 1904, the North Eastern Railway *No.1* became the first electric locomotive built for a British mainline railroad. It was one of two B-Bs designed for Newcastle-upon-Tyne's steep quayside line. *No.1* remained in service up until 1964.

Pantograph collects current at 600 vDC

Locomotive can also collect current from conductor rail

NORTH   EASTERN

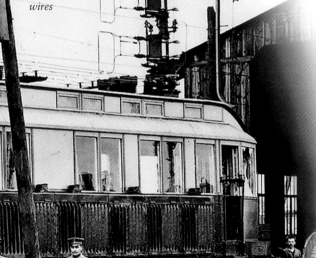

Mast carries conductor wires

SWITZERLAND TAKES THE LEAD

This 2,500 hp, 1-E-1 locomotive was one of 12 built to operate on the 47-mile (75-km) long Bern-Lötschberg-Simplon line, which was the first in the world to be built as an electric railroad over its entire length.

GERMAN RECORD-BREAKER

In October 1903, this Siemens & Halske-built, high-speed, three-phase electric motor coach reached a speed of 131 mph (210 kph) on a military line that ran between Marienfelde and Zossen. This record-breaking run made it far and away the fastest railroad vehicle of the time.

1900-1920 CROCODILE

DURING WORLD WAR I, neutral Switzerland was unable to import the coal its railroads depended upon. The experience prompted the electrification of almost all its main routes. One of the first electric locomotives to be developed in Switzerland was the rod-driven 1-C+C-1. This classic engine, popularly known as the "Crocodile," was used for freight duties on the transalpine Gotthard line, which runs between Zurich and Como in Italy. *No.13254*, featured here, was one of 33 Crocodiles acquired by the Gotthard. It remained in service for over 60 years before it was retired in 1982.

Pantograph draws current from 15 kvAC overhead wires

Collecting

SPECIFICATION

Manufacturer	Swiss Locomotive Works, Winterthur, Switzerland
Classification	Ce6/8 II 1-C+C-1
Date built	1920–22
Number built	33
Fuel	Electric (15 kvAC)
Top speed	47 mph (75 kph)
Length	63½ ft (19.4 m)
Height	14½ ft (4.5 m)
Total weight	124 tons
Tractive effort	66,150 lb (30,000 kg)

Cabs at each end make engine easy to drive in both directions

Engine number

Central section houses transformer

Running board

Truck wheel

Ammeter and voltmeter

Warning bell

Cab light

Security chock

Speedometer

Brake gauge

Notched controller regulates current flow and speed

Front cab window

Handbrake

Air brake

TWO NOSES

The term "Crocodile" derives from the elongated nose sections at each end of the locomotive. In the central section, a heavy transformer is sandwiched between two driving cabs. Crocodiles were very powerful engines for their time, able to develop 2,460 hp.

THE DRIVING FORCE

The driver of the Crocodile uses a notched controller to alter the voltage supplied to the traction motors. Speed and tractive effort vary according to the voltage level. If he takes his foot off the dead man's handle, the brakes engage automatically.

Motor truck

Connecting rod

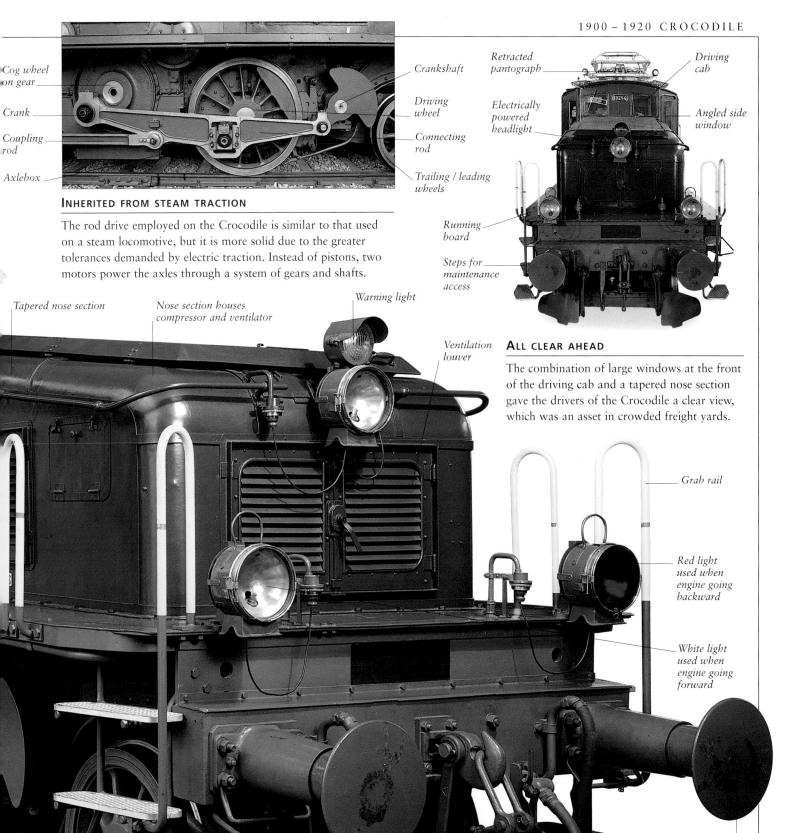

Cog wheel on gear

Crank

Coupling rod

Axlebox

Crankshaft

Driving wheel

Connecting rod

Trailing / leading wheels

Retracted pantograph

Driving cab

Electrically powered headlight

Angled side window

Running board

Steps for maintenance access

INHERITED FROM STEAM TRACTION

The rod drive employed on the Crocodile is similar to that used on a steam locomotive, but it is more solid due to the greater tolerances demanded by electric traction. Instead of pistons, two motors power the axles through a system of gears and shafts.

Tapered nose section

Nose section houses compressor and ventilator

Warning light

Ventilation louver

ALL CLEAR AHEAD

The combination of large windows at the front of the driving cab and a tapered nose section gave the drivers of the Crocodile a clear view, which was an asset in crowded freight yards.

Grab rail

Red light used when engine going backward

White light used when engine going forward

Buffer

Step

Coupling

Brake hose

Skirt

81

1900–1920 WORLD WAR I

BOTH SIDES IN World War I utilized trains to move troops and supplies in large volumes. In 1914, the railroads enabled the rapid mobilization of German forces and also allowed the French Army to escape defeat at the Battle of the Marne. When the German advance halted along the 300-mile (480-km) Western Front between the English Channel and the Swiss frontier, track was laid to carry fresh troops to the front line. Trains transported vast quantities of ammunition and explosives to the front and ferried away millions of wounded soldiers. Trains also gave birth to a new weapon: the rail-borne howitzer.

DEPARTURE INTO THE UNKNOWN

This scene, depicting Hungarian soldiers leaving for the Western Front, is typical of the enthusiastic send-off conscripts and volunteers received across Europe when they embarked for the Front. Throughout most of the course of the war, their friends and families were unaware of the horror awaiting them.

FRONT LINE TRANSPORT

Troops often traveled to the trenches by train. Here Prussian troops, wearing their distinctive spiked helmets, are transported in open-sided freight cars along a narrow-gauge railroad. Narrow-gauge lines were used by both sides because they were relatively quick and inexpensive to build.

GERMAN GUN

Rail-borne howitzers offered the artillery a degree of mobility. The only drawback was that they needed a large support crew and they took a long time to set up. Nonetheless these formidable guns were able to fire 200-lb (91-kg) shells a distance of 70 miles (113 km).

Steel cabin shelters gun crew and the ammunition

Rotating gun platform

Gun transporter is of girder construction

Nameplate   *Safety valves*

Coal tender

N. 673 B.

GOVERNMENT REQUISITION

North British Railway C class 0-6-0 No.673 *Maude* was one of over 600 locomotives requisitioned for military use by Britain's Railway Operating Department. Sent to France in October 1917, it was later named after a British commander, Lieutenant General Sir Frederick Stanley Maude KCB.

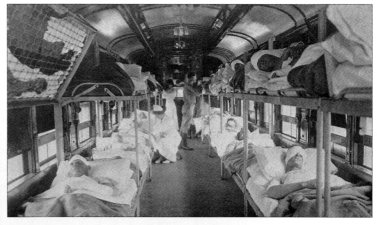

TRANSPORTING THE WOUNDED

As casualties mounted in the trenches, makeshift bunks were fitted into passenger rolling stock to create mobile hospital trains. This British Medical Department ward car shows just how basic the amenities were for seriously wounded soldiers being ferried home for hospitalization.

DEADLY CARGO

Rail and water transport collaborated during the Battle of Arras in April 1917. British gunners ferried pontoon boats to the bank of the River Scarpe at Blangy, where they were loaded with shells from wagons on an adjacent narrow-gauge railroad.

A SYMBOL OF WAR AND PEACE

Restaurant car *No.2419*, which belonged to the Compagnie Internationale des Wagons-Lits (CIWL), entered history on November 11, 1918, when the Armistice ending World War I was signed there. During World War II, the Nazis accepted France's surrender in the same car, which they later destroyed.

Car is over 67 ft (20 m) long

Plaque commemorating 1918 armistice

1900-1920 SPECIAL PURPOSE

AS THEIR ROLE BROADENED at the end of the nineteenth century, railroads built engines to perform tasks outside the range of their everyday locomotive fleets. Small switchers were designed to work in confined areas; maintenance machines such as snowplows became vital; workshops used crane engines to lift heavy loads; and inspection vehicles were built to check on the condition of the track. Whether for work or pleasure, engineers succeeded in designing engines to perform most roles.

Iron ore hoppers

SCOTLAND'S FIRST ELECTRIC ENGINES

The first electrified railroad in Scotland was a little-known line built at Kinlochleven, at the head of Loch Leven in the West Highlands, in 1908. Using locally generated hydroelectric power, the streetcarlike engines hauled hoppers of ore to an aluminum smelter.

ECCENTRIC OUTING

Magnus Volk, a Swiss-born engineer, built the stilted electric trains shown in this poster in 1896 to take vacationers from Brighton in Sussex to Rottingdean. At low tide the platform on these cars towered 23 ft (7 m) above the rails. At high tide the train cruised through 15 ft (4.5 m) of water.

Stack passes through vestibule canopy

Inspection car

Air brake reservoir

Tender valance

READY FOR INSPECTION

In order to examine the condition of the track and signaling along the 546 miles (874 km) of line on the New York, Ontario & Western Railroad in the US, the staff rebuilt one of its 4-4-0s in 1890 to create this self-propelled inspection vehicle. The original locomotive engine dated from 1872 and it remained in its inspection-vehicle guise until 1932.

CHINA'S CIRCLE LINE

Articulated electric locomotives, based upon a 1920s Swiss design, were used to haul ore hoppers at Anshan in China. The trains carried the iron ore to steel-producing blast furnaces along an 50-mile (80-km) circular line.

Operating cab

Sloping front improves visibility from cab

Articulated chassis

STEAM WITHOUT FIRE

Fireless locomotives were used as switchers in locations such as chemical works and refineries where a stray spark could cause an explosion. Instead of generating its own steam, the boiler of these fireless engines is merely used as a vessel into which high-pressure steam is pumped and stored.

TAKING THE WEIGHT

This 0-6-0 crane locomotive was built in England in 1903, and was sold to an Indian sawmill. Its main task was to pick up tree trunks, and it could lift up to 31 tons (31,500 kg). This lifting capacity was much greater than that of the elephants it replaced.

Rotary snowplow

Accommodation for crew

THE KLONDIKE'S MAGNIFICENT SNOWPLOW

This steam-powered rotary snowplow, seen here complete with a caboose at the rear for the crew, was built in 1898 for the White Pass & Yukon Railroad of Alaska. The snowplow was used to clear snow from a railroad that ran supplies to gold prospectors in the Klondike.

1920-1940
THE PURSUIT OF SPEED AND ELEGANCE

RAILROADS EXPERIENCED a "golden age" between the world wars, despite the fact that the broader world picture was far from stable, both economically and politically. The Wall Street Crash of 1929 and the Great Depression that followed proved to be a spur, rather than a barrier, to innovation. In a bid to lure passengers back onto the railroads and to reduce operating costs, elegant streamlined diesel-electric railcars, which matched for speed the existing steam-hauled express trains, were introduced in the 1930s. Similar considerations also spurred advancements in electric traction, culminating in a 126-mph (203-kph) speed record set by an Italian Elettrotreno Rapido in 1939. Steam power continued to thrive on both sides of the Atlantic, however. In the 1930s, André Chapelon in France and Nigel Gresley in Britain created Pacific designs that were free-steaming and fast-running and, in the US, streamlined Hiawathas provided the fastest steam-hauled service in the world.

IN 1938, *MALLARD* SET THE SPEED RECORD FOR STEAM

1920-1940 CLASSIC STEAM

THE POSTWAR OPTIMISM of the 1920s spawned a huge growth in the luxury express services of North America and Europe. Paradoxically, however, it was not until the 1930s, when the world was gripped by the Great Depression, that the apex of steam power was reached. Advances in locomotive design made the 1930s a decade in which dramatic increases in the speed and power of steam engines were achieved. While the 1930s also saw many express passenger engines fitted with streamlined casings, the majority retained their classic appearance, shown here.

Boiler feedwater preheater

A LOCOMOTIVE OF LEGEND

While some railroads in Britain rejected 4-6-0s for express passenger service, the Southern Railway kept faith with the type and introduced the 2-cylinder King Arthur class in 1925. Each of the 74 built were named after characters in the Arthurian legend.

Steps provide easy access to running board

TROPHIES OF WAR

A pair of ex-DR 2-10-0s are seen here fronting a Ukrainian train. The 2-10-0 was adopted by Deutsches Reichsbahn (German Railways) as their standard freight engine in 1938, and an estimated 10,600 were built. These two were seized by the Soviet Union at the end of World War II.

Steam and air brake hoses

Coupler

Stovepipe smokestack

Steam-collecting dome

Running board's safety handrails

A SOVIET SUCCESS STORY

Introduced in 1926, the Su 2-cylinder 2-6-2 was a modified and enlarged version of the S class of 1911. Like many of the Soviet Union's successful locomotive classes, the Su was mass produced. A total of 2,400 were built over a 15-year period.

THE MOUNTAINS OF FRANCE

Locomotives with a 4-8-2 wheel arrangement were first used in the US in 1911 and became known as Mountains. France began using the type extensively from 1925 onward to haul heavy passenger trains, and built more than 90 de Glehn-designed 241A class compound 4-8-2s.

Windowed engine's cab (or footplate)

81-in (206-cm) driving wheels

Water feed to boiler

Double stack

BRITISH RECORD-BREAKER

In terms of horsepower, the four-cylinder Coronation class Pacifics, built in 1937, were the most powerful express passenger steam locomotives ever to run in Britain. Thirty-eight were built by the London Midland & Scottish Railway for its west coast route between London and Scotland.

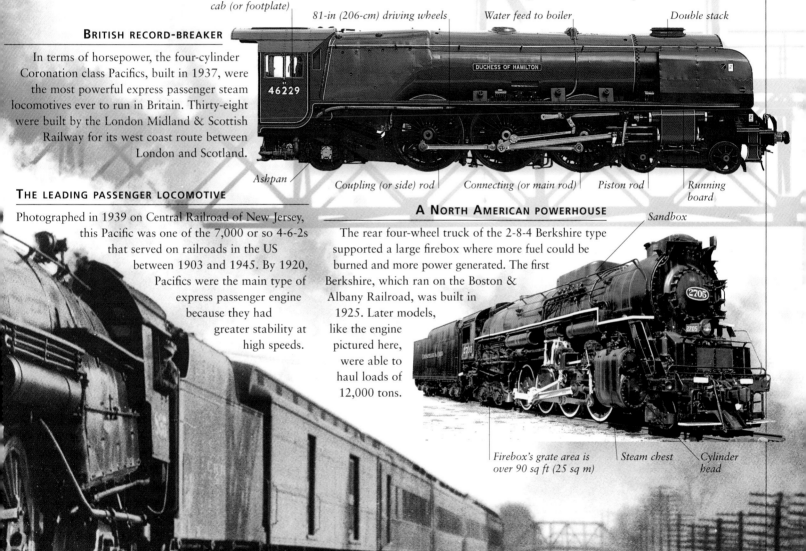

DUCHESS OF HAMILTON

46229

Ashpan

Coupling (or side) rod

Connecting (or main rod)

Piston rod

Running board

THE LEADING PASSENGER LOCOMOTIVE

Photographed in 1939 on Central Railroad of New Jersey, this Pacific was one of the 7,000 or so 4-6-2s that served on railroads in the US between 1903 and 1945. By 1920, Pacifics were the main type of express passenger engine because they had greater stability at high speeds.

A NORTH AMERICAN POWERHOUSE

The rear four-wheel truck of the 2-8-4 Berkshire type supported a large firebox where more fuel could be burned and more power generated. The first Berkshire, which ran on the Boston & Albany Railroad, was built in 1925. Later models, like the engine pictured here, were able to haul loads of 12,000 tons.

Sandbox

2705

Firebox's grate area is over 90 sq ft (25 sq m)

Steam chest

Cylinder head

1920-1940 NORD PACIFIC

BY RADICALLY IMPROVING the drafting, steam circulation, and superheating of the Paris-Orléans Pacific (*see pp.72–73*), André Chapelon inspired one of the greatest steam locomotive designs of the twentieth century. France's prestigious Nord railway acquired 20 P-O Pacifics that had been modified by Chapelon in 1932. They were so impressed with them that Nord built 28 new engines that utilized Chapelon's idea. *No.3.1192* belongs to this batch of 231 E class Pacifics, which remained in service for 30 years.

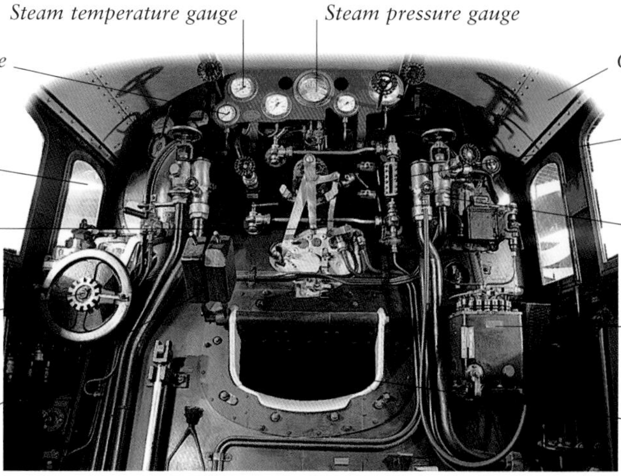

Steam temperature gauge · Steam pressure gauge · Brake gauge · Cab roof · Side window · Water glass gauge · Regulator · Injector control · Wheel reverser · Sight-feed lubricator · Firedoor lever · Firehole

INGREDIENTS FOR SUCCESS

No.3.1192 clearly displays two key external features of Chapelon's design: the lozenge-shaped boiler feedwater heater and the double chimney, which is fitted with a Kylchap blastpipe. Other modifications to the P-O Pacific design include the addition of smoke deflectors, the fitting of new cylinders, and the streamlining of all the steam passages.

EXPRESS PURPOSE

Nord Pacifics handled expresses such as the *Flèche d'Or* (Golden Arrow), the Night Ferry, and the Mediterranean-bound Blue Train. With 3,500 hp available, they were much faster than the P-O Pacifics. This extra power is reflected in the more complex instrumentation.

Rain strip on cab roof · Spectacle glass shroud · Safety valves · Washout plug · Steel firebox · Handrail · Sand dome

CALAIS C7 F7 3.1192

Indicates engine based at Calais depot · Injector · Trailing wheel · Electrical generator powers lights · Driving wheel 77 in (195 cm) in diameter · Connecting rod big end · Return crank

SPECIFICATION

Manufacturer	Chemin de Fer du Nord (Northern Railway), France
Classification	Class 231.E 4-6-2 (4-cylinder compound)
Date built	1936
Number built	28 (plus 20 existing 4500 class Pacifics rebuilt)
Fuel	Coal
Top speed	110 mph (176 kph)
Length	77 ft 7 in (23.7 m)
Height	14 ft (4.3 m)
Total weight	104.9 tons
Tractive effort	28,440 lb (12,912 kg)

Gone from the Chapelon Pacific are the traditional fittings, such as the oil-fired headlights and the warning bell. The single headlight on *No.3.1192* is electrically powered, as is the identification display. The most revolutionary aspects of its design derive from Chapelon's ideas on converting heat into locomotive energy, which were so successful that they were applied to over 1,500 locomotives in France alone.

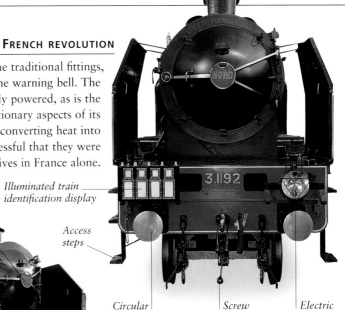

Chemin de Fer du Nord roundel

Angled smoke deflectors

Six-wheeled tender

Illuminated train identification display

Access steps

Circular buffer

Screw coupling

Electric headlight

BUILT FOR SPEED

No.3.1192 had a top speed in service of 87 mph (139 kph), which was below its potential top speed. On a test run, a Chapelon Pacific was recorded traveling at 110 mph (176 kph).

Air-brake compressor

Steam dome

Lubricator

Feedwater heater

Double chimney

Whistle

Steampipe

Smoke deflector

Company name

Connecting rod

Reversing shaft

Gudgeon pin

Piston rod

Combination lever

Oscillating cam

Cylinder steam chest

Valve chest

Leading four-wheel truck

Truck axle

Access steps

1920–1940 THE ORIENT EXPRESS

THE DEPARTURE OF the first Orient Express from Paris's Gare de l'Est on June 5, 1883 launched the first ever trans-European luxury train service and gave birth to a railroad legend. The Orient Express service was run by Compagnie Internationale des Wagons-Lits (CIWL), a (luxury) coach manufacturing company formed by the Belgian-born entrepreneur Georges Nagelmackers. After 1883, the Orient Express trains provided a railroad service from France, Germany, and Austria to Constantinople (now Istanbul), the capital of Turkey.

EARLY STEAM-HAULED ORIENT EXPRESS

An Orient Express is seen approaching Constantinople in 1905, headed by a four-coupled steam locomotive. At this time, Orient Expresses usually included two sleeping cars, a dining car, a luggage car, and a carriage for the crew.

Clerestory roof

Boarding platform

PORTRAIT OF A PARTNERSHIP

In this 1873 photograph, Nagelmackers sits on the boarding platform of a "Boudoir" car that was built by his partner, Colonel William d'Alton Mann, who stands beside him. When the partnership split up in 1876, Nagelmackers acquired 53 of these luxury sleeping cars for CIWL use.

ELECTRIFIED IN THE ALPS

An electrically powered Orient Express is seen framed by the towering Alps as it crosses the Kander viaduct in Switzerland's Lötschen Valley. At its head are two rod-driven 1-E-1 2,500-hp electric locomotives of the Bern, Lötschberg, Simplon railway, which was electrified in 1910.

EASTWARD BOUND IN BAVARIA

In this 1930s photograph, an Orient Express is seen nearing Augsburg, in the southern German state of Bavaria, fronted by a S3/6 class 4-4-0 steam locomotive. At Augsburg, steam power gave way to electric traction for the onward journey to Munich, Vienna, and across Eastern Europe.

1-E-1 locomotive has five powered axles

Baggage car

Supporting mast

THE ORIGINAL ORIENT EXPRESS ROUTE

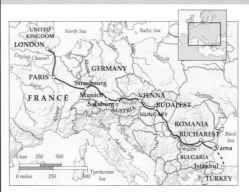

The original Orient Express service traveled from Paris to Constantinople via Munich, Vienna, Budapest, and Bucharest. On this journey, the passengers had to disembark 45 miles (72 km) east of Bucharest at Giurgiu in Romania. Here they boarded a ferryboat, which took them across the River Danube. Once across the Danube, they transferred to a second train, which transported them to Varna, a port on the Black Sea. Here they disembarked again and boarded a second ferry which sailed them to the exotic oriental city of Constantinople.

MYSTERY TRAIN

The allure of a journey on the Orient Express resulted in these trains featuring in six movies and 19 novels. In this scene from *Murder on the Orient Express*, detective Hercule Poirot has gathered all the suspects together for an archetypal Agatha Christie-style showdown.

PROMOTING INTERNATIONAL RELATIONS

This 1889 poster illustrates clearly the complex negotiations Nagelmackers had to undertake in order to run the Orient Express across Europe. A total of four companies, two British and two French, are credited with providing the service, which needed the cooperation of countless rail authorities and several national governments.

A NOSTALGIC RETURN

The original Orient Express service ceased operation in 1977, but one can now travel from London to Venice in the original blue-and-cream CIWL cars aboard the Venice Simplon Orient Express (VSOE). This VSOE train is headed by a German Class 50 2-10-0.

Wagons-Lits car

Overhead catenary

1920-1940 EARLY DIESELS

ALTHOUGH RUDOLF DIESEL demonstrated the first viable compression-ignition (diesel) engine in 1889, it took a further 25 years before a successful diesel railcar was developed. Even after 1913, diesel traction was not widely adopted as an alternative to steam on mainline routes until luxury diesel streamliners, such as the Zephyr, were introduced in the 1930s. It was the United States, with its abundance of cheap oil, that welcomed most the flexibility and savings diesel offered. During trials in 1939, *Electro-Motive No.103*, a 5,400 hp four-unit freight diesel engine, covered 83,000 miles (133,500 km), outclassing its steam-powered rivals. It was the start of a revolution that saw over 19,000 diesel locomotives built for US railroads in under 13 years.

AN AMERICAN FIRST

No.1000 was the first US-built diesel unit to be sold to a US railroad, the Central Railroad of New Jersey. This boxlike switcher, introduced in 1925, remained in service until 1957.

Air intake grille

Sloping roof for minimum wind resistance

SPEED ON SCHEDULE

Flying Hamburger trains, like the ones shown here, were built in Germany to operate the world's first scheduled high-speed diesel service between Berlin and Hamburg. The Flying Hamburgers began service in 1933, and their average speed was 77 mph (124 kph). But on a test run, one of the units was claimed to have reached 124 mph (198 kph).

Wedged-shaped front end

Recessed headlight

Raised cockpit engineer cab

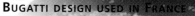

Two 200-hp motors mounted centrally

BUGATTI DESIGN USED IN FRANCE

Between 1933 and 1946, over 80 streamlined Autorails were built for France's État and Paris Lyons Mediterranée railways. They were designed by Ettore Bugatti, who was known for building elegant automobiles. In November 1935, an Autorail broke the world diesel speed record with 122 mph (196 kph).

Cooling fan

Stainless steel body

UNION PACIFIC'S ORIGINAL CITY

The "Cities" were among the most celebrated express trains in the US. However, the three-car M-10000 prototype seen here used a spark ignition engine because diesel power plants were not perfected. It was christened *City of Salina* when it was introduced into service in 1934.

Booster unit

GOING LIKE THE WIND

From the mid-1930s, the development of lightweight diesel engines, alloy steels, and welded construction allowed the Chicago, Burlington & Quincy Railroad to order the Zephyr. The 3,000-hp Denver Zephyr seen here was introduced in 1936. It ran at an average speed of 84 mph (134 kph) and had a top speed of 116 mph (186 kph).

NORTH AMERICAN STREAMLINED STANDARD

The first fully streamlined diesel locomotive, the E type, was introduced in 1937 by the Baltimore & Ohio Railroad in the United States. Electro-Motive built its two engines to generate 1,800 hp, and the twin six-wheel trucks to ensure it remained stable at speeds of over 100 mph (160 kph). For two decades the E type was the standard US passenger diesel.

Flared buffer housing   Casing houses hydro-mechanical transmission

BRITISH ARTICULATED

During the 1930s, the greatest commitment to diesel traction in Britain was by London Midland & Scottish Railway. Its diesel fleet included this three-car articulated train set. Built in 1938, it shuttled between Oxford and Cambridge at a speed of 65 mph (104 kph).

1920–1940 STREAMLINED STEAM

A GENERATION OF VISIONARY industrial designers turned the 1930s into the decade of streamlining. In a time of economic downturn and political uncertainty following the 1929 Wall Street Crash, sleek lines were applied to everything from trains and cars to domestic appliances. Streamlining was both glamorous and futuristic, and inspired a feeling of speed and luxury. On the railroads in both Europe and North America streamlined engines were used to head the flagship express trains that enticed customers back on to the railroads. These designs helped the railroads to survive the Great Depression and created a golden age of rail travel.

GERMAN AMBITIONS

The Nazi party set out to create the fastest streamlined steam locomotives in the world. *No.05.001* (*right*), a 4-6-4, set a speed record of 124 mph (199 kph) in 1936. To improve wind resistance, the 03 engine (*above*), which was built in 1940, was provided with a shrouded casing.

05001

Recessed headlight

THE CAPED CRUSADER

Reading Railroad's Crusader leaves Jersey City in 1937, with a cape of fluted stainless steel. The Crusader was one of more than 100 US streamlined passenger expresses that took on the challenge from the automobile and early airline services during the late 1930s.

SCHEDULED FOR SPEED

The Chicago, Milwaukee, St. Paul and Pacific Railroad introduced its streamlined Hiawatha in 1935. The oil-fired 2-cylinder 4-4-2 Atlantics fronting the Hiawathas provided the fastest scheduled steam-hauled trains in the world. Their average speed was 80 mph (129 kph).

Metal shroud extends almost to rail level

Electric headlight

BRIGHT IDEA

The yellow livery of this streamlined 4-6-4 Hudson, *No.490*, was devised by the US Chesapeake & Ohio Railroad's (C&O) publicity department. Four of these L1 class locomotives were built and became known as "Yellowbellies." They hauled the C&O's passenger streamliners, such as the *Fast Flying Virginian.*

490

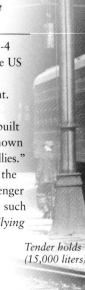

Tender holds 3,300 gallons (15,000 liters) of fuel oil

Streamlined casing is of fluted stainless steel

Steps for crew access

A UNIQUE ACHIEVEMENT

The Pennsylvania Railroad's solitary S1 class four-cylinder 6-4-4-6 "Duplex," *No.6100*, was the largest and fastest high-speed steam locomotive to operate in the US.

The famous designer, Raymond Loewy, utilized wind tunnel tests to create this striking aerodynamic design. Sadly, this unique giant was scrapped in 1949 after only ten years of active service.

Locomotive has two individual four-wheel driver sets

No.6100 is 140 ft (43 m) long

ROYAL CONNECTIONS

This poster promotes the London Midland and Scottish Railway's Coronation Scot passenger service from London to Scotland, which was launched in 1937, the year of King George VI's coronation. The Coronation Scot was hauled by a class of Pacific engines designed by Sir William Stanier.

STREAMLINED SURVIVOR

The J class was the pride of the Norfolk & Western (N&W), the last US railroad to use steam traction on any great scale. Said to be North America's finest 4-8-4, 14 of these streamlined giants were constructed between 1941 and 1950. *No.611*, shown here, is the sole survivor. During service, it hauled the N&W express at an average speed of 90 mph (144 kph).

Smokestack recessed into casing

Air inlet

Hinged flaps give access for lubrication

Hiawatha locomotive weighs 244 tons

1920–1940 MALLARD

MALLARD MADE HISTORY by setting a world speed record for steam traction of 126 mph (202 kph) in July 1938. It is a record that still stands. Designed by Sir Nigel Gresley for Britain's London & North Eastern Railway (LNER), *No.4468 Mallard* was one of 35 A4 class streamlined Pacifics that hauled luxury expresses up until the 1960s. The inspiration for Mallard's sleek exterior came from the streamlined diesel railcars being used in Europe, especially those styled by Bugatti.

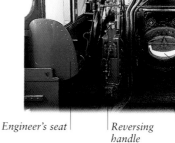

Steam chest pressure gauge
Steam sanding control
Boiler pressure gauge
Vacuum brake gauge
Boiler water level glass gaug
Exhaust steam water injector control
Steam heating pressure gauge
Fireman's seat
Engineer's seat
Reversing handle
Firebox
Firehole

TRUE BLUE

Mallard entered LNER service on March 3, 1938, where it worked for 25 years, covering 1,426,000 miles (2,294,943 km). It has been preserved in its pre-World War II livery.

WHERE RECORDS WERE BROKEN

On its world record run on July 3, 1938 the driver, Joe Duddington, operated the controls on the left and his fireman, Tommy Bray, kept the firebox stocked with coal and maintained the supply of water to the boiler. An inspector, Sid Jenkins, also manned the footplate.

Cab roof ventilator
V-shaped cab front
Washout door
Handrail
Flap gives access for lubrication
Commemorative plaque

4468

Builder's plate
Trailing wheel
Coil spring
Airfoil valance
Coupling rod
Brake rigging
Return crank

FOR THE RECORD

Plaques on the streamlined boiler casing of *Mallard* record its world speed record. The run was logged in a dynamometer car behind the engine. The locomotive was fitted with this Flaman speed recorder.

FLAMAN SPEED RECORDER

Speed gauge

Time dial

Pen recorder charts speed graph

Speed recorder has a sealed brass casing

Details of speed record

LNER

ON 3RD JULY 1938 THIS LOCOMOTIVE ATTAINED A WORLD SPEED RECORD FOR STEAM TRACTION OF 126 MILES PER HOUR

COMMEMORATIVE PLAQUE

Chime whistle

Aerodynamically contoured nose section

Handrail

Hinged smokebox door

Lamp bracket

Nº 4468

CLASS   A4

Truck frame

Screw coupling

Buffer

SPECIFICATION

Manufacturer	L&NE Railway, Doncaster, England
Classification	A4 class 8P6F 4-6-2
Date built	1937
Number built	35
Fuel	Coal
Top speed	126 mph (202 kph)
Length	71 ft (21.6 m)
Height	13 ft (4 m)
Total weight	167 tons
Tractive effort	35,492 lb (16,096.6 kg)

DISTINCTIVE CHIMES

Mallard and the other A4 Pacifics had North American-style chime whistles mounted on the front of their smokestacks. Their distinctive shrill announced the arrival of these elegant engines. Below the whistle, two hinged doors give access to the smokebox.

Streamlined casing

Nameplate

Kylchap double smokestack

LIKE THE WIND

Though based on the French Bugatti railcar, the outline of the A4 Pacific's wedge-shaped front was decided by wind tunnel tests. The streamlining extended to fitting airfoil valances over the wheels. This aerodynamic shape contributed to *Mallard's* fast running, but more significant was its Kylchap double-smokestack exhaust system.

MALLARD

Buffer

Vacuum brake hose

Guard iron

Connecting rod

Eccentric rod

Sand pipe

Drop arm

Union link

Cylinder cock pipes

Leading wheel

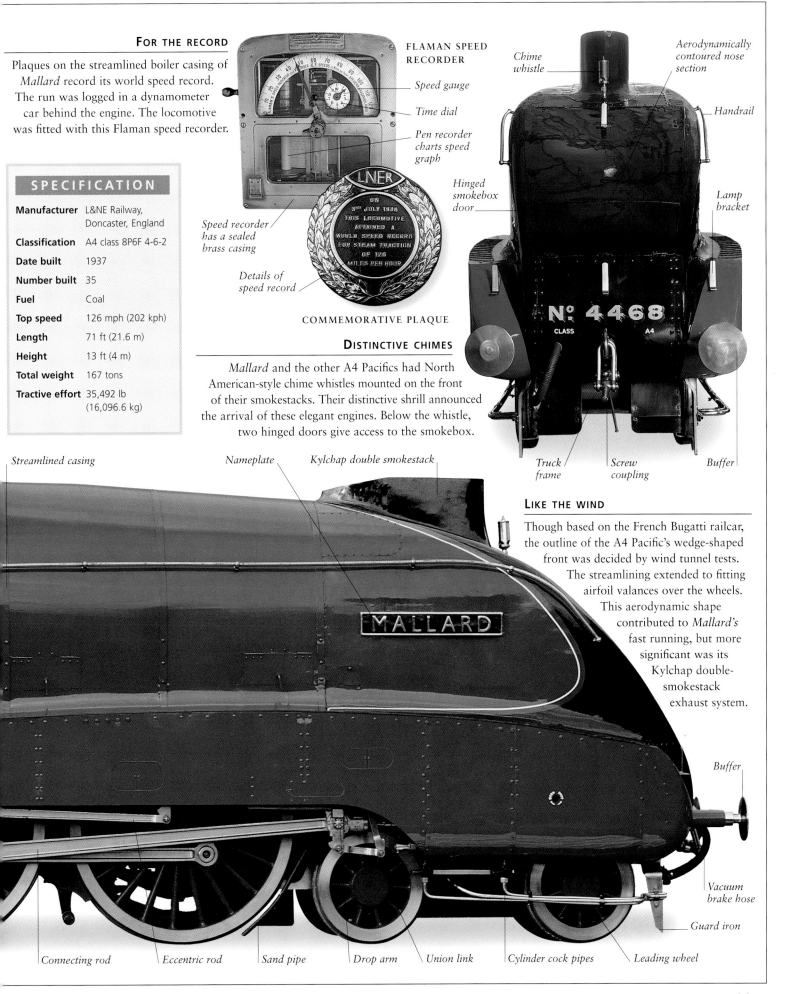

1920–1940 ELECTRICS

PROMPTED BOTH BY ADVANCES in electric technology and the economic consequences of World War I, this period saw a world-wide expansion of mainline electrification. Coal shortages forced countries such as Italy to rely ever more heavily on electric trains. This had its advantages, and by the mid-1930s Italian railroads were amongst the most efficient in the world. Germany and several other countries in Eastern Europe built single-phase AC lines. The first electric railroad in India was also constructed in this period, and huge progress in electric traction occurred on the busiest routes in the eastern US.

Louvered cab window

Panel displays company initials

Diamond-shaped pantograph.

SWISS-BUILT FOR INDIA

This Swiss-built electric locomotive entered service on India's first electrified railroad, the Grand Indian Peninsular, in 1930. Named after a Governor of Bombay, *Sir Roger Lumley* had six axles that were each driven by a pair of motors, which let this 103-ton engine run at six different operating speeds.

Articulated cars

A TWENTY-FIVE-YEAR RECORD HOLDER

In July 1939, this Italian Railways ETR (Elettrotreno Rapido) 200 series demonstrated the high-speed potential of electric traction. On the new mainline between Florence and Milan, it set a new world speed record for electric traction of almost 126 mph (203 kph).

TAILOR-MADE FOR ITS TIME

The 70-seater Rce2/4 Rotorpfeil (Red Arrow) railcar below entered service with Swiss railroads in 1935. These cheap-to-run, lightweight units were built to cope with a decline in passenger rail travel during the depression years of the 1930s. The Rotorpfeil ran on two four-wheel trucks, and had a maximum operating speed of 125 kph (78 mph).

Pantograph folded down

Gangway window

Locomotive number

Square end nose

Engineer's cab located both at front and rear

Large viewing window

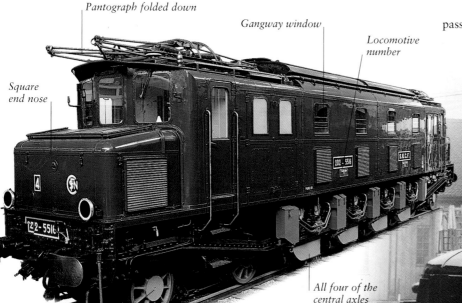

All four of the central axles are powered

AN EARLY FRENCH CLASSIC

Front two sets of axles are unpowered

Following pilot mainline electrification schemes by the Societé Nationale de Chemins de Fers Français (SNCF), *No.5516*, built by Fives-Lille in France, entered service on the 1,500 vDC line between Paris and Vierzon in 1933. This sturdy 2-D-2 electric locomotive was not retired until 1978.

STREAMLINED AMERICAN

With a body styled by Raymond Loewy, the Pennsylvania Railroad's 4,620-hp 2-C+C-2 GG1 of 1935 was the world's first streamlined electric locomotive. GG1s hauled the express service between New York and Washington DC at 90 mph (144 kph). The last GG1 retired in 1983.

Diamond-shaped raised pantograph

Welded bodyshell

Engineer's cab window

Pantograph picks up 15 kvAC current from overhead cable

Body of Ae8/14 is 112 ft (34 m) long

Headlight

Threepane cab window

Oblong buffer

SWISS SUPERPOWER

In 1939, Switzerland's trans-Alpine Gotthard line, which was electrified in 1921, took delivery of what was then the world's most powerful class of electric locomotive, the Series Ae8/14. These aerodynamically-styled 1-B-1-B-1 heavy freight engines developed 8,800 hp.

GERMANY'S ELECTRIC WAR LOCOMOTIVE

This E94 class C-C, *No.1020-037-6*, was one of 145 such engines built in Germany in the 1930s and 1940s. During World War II, these heavy freight engines were nicknamed "Germany's electric war locomotive." After the war, 44 of the class, including this one, were sent to Austria.

Pantograph

Insulator

Body shell made of welded steel sheets

Levered door

Flat partitioned windshield

"Hoods" house railcar power equipment

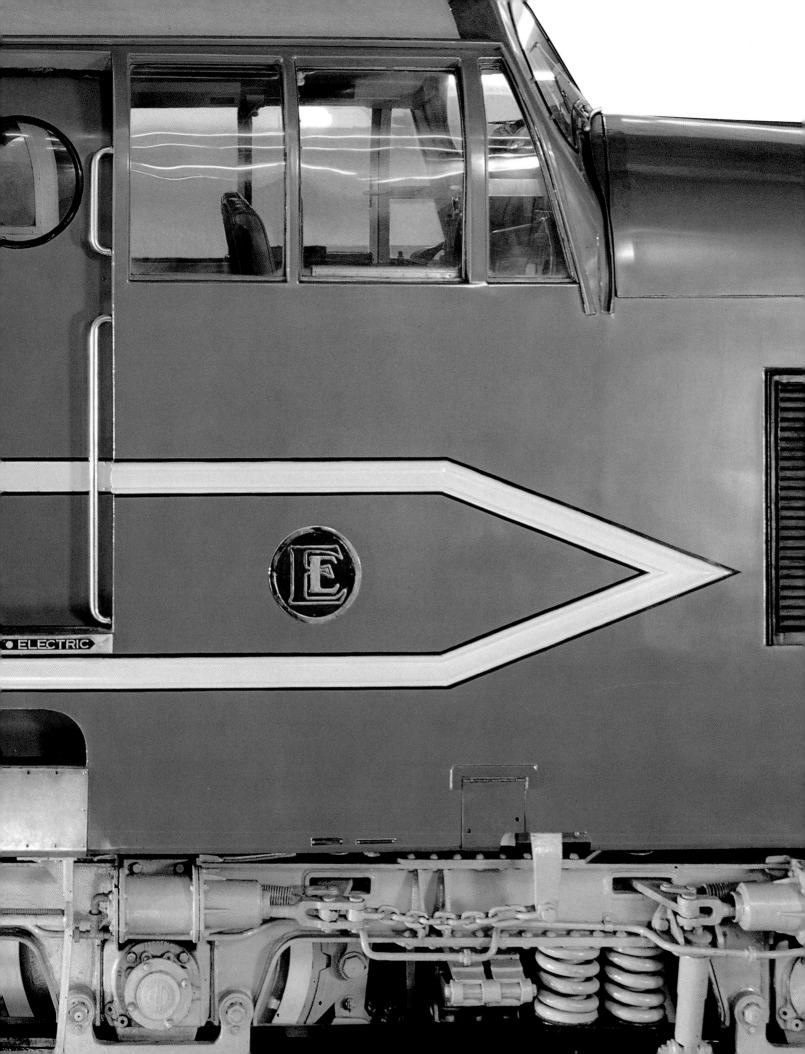

1940-1970
THE NEW POWER GENERATION

STEAM REMAINED THE DOMINANT motive power for the duration of World War II, and thousands of sturdy steam engines were constructed, including Union Pacific's massive articulated Big Boys. When peace came in 1945, the challenges facing steam traction were all too apparent. Engineers in the US had already developed diesel-electric locomotives that both outperformed and were cheaper to operate than their steam rivals, which they quickly replaced. Many countries around the world followed suit, including Britain, which introduced the Deltic diesel prototype in 1955. France had different ideas and opted to invest heavily in electrification. By the 1950s, its Mistral electric trains offered the fastest express service in Europe and inspired the setting up of the Trans-Europ Express. It was Japan, however, that took the bold step of building an entirely new railroad, the Shinkansen, for its high-speed electric trains, and the opening of this line in 1964 marked the start of the modern high-speed era.

TRANS-EUROP EXPRESS LAUNCHED IN 1957

1940-1970 WORLD WAR II

UNLIKE THE GERMAN ADVANCE of 1914, roads not railroads, carried the Nazis' Blitzkreig attacks of 1939 and 1940. Motorized armor headed by tank divisions and supported by aircraft tore through Europe. The railroads only became strategically important as fuel supplies ran low, crucially during Operation Barbarossa, Hitler's ill-fated invasion of the Soviet Union. The Soviets used railroads both to transport entire factories from threatened areas in the west to safety east of the Urals and to move troops. By 1943, aerial bombing had badly damaged the rail networks of Western Europe, and this hampered both sides.

AMERICAN SUPPORT

In 1943, the first of over 2,000 US-built S160 2-8-0s were shipped across the Atlantic to Britain. After the Normandy landings in June 1944, these engines hauled supplies to the Allied troops. This locomotive remained in the US for training purposes.

CAPTURED IN CHINA

In 1937, four years before the attack on the US fleet at Pearl Harbor, Japan invaded China. The capture of China's 7,200 miles (11,585 km) of railroads was a key aim along with a locomotive fleet that included this American-built 2-6-2. By 1949, 12 years of war and revolution had left only 4,000 miles (6,436 km) of track operable.

MILITARY MUSCLE

Locomotives with eight and ten driving wheels, such as this American-built 2-8-2, were the most widely used engines during World War II. This was because their axleloading was light enough to haul heavy cargoes, like this trainload of trucks, on war-damaged or light track.

Electrically powered headlight

Wartime 2-8-2s were known as "MacArthurs" after US general Douglas MacArthur

Walschaerts valve gear

Solid wheels on leading truck

FOOD, SHELLS AND FUEL

MUST

COME

FIRST

If your train is late
or crowded
– DO YOU MIND ?

TOP PRIORITY

Posters, such as this one issued
by Britain's Railway Executive
Committee, brought home to
the traveling public the key
role railroads were playing in
supplying ammunition, and
other supplies vital to the war
effort. The railroads were also
employed to ensure that food
and fuel reached British homes.

THE WORLD'S BIGGEST GUN

Built in 1941, and weighing 1,344 tons,
Germany's rail-mounted Schwere Gustav (Heavy
Gustav) was the largest artillery
weapon ever built. However,
this gun was far too cumbersome
and was used for just 13 days in
June 1942, when it shelled ports
on the Crimean Peninsula in the
Soviet Union.

*31½-in (80-cm)
calibre gun*

*Gun had maximum
range of 29 miles
(46 km)*

TRAIN FERRY

Trials using this converted tank
landing craft to transport steam
engines across the Channel were
conducted on Southampton Water,
in England, in April 1945. The
engine involved, *No.79250*, was
one of 935 British "Austerity"
2-8-0s built between 1943 and
1945 for military duties overseas.
This example remained in Britain
until it was scrapped in 1957.

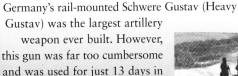

LOST IN FRANCE

This 0-6-0 freight engine was one of many hundreds of
locomotives that were destroyed in France by artillery shells
or during aerial bombing raids, first by the German
Luftwaffe and later by the Allied airforces. A further 6,000
trains were sabotaged by French resistance fighters who
sought to disrupt the German lines of communication
during the four-year-long Nazi occupation of France.

RETURNING TRIUMPHANT

Seen here is the first trainload of soldiers of the victorious
Red Army returning to the Soviet Union from Germany in
the late spring of 1945. They had fought their way across
Eastern Europe to take Berlin in what was the bloodiest
conflict of the war. The Soviet railroad system played a vital
role in the nation's four-year struggle against the Nazis.

1940–1970 ARTICULATED STEAM

ARTICULATED LOCOMOTIVES have two sets of driving wheels, which give these huge steam engines the flexibility to negotiate sharp curves and the power to haul the heaviest trains. The original Mallet design was pioneered by French engineer, Anatole Mallet. Herbert Garratt, a British engineer, came up with a variation that was built by Charles Beyer and named after them. Beyer-Garratts are still used in Africa. By 1940, however, the largest articulated locomotives were being constructed by, and deployed in, the United States.

KEEPING FAITH IN STEAM POWER

The Norfolk & Western Railroad built its first 2-8-8-2 Mallet in 1918 and kept faith with the type until dieselization was unavoidable. This locomotive was built in 1952 and was the final member of the last Mallet class, classified Y6b, built in the US. It remained in service until 1960.

Central air compressor

Boiler rests on girder frame

NORTH AMERICA'S HEAVYWEIGHT CHAMPION

This 2-8-8-4 Mallet, which operated on the Duluth, Mesabi, & Iron Range Railroad in Minnesota, was one of 18 of the class built between 1941 and 1943. Known as Yellowstones, these 2-8-8-4s hauled the heaviest steam trains ever regularly operated in the world.

Cylinder is 24 in (61 cm) in diameter

Strengthened cab at front of engine

Oil fuel tank

FORWARD-LOOKING LOCOMOTIVE

Southern Pacific Railway, in the US, built 256 of these oil-fired "Cab Forward" 4-8-8-2s by 1944. They were developed because the smoke exhaust of the conventional Mallet-type engines was overpowering for the crew in the tunnels and snowsheds on the Sierra Nevada route.

Safety valves

69-in (175-cm) driving wheel

Main air reservoir

No.3985 is the only surviving Challenger

Tender has 14 wheels

CHALLENGING CONVENTION

While most US articulated locomotives were designed for relatively slow-speed heavy freight work, Union Pacific's 4-6-6-4 Challengers proved they were capable of fast running as well as prodigious feats of hauling.

Tender holds 25½ tons of coal

No.4012 is one of six preserved Big Boys

Sandbox

THE US'S SUPREME STEAM ENGINE

Steam power attained its peak in 1941 with the Big Boy 4-8-8-4 Mallets of Union Pacific (UP). Built for speeds up to 70 mph (112 kph), these coal-burners generated 6,290 hp and were able to haul up to 6,000 tons on a ruling grade of 1-in-122. UP built 25 Big Boys in total.

Boiler

Exhaust pipe to smokebox

Engine unit

Water tank

AFRICA'S WORKHORSE

British Beyer-Garratts saw service on many of Africa's railroads. This Beyer-Garratt 14/14A class 2-6-2+2-6-2 was sent to Rhodesia (now Zimbabwe) in about 1953. Despite its size, it had an axleloading of only 13¾ tons, which enabled it to work on lightly laid track.

1940-1970 UNION PACIFIC BIG BOY

THE ULTIMATE ARTICULATED steam locomotive to operate in the United States was Union Pacific's (UP) 4-8-8-4, the Big Boy. It was the world's longest steam engine, and was designed for the arduous route through Wyoming and over the Wasatch Mountains in Utah. A total of 25 Big Boys, officially called the 4000 class, were constructed by the American Locomotive Company (ALCO) from 1941 to 1944. It was there that a worker chalked "Big Boy" on the smokebox of a 4000 class under construction. The name stuck.

A BIG BOY FIRING UP FOR ACTION IN UTAH

Handrail

Windshield wings on cab windows

Cab roof ventilator

Ventilators on front windows

Boiler wash-out plug

Cab insulated with fiberglass

No.4006 was the seventh Big Boy built, in 1941

4006
4-8-8-4-1-68 23¼ 23x 540M B

Cab handrail

Boiler blow-off muffler

Truck frame

Journal boxes have roller bearings

Pneumatic boiler blow-off cock

Trailing truck wheel 42 in (107 cm) in diameter

Ashpan

Riveted firebox

Ashpan operating wheel

Tender is 47 ft (14.4 m) long

Locomotive is 86 ft (26 m) long

UNION PACIFIC

4006

Tender water space holds 24,000 gallons (90,920 liters)

Tender coal space holds 32 tons

Four–wheel pivoting guide truck

A GIANT BUILT FOR COMFORT

The engineering of *No.4006* Big Boy is on a massive scale. The firebox, for instance, is 20 ft (6 m) long. Features such as roller bearings, fiberglass insulation, cab window defrosters, and Boxpok wheels made the ride more comfortable, but the design is conventional.

BIG BOY, BIG APPETITE

The huge boiler of this Big Boy was made up of three rings and could sustain pressures of 300 psi (21 kg/cm²). The tender feeding its huge appetite for coal and water rode on 14 42-in (107-cm) diameter wheels, the front four of which formed a swiveling truck. The combined length of the locomotive and tender is an impressive 133 ft (40.4 m).

Sand dome

Handrail

Reversing shaft lever

Safety valve

Driving axle

Boxpok driving wheel

Coupling (side) rod

Eccentric rod

Connecting rod

Expansion link

Rod made of heat-treated, low-carbon nickel steel

Radius rod

KINGS OF THE MOUNTAINS

Climbing to a height of 8,013 ft (2,443 m), Big Boys were powerful enough to haul 100-car, 3,600-ton trains unaided on the 1-in-65 grade of Sherman Hill in Wyoming. When a new route reduced the ruling grade to 1-in-122, these 4-8-8-4s, which were able to develop up to 6,290 hp, hauled trains of up to 6,000 tons. After they were retired, UP found that it took five diesel units to do the work of one Big Boy.

Exhaust pipe to smokebox

Handrail at front of smokebox platform

Enclosure houses aftercooler

Pilot beam

Pilot coupler

Pilot

Articulation hinge

Walschaerts valve gear

Cylinder is 24 in (60 cm) in diameter

Four-wheel leading truck

Running board · Steam dome · Air reservoir · Sand dome · Handrail · Regulator rod · Front-end regulator valve in smokebox

Cylinder cocks · Cylinder steam chest · Brake hanger · Driving wheel 68 in (173 cm) in diameter · Sanding pipe · Coupling (side) rod · Connecting rod big end · Return crank · Guard for lubricator chain drive · Reverse link

SPECIFICATION

Manufacturer	American Locomotive Company (ALCO)
Classification	4000 class 4-cylinder 4-8-8-4
Date built	1941–44; No.4006 built in 1941
Number built	25
Fuel	Coal
Top speed	80 mph (128 kph)
Length	133 ft (40.4 m)
Height	16.4 ft (5m)
Total weight	539.6 tons
Tractive effort	135,375 lb (61,460 kg)

UNIQUE TO UNION PACIFIC

Even from the front, the Big Boy is an imposing locomotive, towering about 16½ ft (5 m) above the tracks. Big Boys were too long and heavy to operate on most railroads, so only UP used them. To accommodate the Big Boy, UP installed the world's longest turntables at their depots. The class was retired from service in the late 1950s. No.4006 is one of eight Big Boys to have been preserved.

Traditional warning bell

Smokebox-securing lugs or "dogs"

Headlight

Steps up to smokebox

Pilot beam is 10 ft 10 in (330 cm) wide

Air brake and signal hoses

Numberplate (X indicates "Extra" train)

Cylindrical smokebox

Union Pacific shield

Air intake grille

Retractable coupler cover

Footboard

Pilot

Double chimney

Smoke hood

IT'S ALL IN THE SWING

At the front end, a "lever" arrangement controlled the lateral motion of the Big Boy, enabling it to negotiate curves. On a curve of 10° radius, the front end of the boiler swung out 2 ft (60 cm) from the center of the track. The sharpest curve it could negotiate was a 20° radius.

Steampipe

Aftercooler

Crosshead

Union link

Wheel tire

Piston rod

Valve spindle

Piston head

Cylinder steam chest

Cylinder cocks

Leading wheel has a diameter of 36 in (91.5 cm)

1940-1970 THE BLUE TRAIN

NOW WIDELY REGARDED as offering the most luxurious train journey in the world, South Africa's Blue Train can trace its origins back beyond the Union of South Africa in 1910. At that time, the luxury rail service between Cape Town and Johannesburg was named the Union Limited when it journeyed northward and the Union Express when southbound. In 1928, new sapphire-blue articulated cars were introduced on all Union services, but it was not until 1946 that the title "Blue Train" was officially adopted. The trains run on narrow 42-in (107-cm) gauge track.

BEFORE THE BLUE TRAIN

A forerunner of the Blue Train, the Union Express is seen en route from Cape Town to Johannesburg, with a South African Railways large-boilered 4-8-2 at its head. The Blue Train continued to use steam locomotives for part of the journey right up until 1973.

LAYING DOWN THE TRACK

Mules hauled materials and this crane wagon into position during the building of the line northward from Cape Town in the nineteenth century. The discovery of diamonds in 1870 provided Cecil Rhodes with the impetus to construct the railroad, which by 1895 had reached Johannesburg.

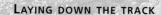

Articulated stainless steel carriages

AWESOME VIEW

A Blue Train is seen crossing the 400-ft (122-m) deep Zambesi River gorge in front of the Victoria Falls. The 500-ft (152-m) long steel bridge that it uses to cross into Zambia was built in 1905 as part of Cecil Rhodes' Cape-to-Cairo railway. This trans-African line was never completed.

THE BLUE TRAIN ROUTE

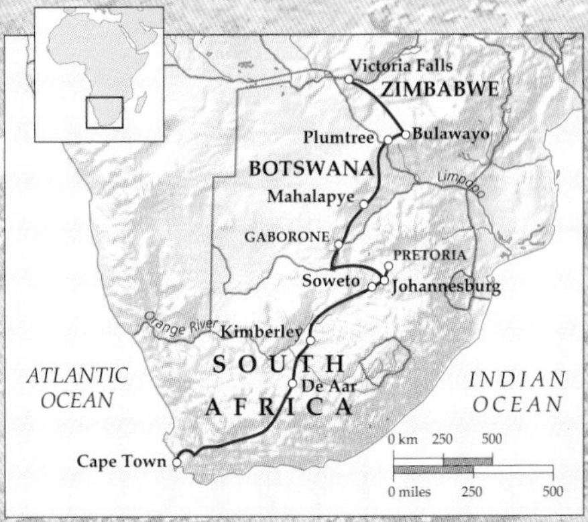

After leaving Cape Town, the Blue Train travels through the wine-growing area of the Western Cape before crossing the Hex River Mountains and the Great Karoo desert. It then journeys through the mining country of the Orange Free State before reaching its destination of Pretoria in the Western Transvaal, a distance of 1,005 miles (1,608 km). Excursions also run north through Botswana and Zimbabwe to the Victoria Falls.

HOTEL ON WHEELS

Despite the cars being narrower than on most luxury trains, the standard of service is unsurpassed. Along with the bar-lounge seen here, the Blue Train also offers four classes of accommodation, excellent cuisine in the dining car, and 28 staff to look after 100 passengers.

ELECTRIC ATTRACTION

The Class 6E B-B electric units seen climbing through mountain country at the head of this Blue Train muster over 3,000 hp. The average speed of the Blue Train is kept to a sedate 36 mph (58 kph), however, to allow its passengers to appreciate the views en route.

Masts support electric cable

Catenary

Locomotive has twin pantographs

AN ENGINEERING WONDER

Hauled by three 6E class electric locomotives, a Blue Train passes through the verdant Hex River Pass in the Western Cape. Here, in 1876, the line was built through what were deemed to be unbreachable mountain ranges. Gradients as steep as 1-in-31 were surmounted along this steep stretch of line, which climbs from 1,565 ft (477 m) to 3,150 ft (960 m) above sea level.

1940–1970 DIESELS

CHANGE SWEPT ACROSS North American railroads during the 1940s and 1950s, as diesel units replaced steam engines. New designs, such as the ALCO (American Locomotive Company) PA and General Motors' EMD F class, proved conclusively the superior efficiency and economy of diesel traction, as well as the advantages of their relatively smoke-free running. In the years after World War II, the higher construction cost and complex maintenance requirements of diesel units deterred the majority of countries from adopting them. However, by 1970 diesel had replaced steam in much of Europe, Australasia, Africa, and South America.

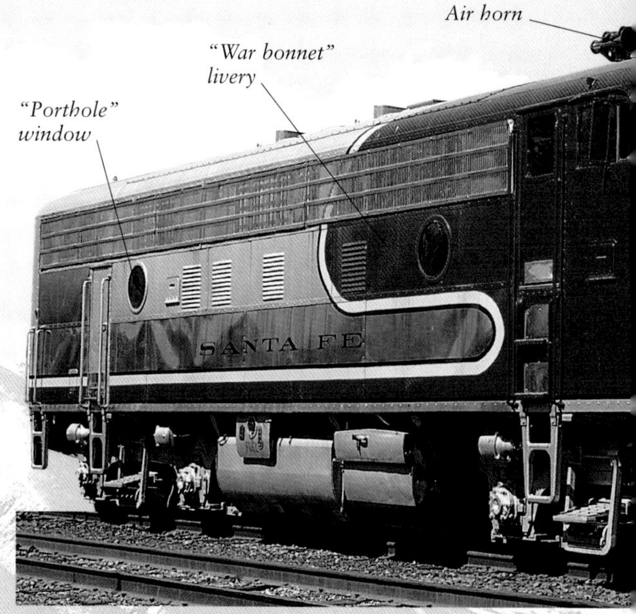

"War bonnet" livery

Air horn

"Porthole" window

FIRST OF A KIND

General Motors launched its GP (General Purpose) F series of diesel-electric B-B road units in 1939. No.347C, seen above in "war-bonnet" livery, was the first 1,500-hp F7 series and was built in 1949. By 1954, a further 3,681 F7 series diesel-electric units were in use in the US alone.

Fuel tank

Air inlet

Class identification and number plate

Two-axle truck

GERMAN DIESEL-HYDRAULIC

The V200 12-cylinder 2,200-hp B-B shown above was developed by the Deutsches Bundesbahn (DB) in Germany. V200s were first used in 1953, and were one of the most successful diesel-hydraulic classes to be designed by DB. V200s continued to be built until 1963 and one of this class remained in regular service up until 1988.

Locomotive is a hood unit

Driving cab

Peruvian Railways logo

Radiator air intake

Radiator

GASPING FOR AIR

High in the Andes, on the Central Railway in Peru, a US-built C-C diesel-electric pauses at Meigg's loop between Casapalca and Ticlio. As the line ascends to 15,000 ft (4,572 m), the US-designed locomotive had to be fitted with a turbocharger to force oxygen into the cylinders.

Three-axle powered truck

Ladder

Snub nose

Headlight

47C

SANTA FE

Name of railroad

Jumper cables

"Carbody" body shell

Passenger car

Boxcar

ARGENTINA'S CLOUD TRAIN

Headed by C-C diesel-electric, the *Tren a Las Nubes* (The Train of the Clouds) climbs through the Andes at Abra Muñano, in the Salta province of Argentina, on a stretch of the Transandine line that climbs to an altitude of 13,252 ft (4,039 m). The diesel unit belongs to a class developed in the US for export purposes.

Raised "cockpit" cab

GERMANY UNITES EUROPE

Germany's first Trans-Europ Express services used Class 601 diesel multiple units like the one here. These trains were introduced in 1957 and were powered by two 1,100-hp engines. These seven-car sets could operate at speeds of up to 88 mph (140 kph) and they remained in international service as TEE trains until the 1970s.

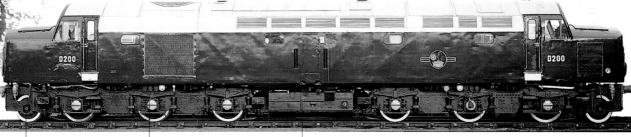

Leading guide axle   Three-axle truck   Fuel tank

A SUCCESS IN BRITAIN

One of the most successful classes of mainline diesel locomotives to replace steam on Britain's railroads during the 1950s and 1960s was the 16-cylinder 2,000-hp Type 4 (later Class 40) 1-C-C-1 diesel-electric. The prototype D200, seen here, entered service in 1958 and had a top operating speed of 90 mph (144 kph).

LONG-NOSED EASY RIDER WITH BOOSTER

A PA cab unit and a PB booster unit head the Delaware & Hudson Railroad's Adirondack Express as it awaits departure from Montreal, Canada. The PA and PB series, built by ALCO, first saw service in 1946. Their two three-axle trucks rode at up to 100 mph (160 kph).

1940–1970 DELTIC

THE WORLD'S MOST POWERFUL single-unit diesel locomotive during the 1950s and early 1960s was not North American, but British. The 3,300-hp Deltic C-C diesel-electric prototype was built by the English Electric Company in 1955. It then spent six years working on the West Coast Main Line and the East Coast Main Line in Britain. At a time when steam traction was still dominant in Britain, the streamlined Deltic made an enormous impact. On both routes, the Deltic was easily a match for the Pacific-type steam locomotives. On one run between London and Edinburgh it averaged a speed of over 72 mph (115 kph).

HIGH MILEAGE, HIGH IMPACT

During six years of trials, the Deltic prototype covered over 400,000 miles (640,000 km) in public service. Its success prompted British Railways to order 22 production Deltics, one of which hauled Britain's fastest locomotive service at an average of 91 mph (146 kph).

SPECIFICATION

Manufacturer	English Electric, Preston, England
Classification	Deltic-type C-C diesel-electric
Date built	1955
Number built	1 prototype; 22 production series
Fuel	Diesel
Top speed	105 mph (167 kph)
Length	64 ft (19.5 m)
Height	13 ft (4 m)
Total weight	107½ tons
Tractive effort	60,064lb (27,240 kg)

Engine room vent   Exhaust port   Inspection hatch   Radiator fan   Engine room window   Engine room vent

1,080-gallon (4,090-liter) fuel tank   Inspection socket   Folding step   Drain for radiator coolant   Radiator coolant hatch   Sandbox   Telescopic damper

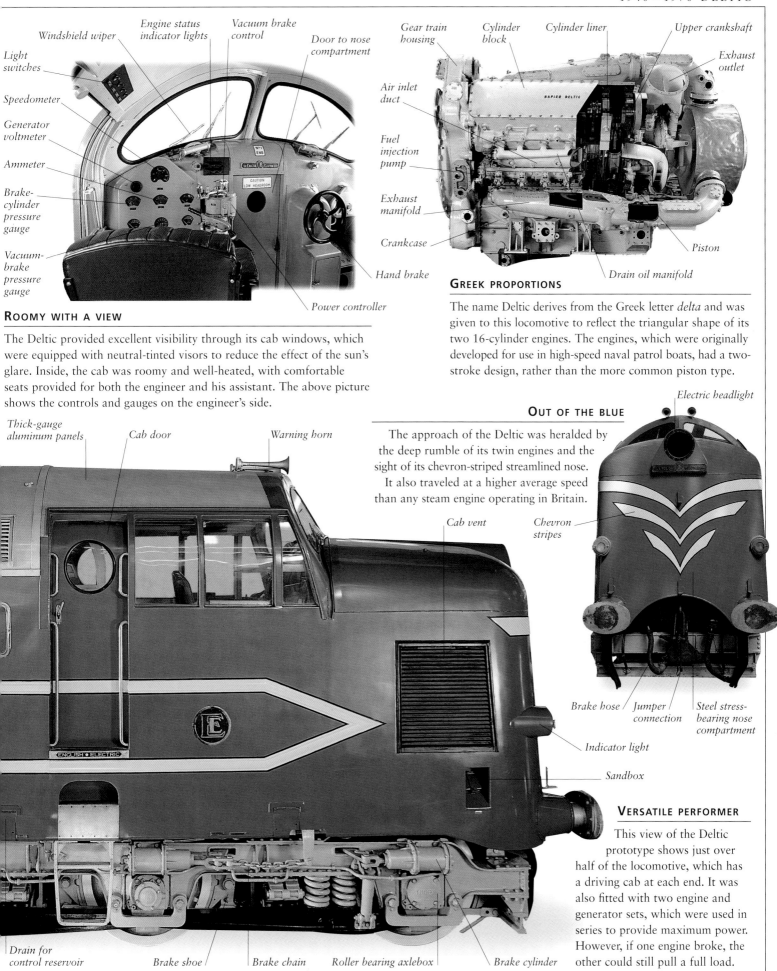

Light switches

Windshield wiper

Engine status indicator lights

Vacuum brake control

Door to nose compartment

Speedometer

Generator voltmeter

Ammeter

Brake-cylinder pressure gauge

Vacuum-brake pressure gauge

Hand brake

Power controller

Gear train housing

Cylinder block

Cylinder liner

Upper crankshaft

Air inlet duct

Exhaust outlet

Fuel injection pump

Exhaust manifold

Crankcase

Drain oil manifold

Piston

ROOMY WITH A VIEW

The Deltic provided excellent visibility through its cab windows, which were equipped with neutral-tinted visors to reduce the effect of the sun's glare. Inside, the cab was roomy and well-heated, with comfortable seats provided for both the engineer and his assistant. The above picture shows the controls and gauges on the engineer's side.

GREEK PROPORTIONS

The name Deltic derives from the Greek letter *delta* and was given to this locomotive to reflect the triangular shape of its two 16-cylinder engines. The engines, which were originally developed for use in high-speed naval patrol boats, had a two-stroke design, rather than the more common piston type.

OUT OF THE BLUE

The approach of the Deltic was heralded by the deep rumble of its twin engines and the sight of its chevron-striped streamlined nose. It also traveled at a higher average speed than any steam engine operating in Britain.

Electric headlight

Thick-gauge aluminum panels

Cab door

Warning horn

Cab vent

Chevron stripes

Brake hose

Jumper connection

Steel stress-bearing nose compartment

Indicator light

Sandbox

Drain for control reservoir

Brake shoe

Brake chain

Roller bearing axlebox

Brake cylinder

VERSATILE PERFORMER

This view of the Deltic prototype shows just over half of the locomotive, which has a driving cab at each end. It was also fitted with two engine and generator sets, which were used in series to provide maximum power. However, if one engine broke, the other could still pull a full load.

1940–1970 LATE STEAM

AFTER WORLD WAR II, competition from the aviation and motor industries forced railroad operators to cut the cost of their service. This led designers to look at ways of making steam locomotives more efficient. Despite these endeavors, however, cleaner and more cost-effective diesel- and electric-powered locomotives were increasingly preferred, and by the mid-1950s mainline steam traction was rare in the US. By 1965, it was also dying out in Europe, but in other regions such as China, where labor is cheaper and coal supplies are plentiful, steam still survives.

COLORFUL CALIFORNIAN

Smart in their black, orange, and red livery, Southern Pacific Railroad's semistreamlined GS-4 4-8-4s hauled the Daylight service between Los Angeles and San Francisco. In all, 30 of these two-cylinder oil-fired machines were built at the Lima Locomotive Works in Ohio between 1941 and 1942.

AMERICANS IN PARIS

After World War II, France turned to North America to restock its depleted locomotive fleet. Between 1945 and 1947, 1,323 141R Liberation class 2-8-2s were imported. Known as Les Americains, they were the last mainline steam locomotives in regular service in France.

Boxed-in steampipe

Smoke deflector

Decorated for competition

Handrail

Torpedo-shaped smokebox

स्वयंवर

7247 WP

STAR OF INDIA

This ornately decorated Indian WP Pacific was entered into a locomomotive "beauty contest" in Delhi. The WP Pacific class, which was developed by India and America's Baldwin Locomotive Works, was the standard express passenger class in India after World War II.

Display board

Buckeye coupler

Cylinder valve chest

Air brake cylinder

SOUTH AFRICAN SURVIVOR

For over 40 years from the early 1940s, the class 15F two-cylinder 4-8-2 was a mainstay of South African Railways, which used 255 of these engines. The 15F has 60-in (150-cm) diameter driving wheels and its large tender is able to carry 14 tons of coal and 6,050 gallons (27,500 liters) of water.

Casing encloses steampipe

Safety valves

"Boxpox" driving wheel

Space for easy maintenance access

Firebox

Trailing truck supports cab

POST-WAR PRACTICALITY

The design of this Russian 2-10-2 clearly demonstrates a feature of post-1945 steam locomotive design – ease of maintenance. The high-pitched boiler allows easy access to the running gear and the other moving parts that need daily lubrication.

TRANS-SIBERIAN STREAMLINER

The P36 class 4-8-4s were the last mainline express passenger locomotives built in the Soviet Union. The prototype appeared in 1950, and by 1954 250 P36s had been built. These streamlined machines remained the backbone of the Trans-Siberian service for 15 years.

STEAM'S LAST EMPEROR

Today, China is by far the world's largest user of steam traction and around 3,000 Qian Jin (March Forward) 2-10-2s are still thought to remain in service. The QJ class was introduced in 1957 and continued to be constructed until 1982 at the rate of about 300 engines a year.

Eight-wheeled truck car

A GRAND FINALE

Introduced in 1954, the 9F 2-10-0 was the finest freight steam locomotive ever built in Britain, the country which developed the world's first steam engines. It is therefore fitting that the last 9F to be built, *Evening Star*, was also the last mainline steam engine built in Britain. It was constructed at the ex-Great Western Railway works at Swindon in Wiltshire in 1960.

Double smokestack

Steam dome

Flangeless central pair of driving wheels

Walschaerts valve gear

EVENING STAR

92220

1940–1970 ELECTRICS

THE CONCLUSION OF WORLD WAR II saw an era of widespread mainline electrification. The process, which began in Italy and Switzerland at the beginning of the century, was soon under way in France and Germany. The rebuilding of the lines destroyed during the war offered a unique opportunity for innovation. The French Mistral Express, which came into service in 1950, launched the era of high-speed intercity rail travel. French electric engines were also the first to exceed the 200-mph (320-kph) barrier. Extensive electrification was also adopted by countries outside Europe such as Russia and Japan, where the first dedicated high-speed electric railway, the Tokaido Shinkansen, was opened in 1964.

FRENCH FLIER

During the 1950s, the Mistral was Europe's fastest train. This first-class-only service ran between Paris, Lyons, and Nice and was hauled by 9200 series B-B electric engines, like the one above, which cruised at 80 mph (121 kph).

ITALY'S LUCKY SEVEN

The Settebello, or Lucky Seven express as it was dubbed because it hauled seven coaches, was the finest train in Italy. Launched in 1953, this train covered the 394 miles (630 km) between Rome, Florence, Bologna, and Milan in under six hours, at an average speed of 67 mph (106 kph).

Cockpit operator's position

Train is soundproofed with double-glazed windows

Aerodynamically molded front end

Panoramic observation saloon

CROSS-FRONTIER TRAIN

The Edelweiss, seen here, traveled from Brussels, in Belgium, to Zurich in Switzerland as part of the Trans-Europ Express (TEE) fleet. These trains needed to be able to operate on all four AC and DC electrification systems employed in western Europe. The service was launched in 1957.

JAPANESE HIGH-SPEED PIONEER

Seen here between Osaka and Kyoto is a 485 series electric multiple unit, Japan Railways' principal express type before the inauguration of the high-speed "Bullet Train" in 1964. Electrification was adopted in Japan because it had no oil.

GERMAN FLAGSHIP

Class 103s, like the one here, were the flagship electric engines of the Deutsches Bundesbahn (German Federal Railways) for almost 30 years. Developed in the 1960s, they had a top cruising speed of 125 mph (200 kph).

Aerodynamically shaped nose fairing

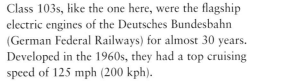

Pantograph collects current

Train weighs 364 tons

CONTINUING DOWN THE LINE

Following the success of the ETR prototype in 1939 (*see p.100*), Italy continued to develop several generations of Elettrotreno Rapido (High-Speed Electric Train) after World War II. The design for this ETR 223 multiple unit, pictured at Perugia in 1994, was developed in the 1960s.

CROSSING THE CAPE

Two South African Railways 6e class B-B electric locomotives prepare to double-head the Trans-Karoo Express across the flatlands of the Karoo in Cape Province. Electric locomotives took the place of steam engines after the line was electrified in the 1970s.

1940-1970 TOKAIDO SHINKANSEN

AFTER WORLD WAR II, Japan began electrifying its major routes but found that the speed its new electric trains could go was limited by the existing track conditions and by slow freight traffic operating on these lines. In 1958, the Japanese government took the bold step of authorizing the construction of a separate passenger-only railroad, the Tokaido Shinkansen. The first high-speed electric multiple units, soon to be known throughout the world as "Bullet Trains," came into service on this line on October 1 1964. Their top operating speed of 131 mph (210 kph) broke all records for a scheduled train service and won them instant fame both at home and abroad. By July 1967, over 100 million passengers had traveled on the Tokaido Shinkansen.

BEFORE THE BULLET TRAIN

In November 1956, celebrations accompanied the departure from Tokyo of the first electrically hauled Kodama (Echo) express along the original Tokaido line. The level of traffic operating on this route, the busiest in Japan, restricted the speed of the Kodama express and prompted the Japanese to build a new high-speed line between Tokyo and Osaka.

AN OLYMPIC FINISH

The 1964 Tokyo Olympics were an important showcase for Japan's post-war regeneration and so the opening of the Tokaido Shinkansen was scheduled to coincide with this event. To meet the deadline, work on the 322-mile (515-km) new railroad continued day and night.

BUILDING PARALLEL LINES

Although the Shinkansen follows a similar route to the original line, they never meet because it uses a wider gauge. In built-up areas the Shinkansen is elevated on trackway and soundproofed with inverted L shaped walls.

Track gauge is 4 ft 8½ in (143.5 cm)

Lightweight steel construction

Pantograph

Registration rod

Mast

THE ROUTE OF THE TOKAIDO SHINKANSEN

For most of its length the Tokaido Shinkansen (New Railroad) follows the southern coast of Honshu, the largest island in Japan. It links the Japanese capital of Tokyo with the major industrial city of Osaka. The "Bullet Trains" stop at ten other destinations en route, including Yokohama, Japan's largest port, Atami, Hamamatsu, Nagoya, and the ancient capital of Kyoto. The success of the Tokaido Shinkansen led Japanese Railways to extend this high-speed line to link up with cities on the other main Japanese islands of Hokkaido, Kyushu, and Shikoku.

ALWAYS LOOKING FORWARDS

In a "Bullet Train," the Green Car, seen here, is akin to the European "First Class." It seats 68 in a two-by-two arrangement. All the cars are air-conditioned and sealed against the pressure pulses generated as the train rushes in and out of tunnels, or passes another train. In the latest "Bullet Trains" seats can turn automatically to face the direction of travel.

FAST MEETS SLOW

Contrasting with the busy scene below, a sleek Shinkansen train glides serenely across a road bridge in Tokyo. Japan was far ahead of Europe and North America in introducing an advanced railroad alternative to motor transport in 1964.

300 series Nozomi

Flattened nose section

Series 100 Nozomi   *Series 0*

Bullet-shaped nose section

PEAK PERFORMANCE

Since its inception, the popular image of the Shinkansen has been of a "Bullet Train," or *Dangan Ressha*, speeding past the snow-capped peak of Japan's highest mountain, Mount Fuji. The train below is a 100 series, introduced in 1986, which cut the journey between Tokyo and Osaka to under three hours.

SPANNING THREE GENERATIONS

Over 25 years of development on the Shinkansen are represented by these three trains. The original Series 0 "Bullet Train" (*right*) was introduced in 1964, and was replaced in 1986 by the Series 100 Nozomi (*centre*). This was overtaken by the Series 300 Nozomi (*left*) in 1992, which has a top speed of 168 mph (270 kph) and is made of lightweight aluminum.

Traction motors slung below car

Passenger compartment on leading car

Cockpit driving position

Horizontal aperture for marker lights

1970-2000
FAST-FORWARD INTO THE FUTURE

IN THE PAST 30 YEARS the railroads have faced relentless competition from road and air transportation, and have had to adapt to survive. The success of the steps taken by railroad operators can be gauged by the revived fortunes of rail transportation. The networks of specially built, passenger- carrying, high-speed electrified lines constructed in Japan, France, and several other European countries have been highly successful. The Channel Tunnel, opened in 1994, now provides a high-speed railroad link between London, Paris, and Brussels. These success stories are now being emulated both in the US, where the automobile has most seriously depleted passenger traffic levels, and in several Asian countries. Faster diesel- and electric-powered locomotives, combined with radically improved handling facilities, have also won freight traffic back from the roads. Equally impressive is the large number of cities involved in building new rapid transit systems to curb traffic congestion. The latest innovations are the magnetic levitation trains being actively developed in Germany and Japan to provide "superspeed" transportation.

TGV SUD-EST WAS THE FIRST
HIGH-SPEED SERVICE IN FRANCE

1970-2000 PASSENGER DIESELS

ADVANCES IN THE ENGINES, transmission systems, and traction motors of diesel locomotives during the 1970s spurred the development of passenger diesel services. This new generation of diesels proved popular in countries such as the United States, Canada, and Australia, where electrification was not a realistic option because of the large distances over which the trains had to travel. However, it was in Britain that the high-speed diesel reached its zenith in 1973 with the arrival of the 125. Despite these advances, diesel units will never be able to match the pace of electric trains due to their weight and other limitations.

CHINA CELEBRATES

Festivities accompany the departure of the first passenger train service to use the newly opened 1,562-mile (2,500-km) Jialong (Kowloon) to Beijing railway in May 1997. Trains on the line, which cost nearly US$5 billion to build, are hauled by Chinese DF4 class diesel-electrics that were first constructed in 1969.

US DIESEL-ELECTRIC TECHNOLOGY IN CANADA

The Intercontinental enters Jasper, Alberta, on its journey across Canada, with a Electro-Motive (EMD) 1,750-hp, F9-type diesel-electric at its head. The F series was first developed in 1939, but it was not until after World War II that these snub-nosed locomotives became a worldwide success.

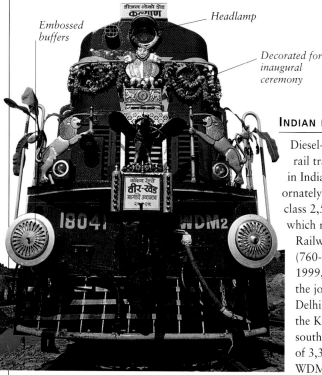

Embossed buffers

Headlamp

Decorated for inaugural ceremony

Disc brakes on all wheels

Housing for electrical and air-conditioning equipment

INDIAN DIESEL POWER

Diesel-powered high-speed rail travel has come of age in India in the form of this ornately decorated WDM2 class 2,536-hp diesel-electric, which runs on the Konkan Railway. The 475-mile (760-km) line, opened in 1999, has greatly reduced the journey times between Delhi in northern India and the Kerala district in the southwest of India. A total of 3,385 American-designed WDM2s operate in India.

AUSTRALIA'S FASTEST TRAIN

Seen running between Perth and Kalgoorlie is a Prospector. These trains are powered by 380-hp, German-built, MAN diesel-hydraulic engines, which maintain an average speed of 53 mph (84 kph) over the length of this 408-mile (653-km) route.

Air-conditioning units

AMERICAN DOUBLE-DECK COMMUTER EXPRESS

Seen passing Lake Street Tower, Chicago, hauling a double-deck suburban train, is a General Motors Electro-Motive Division F40 diesel unit. Chicago's Metro system is one of many US commuter networks employing these 3,000-hp turbo-charged locomotives. The F40 series greatly reduced journey times when it was introduced in 1976 and several hundred of them still operate in the US and Canada.

Semi-streamlined front end

Monocoque (frameless) body shell

FAST SERVICE FOR THE US

Fresh off the General Electric production line, an AMD103-class Genesis diesel-electric powers through Cold Spring in New York State. It is one of the fleet of semi-streamlined Genesis units that Amtrak introduced into service during the 1990s to spearhead its intercity passenger services.

Flexible gangway links coaches

Air intake

Radiator fan

Original Intercity livery

Exhaust outlet

Streamlined driving compartment

INTERCITY

43049

BRITISH MASTERPIECE

British Railways unveiled its High-Speed Train, now known as the 125, in 1973. It promptly set a new world speed record for diesel traction of 143 mph (230 kph). The 125, so called because its normal operating speed is 125 mph (238 kph), revolutionized intercity services in Britain, where it still operates today.

1970-2000 INDIAN PACIFIC

A CONTINUOUS TRAIN JOURNEY across Australia was impossible until a 2,461-mile (3,938-km) single-gauge line was completed in 1969, connecting Perth, situated on the Indian Ocean, with Sydney, on the Pacific Ocean. The Indian Pacific became the first luxury transcontinental passenger express to operate on this route in February 1970, 120 years after the first locomotive was imported into Australia. The delay in providing this railway service is attributable to the regional variations in line gauges that had hampered rail travel in Australia up to this point. The Indian Pacific continues to provide one of the most epic and luxurious railroad journeys in the world.

BUILDING THE LINE

When railroads were first built across Australia's arid interior, camels, imported from India and Afghanistan, transported the track and crossties, as they were the only means of transport able to endure the conditions (*left*). Even when the final length of track was laid from Kwinana to Koolyanobbing, in 1969, the crew labored under harsh conditions (*above*).

A LONG-AWAITED CELEBRATION

The inaugural Indian Pacific bursts through a banner and streamers on arriving in Perth, Western Australia, on February 27, 1970. A crowd of 10,000 welcomed the train that had set out from Sydney five days earlier.

CLP class based on American F class

Diesel-electric engine develops 3,000 hp

INDIAN PACIFIC ROUTE

To travel 2,461 miles (3,938 miles) between Sydney and Perth on the Indian Pacific service is to experience the contrasts that exist in Australia. In the east, the Indian Pacific train negotiates a series of mountain ranges, including the spectacular Blue Mountains. It then crosses the fertile plains of New South Wales, reaching a string of former mining towns, such as Broken Hill. Later comes the vast, arid Nullarbor Plain, which extends into Western Australia, where desert stretches almost to Perth.

ON A STRAIGHT LINE

An Indian Pacific diesel engine is pictured here along the 287-mile (459-km) straight stretch of line that was built to cross the barren limestone plateau of the Nullarbor (No Tree) Plain. This section of line is the longest dead straight stretch of track in the world.

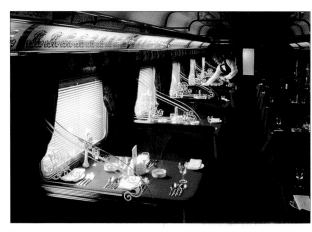

EASTBOUND IN THE AVON VALLEY

The Indian Pacific trains display a strong North American influence that recalls the luxury US streamliner services of the 1950s. The C-C diesel-electric at the head of this train belongs to the CL class that was introduced in 1970. The design originated in the US, but it was built in Sydney.

EVERYTHING ABOARD

The Indian Pacific trains are well equipped for the 65-hour journey across Australia. In addition to the classy dining car seen here, the trains also have a cafeteria, a lounge, club cars, and two classes of accommodation. They are even equipped with a honeymoon suite and a sick bay.

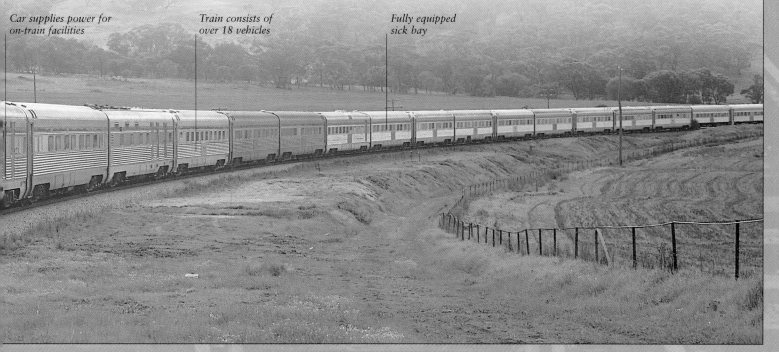

Car supplies power for on-train facilities

Train consists of over 18 vehicles

Fully equipped sick bay

1970-2000 WORLD FREIGHT

BY 1970, STEAM TRACTION had been displaced across most of the world, and the vast majority of freight traffic was hauled by diesel engines. US manufacturers, such as General Motors, came to dominate the production of reliable, cost-efficient diesel units. However, at this time many freight diesel engines were still ponderously slow. Faced with stiff competition from road and air haulers, the railways were forced to streamline their freight service, introduce purpose-built rolling stock, and increase the speed of their engines. The newest types of diesel and electric freight engines are able to haul heavy loads at sustained speeds of more than 70 mph (112 kph).

Air horns in cab roof

Air intake grill

AMERICAN REVOLUTION IN BRITAIN

The new Class 66 C-C diesel-electric shown is one of 250 being shipped over to Britain from the US by the American-owned English, Welsh & Scottish Railways. It can haul a 1,829-ton freight train at a speed of 75 mph (120 kph).

C-C wheel arrangement

Fuel tank

Radiator fan

Powered axles

Each locomotive weighs 118½ tons

NORTH AMERICAN STEEL MOVERS

The two brightly painted GM Electro-Motive SD (Special Duty) series diesel-electrics, pictured in Kirk Yard, Gary, Indiana, haul steel along lines operated by Elgin, Joliet, & Eastern Railway to the mainline routes serving Chicago. These large, 2,000-hp units have 16-cylinder engines.

Air-conditioned driving cab

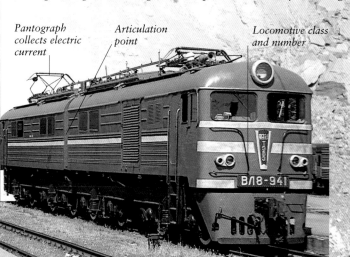

Pantograph collects electric current

Articulation point

Locomotive class and number

Connecting cables for multiple operation

RUSSIAN HEAVYWEIGHT

WL8.941, here in the Ukraine, belongs to the most powerful class of electric engines in the world. Much of the 3,000 million tons of rail freight moved in the former Soviet Union each year is hauled by this class.

HITCHING A RIDE

Two B-B diesel-electric units lead a Wisconsin Central "piggy-back" train out of Chicago. Such trains, which transport trailers on flatcars, are a good example of road-rail cooperation in the US.

Iron ore —————

AUSTRALIA'S IRON ROAD

Three American-designed, Australian-built 3,600-hp diesel-electrics working in multiple haul up to 240 cars of iron ore across the northern region of Western Australia. On an average day, 90,000 tons of ore is transported from the mines at Mounts Newman and Tom Price to coastal ports.

Radiator

Fuel tank

Three-axle bogie

16 cylinder engine delivers 3,600 hp

HIGH-TECH EUROPEAN ELECTRIC

One of the most advanced general-purpose electric locomotives is the Swiss-built LOK2000 B-B, launched in 1991. These 8,180-hp engines are capable of hauling trains at speeds of up to 143 mph (230 kph). The two shown here are in Austrian Railways livery.

DOUBLE THE LOAD IN HALF THE TIME

Three General Electric C-C diesel-electrics head a double-stacked container train on the Aitchison, Topeka, & Santa Fe Railroad in the US. Operating like this they haul freight at average speeds of 70 mph (112 kph).

The nose unit protects the crew in the event of a collision

"Ditch" lights illuminate track

"Well" car carrying two containers

1970–2000 SD-45 FREIGHT DIESEL

A GROWING AWARENESS OF THE ECONOMIES achieved by using fewer high-powered diesel locomotives to haul heavy freight trains, rather than a string of less powerful machines, led to the introduction in 1965 of the 3,600-hp SD-45. The SD-45, the first diesel-electric in the US to employ a 20-cylinder engine, proved powerful enough to do this. By 1972, 1,260 SD-45s were working in the US, and a less powerful SD-40 was developed that sold in even greater numbers. Until this time, four-axle B-B units had reigned supreme as they were cheaper to maintain, but these six-axle C-C engines changed the shape of freight diesels.

UNDER THE HOOD

The SD-45 belongs to a group of locomotives known as "hood" units because its engine and other components are enclosed in a box-like superstructure. This design left space around all four sides for walkways, which facilitated the maintenance and lubrication of the engine.

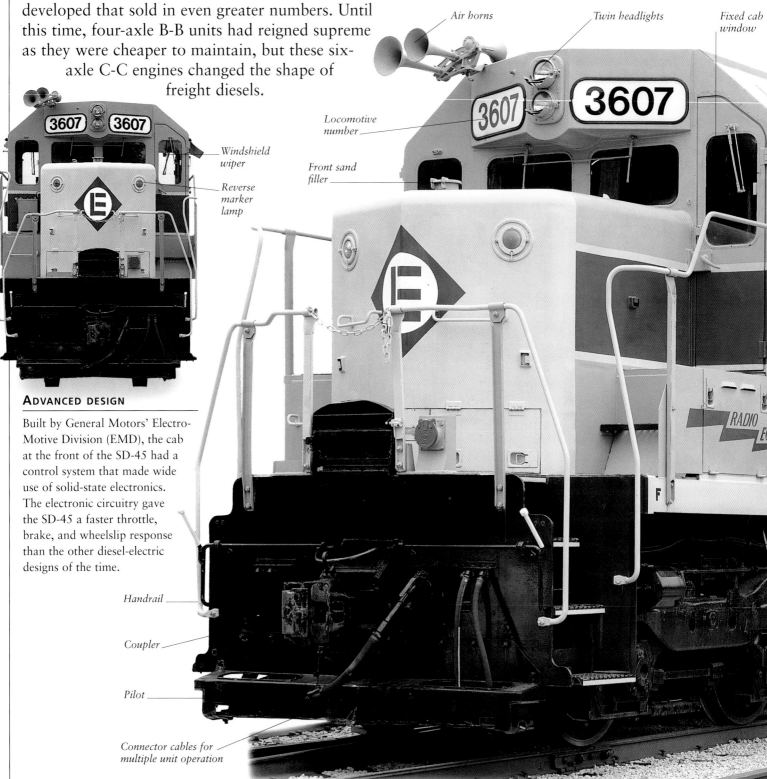

Air horns

Twin headlights

Fixed cab window

Locomotive number

Windshield wiper

Reverse marker lamp

Front sand filler

ADVANCED DESIGN

Built by General Motors' Electro-Motive Division (EMD), the cab at the front of the SD-45 had a control system that made wide use of solid-state electronics. The electronic circuitry gave the SD-45 a faster throttle, brake, and wheelslip response than the other diesel-electric designs of the time.

Handrail

Coupler

Pilot

Connector cables for multiple unit operation

Control cabinet behind cab

Inertial air separator

Dynamic brake

Dynamic brake grid

Radiator cores behind air inlets

SD-45 has six traction motors

3607

ERIE LACKAWANNA

STICKING TO THE TASK

The six-axled C-C format of the SD-45 appealed to railroads that, due to geographical and climatic conditions, needed locomotives that gave the greatest grip on steep grades and damp, slippery rails.

Truck wheelbase is 13 ft 7 in (4.14 m) long

Running board

Fuel tank

Three-axle truck

Flared radiator mounting

Side window awning

Inertial air separator

Dynamic brake

Access doors to engine

KEEPING A COOL HEAD

The flared radiator mounting, conspicuous in this rear-end view of an SD-45, maximized the space for cooling equipment and air circulation. This design allowed the SD-45 to be fitted with a novel kind of traction motor that performed best at high power.

Cooling fan

Herald of the Erie Lackawanna Railroad

3607 3607

Air intake

607

ERIE LACKAWANNA

Rear sandbox

Rear platform

Compartment housing main generator and alternator

Flexicoil truck improves ride

Air reservoir

4,800-gallon (18,184 liter) fuel tank

Roller bearings

SPECIFICATION

Manufacturer	General Motors EMD, US
Classification	SD-45 C-C
Date built	1965–1971; *No.3607* built 1967
Number built	1,260
Fuel	Diesel
Top speed	65 mph (105 kph)
Length	65 ft 8 in (20 m)
Height	15 ft 5 in (4.7 m)
Total weight	175 tons
Tractive effort	83,189 lb (37,727.4 kg)

1970-2000 HIGH-SPEED ELECTRICS

FOLLOWING THE SUCCESS of the Japanese Tokaido Shinkansen (New Railway), which opened in 1964, many countries in Europe began to develop new lines dedicated exclusively to high-speed passenger trains. The most successful of these are the French Lignes à Grand Vitesse (High Speed Lines), the first of which was opened between Paris and Lyons in 1981. Improvements in the design of electric trains, power supply, and computer technology have greatly increased the speed of rail travel on these new lines. Currently, France is the leading producer of high-speed electric trains and is now exporting their Trains à Grand Vitesse (TGVs) around the world.

HIGH-SPEED SPANIARDS

Pictured at Santa Justa station, Seville, this pair of handsome trains operate on Spain's first high-speed line, the Alta Velocidad Espana (AVE), which opened between Madrid and Seville in 1991. Their design is based on France's TGV and they travel at an average speed of 132 mph (209 kph).

JAPAN'S RECORD-BREAKER

The 500 series "Bullet Train," named Nozomi (Hope), was introduced in 1997 and set a new Japanese speed record of 277 mph (443 kph). The 16-car Nozomi shown operates at a top commercial speed of 169 mph (270 kph) traveling on the Tokaido and Sanyo railroads on Japan's main island of Honshu.

Power cable support mast

ADAPTED FOR INTERNATIONAL USE

The international Thalys is a "quadrivoltage" version of France's TGV, which has to work off four different current supplies: the AC systems of Belgium, France, and Germany and the DC supply of the Netherlands. Between Paris and Brussels, the Thalys averages 148 mph (237 kph).

Bubble-shaped canopy houses driving cab

Headlight cover

Extended aerodynamic nose minimizes pressure effect in tunnels

AMTRAK'S TOP-SPEED PERFORMER

The Acela, to be launched in 2000, will be the first US train capable of matching the performance of France's and Japan's high-speed trains. The eight-car, 12,500-hp trains will have a top speed of 150 mph (240 kph) and run in the eastern US.

GERMANY'S LUXURIOUS EXPRESS TRAIN

Germany's ICE (Inter-City Express) is believed to be the most luxurious high-speed train. However the ICE service is not that fast since the trains run mostly on regular track at 125 mph (200 kph).

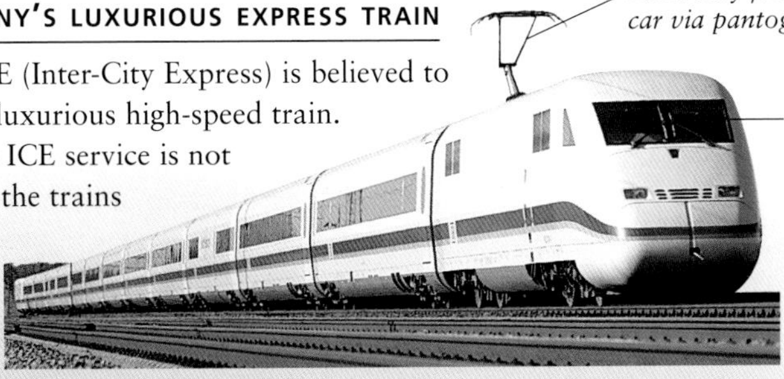

Electricity fed to power car via pantograph

6,400-hp power car

ITALY'S TILTING TRAIN

Elettrotreno Rapido (ETR), also known as the Pendolino, is an Italian train whose cars tilt when going round a curve at high speed. The 6,300-hp ETR 450 seen here has a top speed of 155 mph (250 kph) and was built in 1987.

Pantograph

Crumple zone protects crew

THE FASTEST OF ALL

This TGV Atlantique is one of the latest generation of TGVs introduced onto France's Atlantic line in 1989. On May 18, 1990 one of these high-speed units set the current world speed record for a wheeled train of 320 mph (515 kph). In service, their top speed is 155 mph (250 kph).

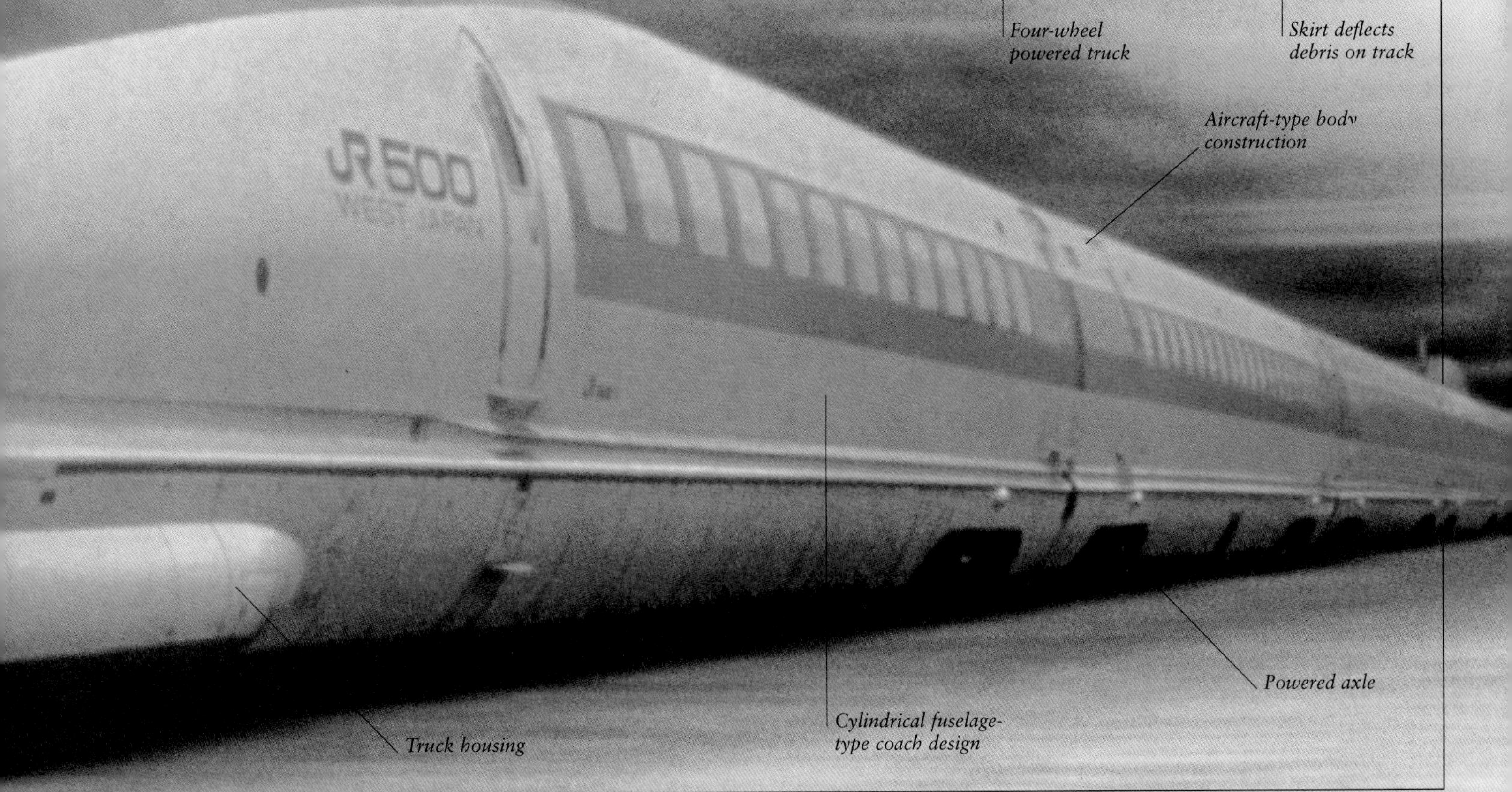

Four-wheel powered truck

Skirt deflects debris on track

Aircraft-type body construction

Truck housing

Cylindrical fuselage-type coach design

Powered axle

1970-2000 THE CHANNEL TUNNEL

PROPOSALS TO CREATE A TUNNEL running beneath the English Channel between Britain and France date back almost 200 years. The first attempt to build one began in the 1870s, but British fears that it would make a foreign invasion of Britain easier led to work being halted. Another attempt was made in the 1970s, but was also abandoned. Finally, in 1987, an Anglo-French company, Eurotunnel, was set up to raise the money, build, and operate a train service though a 31-mile (50-km) long tunnel running under the Channel between Calais and Dover. This tunnel opened in May 1994.

TUNNEL DIGGERS

Eleven of these massive tunnel-boring machines were used to dig out three interlinked tunnels and line them with rings of reinforced concrete. The rail services now run through two of the tunnels and the third is used as a service tunnel.

LE SHUTTLE

The locomotives that handle the vehicle-carrying service Le Shuttle are 7,500-hp B-B-B electric-powered engines. They are powerful enough to haul a 2,400-ton train at a maximum speed of 88 mph (140 kph).

TRAVELING THROUGH THE CHANNEL TUNNEL

The journey through the Channel Tunnel between Folkestone in England and Calais in France takes about 30 minutes. Freight trucks are provided with their own Le Shuttle trains, which travel at an average speed of 62 mph (100 kph).

Red lights on at back of train

Sliding doors close off adjoining tunnels

Lattice-sided truck transporter car

Emergency crossover between tunnels

Battery rack

EUROSTAR ROUTES

The construction of the Channel Tunnel enabled a passenger service to be set up linking London to Paris and Brussels. Eurostar trains take roughly four hours to make these journeys. In England the speed of the trains is limited by the old, crowded tracks. Only in France can they accelerate up to 186 mph (298 kph).

THE PASSENGER SERVICE

The Eurostar trains, three of which are seen here awaiting departure from Waterloo International in London, are based on the French TGV. Each train has two 8,175-hp engines along with 18 coaches that can carry up to 800 people.

GATEWAY TO EUROPE

Folkestone terminal in England is the departure point for all types of motor vehicle traveling through the Channel Tunnel. Up to 120 cars and 12 buses can fit on board each of the 20 or so Le Shuttle trains leaving England each day. Freight trucks also use this terminal.

FREIGHT SERVICE

Forty-six Class 92 C-C electric locomotives were built to haul freight trains through the Channel Tunnel. All of these trains carry the names of major European artistic figures. The two locomotives double-heading this container train honor the composers J.S. Bach and Benjamin Britten.

Total length of Shuttle train is 2,461 ft (750 m)

Nose cone made of a resin and fiberglass molding

le Shuttle

9012

EURO TUNNEL

1970-2000 RAPID TRANSIT

SINCE 1970, many city authorities around the world have been forced to upgrade their urban and suburban transportation networks to cope with worsening congestion. Rapid transit or light rail systems are the preferred solution because the vehicles that run on them are clean and efficient and are comparatively cheap to operate. Most rapid transports run along electrically powered surface lines, but a growing number of cities – especially in Japan – have built overhead monorails and are developing elevated, high-speed, magnetic levitation (maglev) systems.

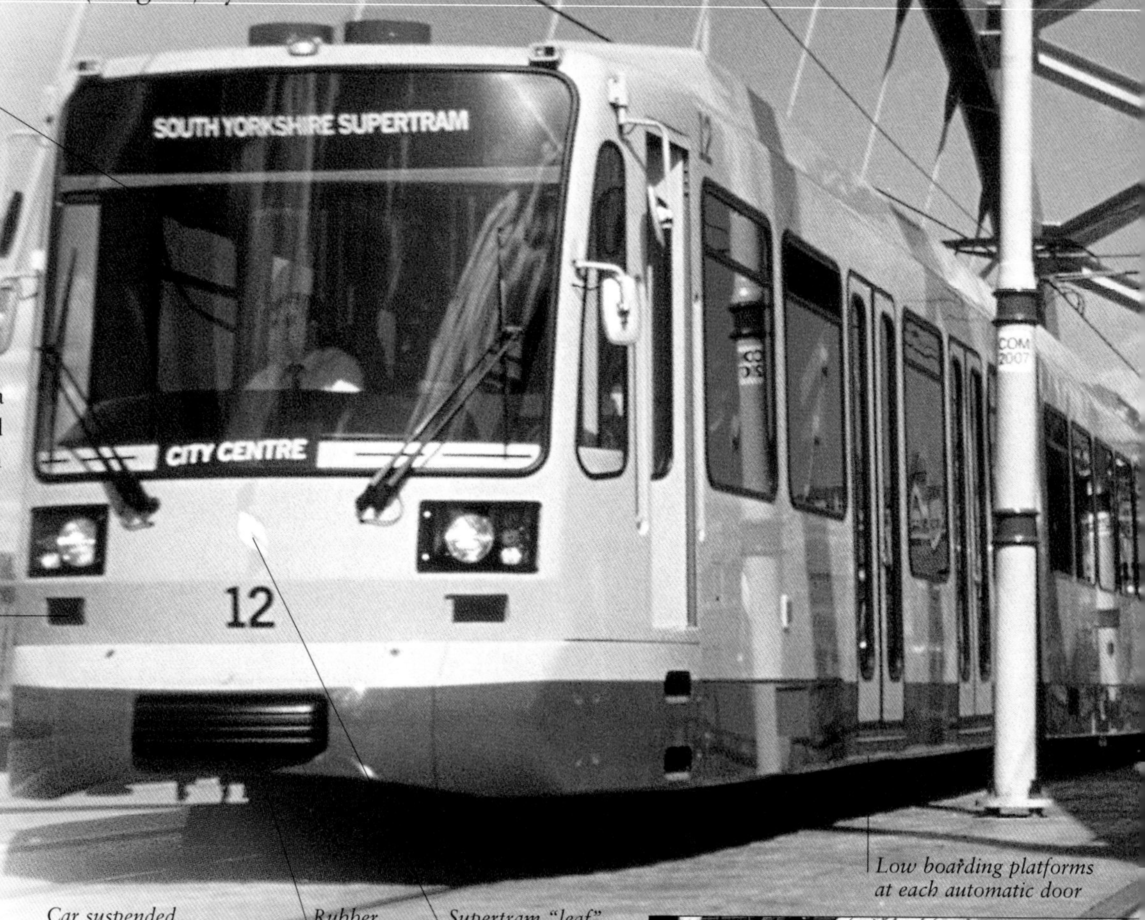

Wide screen for greater visibility

SHEFFIELD'S SUPERTRAM

The supertram, seen crossing the 360-ft (113-m) long Commercial Street bridge, is one of a fleet of German-built articulated trams serving the city of Sheffield in Britain. These trams, which came into service in 1995, have a top speed of 50 mph (80 kph) and climb gradients of up to 1-in-10 on the 18-mile (29-km) long Sheffield tramway system.

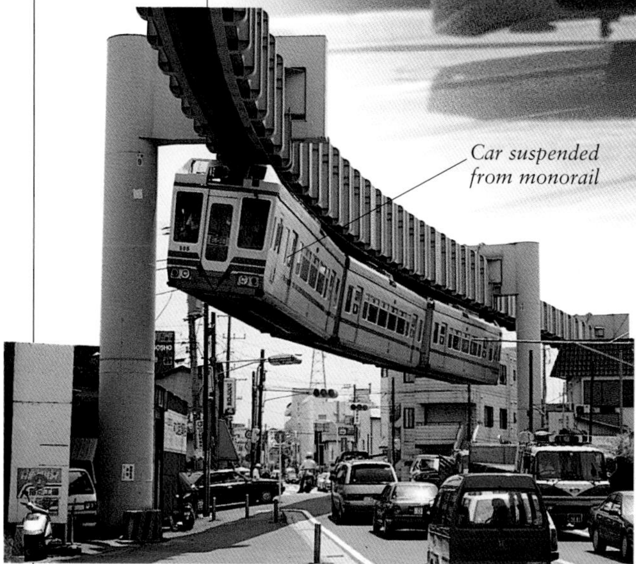

Indicator light

Electrically powered monorail

Car suspended from monorail

Rubber bumper

Supertram "leaf" monogram

Low boarding platforms at each automatic door

SUSPENDED ABOVE THE TRAFFIC

Running above the streets of Ofuna in Japan, three suspended electric cars convey passengers along the Shonan monorail. The system, which was opened in 1970, links the high-speed Tokaido Shinkansen mainline station at Ofuna, south of Yokohama, with the resort area of Enoshima.

Direct current electromagnets are located on underside of each car

JAPAN'S MAGNETIC ATTRACTION

Photographed on a demonstration track in Yokohama in 1989, this magnetically levitated HSST-05 is a product of HSST (High Speed Surface Transport). Powered by a linear induction motor, it is hoped these maglevs will glide at speeds of up to 125 mph (200 kph).

RIDING HIGH IN AUSTRALIA

One of the six train sets belonging to the Darling Harbour monorail in Sydney, Australia weaves its way between the skyscrapers on the 2⅓-mile (3.5-km) long elevated route. The monorail provides a link between the city center and the modern harborfront development shown here.

Concrete guideway

Housing for set of guide wheels

MONORAILS MEET IN OSAKA

A train bound for the airport crosses with a train bound for Kodama City on the Newtram Monorail in Osaka, Japan's third largest city. These remote-controlled trains, which are powered by electricity, have rubber-tired guide wheels and a body which straddles the concrete guideway.

Streamlined carriages

Overhead catenary power supply

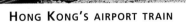

Aerodynamic nose

JAPANESE DOUBLE-DECKER

Japan Railways' new Class 250 electric multiple units consist of double-deck cars that substantially increase passenger capacity on the busiest urban lines. Passengers on the upper deck of the leading car have the excitement of sharing the driver's view of the line ahead.

HONG KONG'S AIRPORT TRAIN

This electric multiple unit operates on the 21-mile (34-km) long railroad linking Hong Kong's Chek Lap Kok airport with downtown Kowloon. It has a top operating speed of 84 mph (135 kph). The railroad opened in 1998.

1970–2000 TRANSRAPID TR07

THE TRAIN'S RELIANCE ON STEEL WHEELS running on steel rails may soon end. From 2005, it should be possible to travel between Germany's two largest cities, Berlin and Hamburg, on board the first superspeed maglev (magnetically levitated) train, the Transrapid. Development began in the 1970s and the prototype Transrapid featured here, TR07, made its debut at a test facility in the German state of Emsland in 1989. Here it reached 281 mph (450 kph) in 1993, and succeeded in accelerating from zero to 250 mph (400 kph) in three minutes. Transrapids have been designed to make no contact with the guideway; they operate on and they are therefore unhampered by contact friction. This makes them faster than wheeled trains, and gives them the advantages of being quieter, and using less energy.

Safety rail supports TR07 if levitation fails

Specially toughened glass

Reinforced nose cone

Guideway contains cable windings

Guideway elevated on concrete pillars

SCIENCE FICTION TO SCIENCE FACT

Once the subject of science fiction, the "floating train" is now a reality at the Emsland test center in northern Germany. Here, Transrapids run on 20 miles (32 km) of guideway.

MOVING FORWARD

Electricity passing through cable windings in the guideway generates a traveling electromagnetic field that pulls the TR07 forward. To achieve this, the levitation magnets fitted to the bottom of the TR07 have to be constantly maintained at a distance of ½ in (10 mm) from the guideway.

Magnets in the pod interact with steel "stator packs" in the guideway

Each car can carry 92 passengers

TR07 is propelled by "traveling" electromagnetic field in guideway

Each pod contains a levitation and lateral guidance system

Body shell based on the fuselage of a jet aircraft

Telephones link monitoring console to the control center

Panel displays gap between magnets, as well the power output and train speed

JUST FOR TESTING

Although the TR07 was built with a cab, in which technicians monitor current levels and fluctuations in the magnetic fields, Transrapids are operated from a remote control center. Transrapids on the Berlin-Hamburg route will also be driverless. Travelling at up to 269 mph (430 kph), the journey will take no more than one hour.

SPECIFICATION

Manufacturer	Thyssen (Transrapid Systems), Kassel, Germany
Classification	TR07 magnetic levitation train
Date built	1989
Number built	8 test vehicles
Fuel	Electrically induced magnetic field
Top speed	281 mph (450 kph)
Length	2-section train 170 ft 6 in (51.7 m)
Height	13 ft 8 in (4.2 m)
Total weight	110 tons
Tractive effort	Zero

Cables conduct test data to recording equipment

Communications headset

ATTRACTION UNDER THE GUIDEWAY

The above view shows how tightly the "hanging system" of a Transrapid wraps around the guideway. The close up (*right*) shows the position of the levitation and guidance magnets in the train's "hanging system," in relation to the stator pack fitted to the guideway. The Transrapid is levitated and guided by the attraction between its own magnets and the stator packs in the guideway.

Communications antenna

Tinted windows

Guideway

Guidance magnet

Stator pack is attached to the guideway

Levitation magnet

"Pod" protects the magnetic equipment and cuts noise emission

Aerodynamic front cab

LOW-FLYING TECHNOLOGY

The TR07 is the seventh Transrapid to be built in Germany. Designed for superspeed running, its streamlined body is based upon the fuselage of a Boeing 737. Along its base, a succession of pods house electromagnets that enable the train to be propelled along by magnetic levitation.

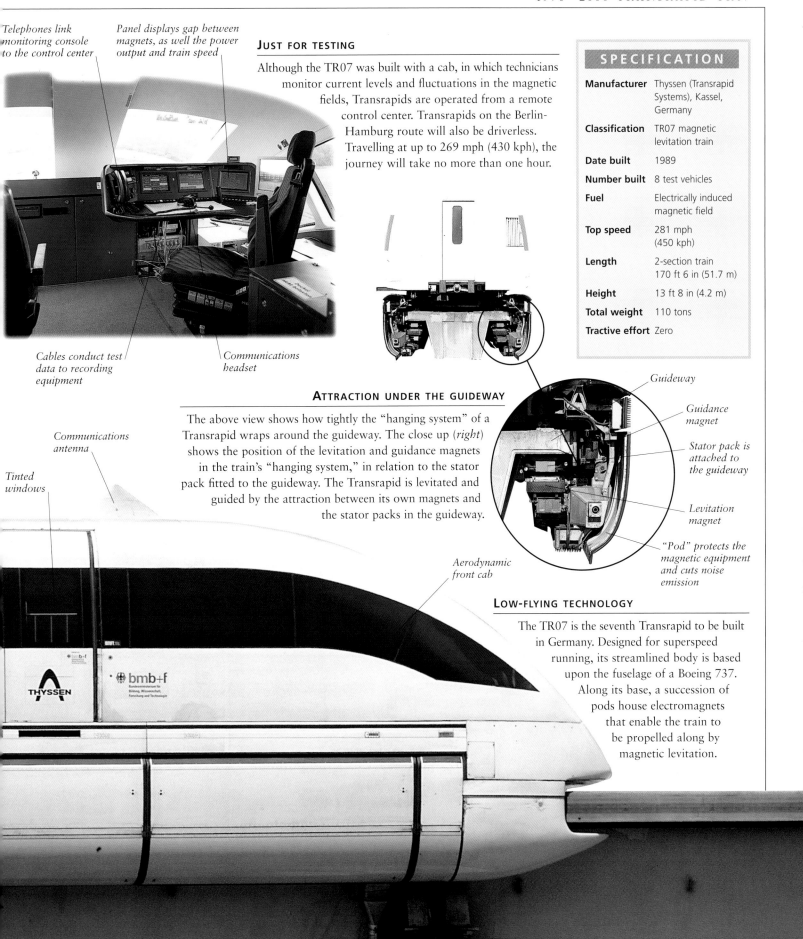

THYSSEN

bmb+f
Bundesministerium für Bildung, Wissenschaft, Forschung und Technologie

2420

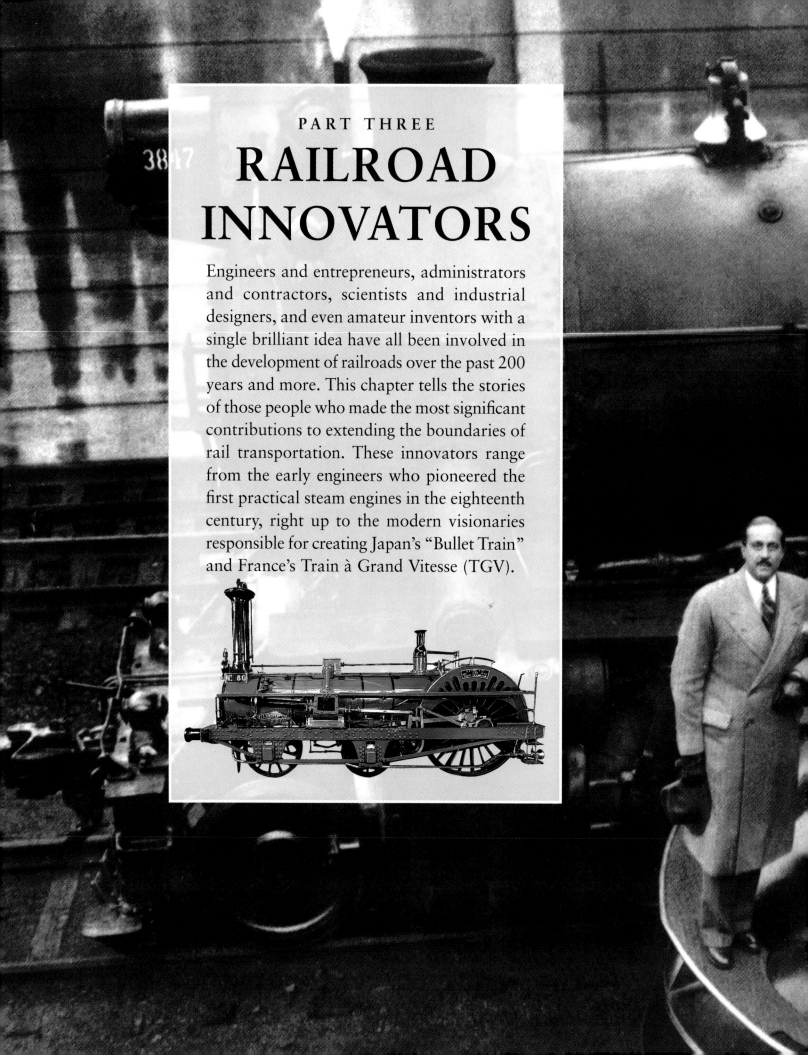

PART THREE

RAILROAD INNOVATORS

Engineers and entrepreneurs, administrators and contractors, scientists and industrial designers, and even amateur inventors with a single brilliant idea have all been involved in the development of railroads over the past 200 years and more. This chapter tells the stories of those people who made the most significant contributions to extending the boundaries of rail transportation. These innovators range from the early engineers who pioneered the first practical steam engines in the eighteenth century, right up to the modern visionaries responsible for creating Japan's "Bullet Train" and France's Train à Grand Vitesse (TGV).

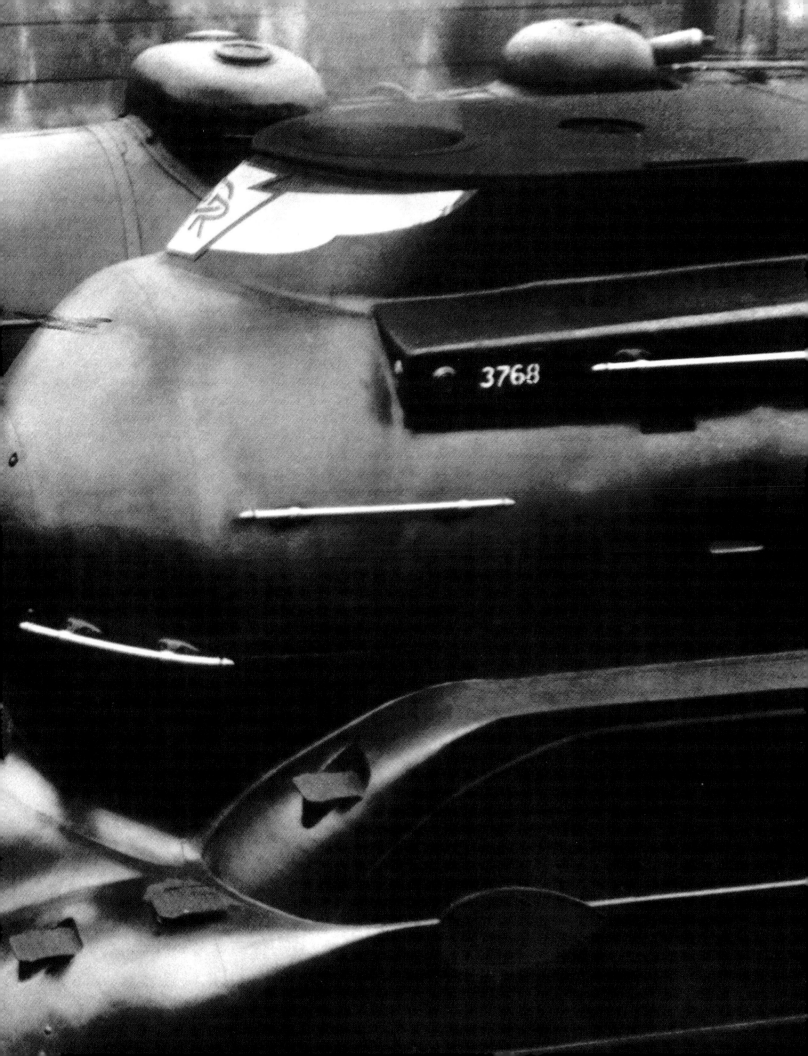

A

ROMAN ABT
1850–1933

The Swiss-born engineer Roman Abt gave his name to one of the most widely used tooth-and-rack systems developed for mountain railroads. Born at Bünzen, in Canton Aargau, in July 1850, Abt studied engineering in Zurich, and from 1872 worked for another pioneering Swiss railroad technician, Nikolaus Riggenbach, at the Swiss Central Railway's works at Olten.

It was in 1882, while working in Paris, that Abt designed and patented his rack-rail system that enabled at least one tooth of the rack to be permanently engaged. The system was first put to use on the Blankenburg to Tanne narrow-gauge railroad in the German Hartz Mountains. In 1891, the system was installed on the standard-gauge Erzberg Railway in Austria and, by 1914, 66 railroads were employing Abt's invention.

After World War I, between 1920 and 1929, a further six railroads were built using the Abt tooth-and-rack system. The most famous of these runs between Arica and La Paz in Bolivia, which rises at a gradient of 1 in 12. Abt died in Lucerne on May 1, 1933, at the age of 82.

WILLIAM ADAMS
1823–1904

William Adams was born in London in 1823. After taking up posts in Britain, France, and Italy, he joined the North London Railway (NLR) in 1855. As well as designing tank locomotives for the NLR, Adams supervised the construction of the company's locomotive assembly works at Bow in East London.

In 1873, he moved to the neighboring Great Eastern Railway, before crossing the River Thames to accept the post of locomotive superintendent of the London & South Western Railway (L&SWR), in 1878, where he worked until 1895. Adams's best work was done for L&SWR, and the engines he designed there were noted for their elegance and economy. The most celebrated of

these were the 60 4-4-0s, built between 1891 and 1896, that headed the express services between London and the south coast, and westward to Salisbury and Exeter.

Adams's main contribution to locomotive design was his long-wheelbase truck that used springs to control the movement of the pivot. This pivot action allowed his truck a smoother, more secure entry into curves at high speeds and overcame the oscillation problems suffered by other trucks.

HORATIO ALLEN
1802–1890

A highly influential figure in the development of the earliest US railroads, Horatio Allen started his professional life as a lawyer after graduating with an honors degree in mathematics in 1823. When, in 1825, the chance arose to become an engineer for the Delaware & Hudson canal project, he seized it. Delaware & Hudson had ambitions to construct and operate a steam railroad, so in 1826 Allen was sent over to England to secure the track and steam engines needed.

HORATIO ALLEN

In England, a contract was placed by Allen with a locomotive company based at Stourbridge in the West Midlands, called Foster, Rastrick & Co, for three of their locomotives. One of this trio of steam engines, named *Stourbridge Lion*, became the first operational locomotive in North America when it ran at Honesdale, Pennsylvania, in 1829. That year, Allen became chief engineer of the South Carolina Railroad and, in 1832, he made railroad history by designing the world's first ever articulated steam locomotive, a 2-2-0+0-2-2.

He also worked for a number of years as a consulting engineer for the New York & Erie Railroad. However, in his later years, Allen decided to retire from commercial life and to devote his energies to research. He died in 1890.

WILLIAM ADAMS'S 02 CLASS 0-4-4 PASSENGER TANK

LOUIS ARMAND
1905–1971

A visionary European railroad administrator of the post-World War II period, Louis Armand was born in France in 1905. He began his career as a mining engineer in Clermont Ferrand in 1926, but

LOUIS ARMAND

left to join the Paris, Lyons, Mediterranée (PLM) Railway in 1934. By 1944, Armand had become director of works for the Societé Nationale des Chemins de Fer Français (SNCF), the French national railroad administration, graduating to the post of director general in 1946. His research into two areas proved particularly rewarding: the employment of alternating current (AC) for electric traction, and the chemical treatment of feed water in steam locomotive boilers to reduce deterioration through scaling and corrosion.

Louis Armand became president of the board of directors of SNCF in 1955 and president of the Channel Tunnel Company in 1961. He was also appointed president and general secretary of the International Union of Railways. Among many honors, he was awarded the Legion d'Honneur by the French Government in 1956.

Armand predicted that railroads would once again become the world's principal transport system in the twenty-first century. The notion was generally dismissed during his lifetime, but diminishing energy resources and environmental pressures could yet see his prophecy fulfilled.

B

MATTHIAS BALDWIN
1795–1866

Born in Elizabeth, New Jersey, Matthias Baldwin began his working life as a jeweler. In 1830, he founded what was to become the world's largest locomotive assembly factory in Philadelphia, Pennsylvania. Two years later he delivered his first

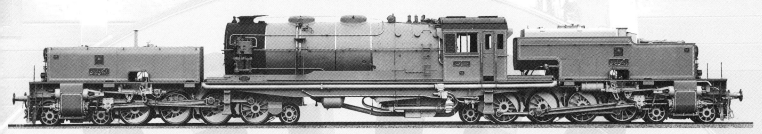

A BEYER-GARRATT ARTICULATED 4-8-2+2-8-4 BUILT BY BEYER PEACOCK IN MANCHESTER, ENGLAND

steam engine to the Philadelphia, Germantown, & Norristown Railroad, a 2-2-0 named *Old Ironsides*. The next locomotive, a 4-2-0 *E.L. Miller*, was much more advanced than its predecessor and had a profound impact on future locomotive design. Several features, such as the leading pivoted guide wheels, were adopted as standard design features in the US.

By 1837, despite success, the company was facing a financial crisis. Fortunately, Baldwin's creditors had confidence in his ability to restore the company to its previous fortunes. He managed to achieve this goal within six years. By the time of Baldwin's death in 1866, his factory had built around 1,500 locomotives and the annual average output stood at 120. The Philadelphia factory continued to prosper until the end of the steam age. It built its last steam locomotive in 1955 for Indian Railways. In total, Baldwin's plant constructed more than 60,000 engines in the course of its 125-year history.

MATTHIAS BALDWIN

ALFRED BELPAIRE
1820–1893

The Belgian engineer Alfred Jules Belpaire was born in Ostend and, after gaining his engineering diploma in Paris, was swiftly recruited by Belgian State Railways. Initially placed in charge of the locomotive workshops at Malines, he had been promoted to the position of director of the rolling stock department in Brussels by 1850.

Belpaire was concerned with the effect of low-grade fuel on the performance of locomotives, and so he sought to improve the combustibility of the fuels used. Driven by this concern, he developed a flat-topped firebox that utilized the maximum space inside the firebox for heating water.

His final version of the firebox was produced in 1864, and during the following 20 years it was incorporated into all new Belgian engines. It was widely adopted across the world, most notably on the Great Western Railway in Britain. The Belpaire firebox is its eponymous inventor's most significant achievement, but he continued to be innovative until his death in 1893. His designs include an engine reversing system and numerous locomotives.

CHARLES BEYER
1813–1876

Though German by birth, Charles Beyer made his name as a locomotive engineer in England. During his studies at Dresden Polytechnic, he traveled to Manchester and was impressed by the work of engineer Richard Roberts of Sharp, Roberts & Co. He returned to Manchester in 1834 to work as a draftsman with Roberts' firm. In 1837, the firm went into locomotive manufacture, and Beyer produced designs for the Sharp Standard 2-2-2s and for a range of 0-4-2s. Following Roberts' retirement in 1843, Beyer assumed responsibility for all locomotive designs. Beyer left Sharp, Roberts & Co in 1853 to set up a new company, Beyer Peacock, with English engineer Richard Peacock. They began to construct locomotives in a factory in Gorton, Manchester, close to the engine works of the Manchester, Sheffield & Lincolnshire Railway where Peacock had been locomotive superintendent. Destined to become one of the world's most illustrious locomotive builders, Beyer Peacock delivered its first locomotive in July 1855, the first standard-gauge steam engine to operate on the Great Western Railway. Many notable engines were constructed at the Gorton plant during its 111-year history. The most famous of all was the Beyer-Garratt articulated locomotives. Production ceased in 1966, but Beyer-Garratts can still be seen working in southern Africa.

JOHN BLENKINSOP
1783–1831

As a result of the Napoleonic Wars, the price of horse fodder rose steeply. British industrialists who depended on horse transport began to examine the alternatives. Yorkshireman John Blenkinsop was quick to see the potential of steam traction.

Blenkinsop rose to the position of agent for the Middleton Colliery in Leeds. Coal traveled 3½ miles (5.6 km) from the pit to be loaded into

barges, a task requiring 50 horses. Eager to replace the horses, Blenkinsop devised, and in 1811 patented, a rail that relied upon a toothed wheel-and-rack system, similar to those still used later on mountain railroads. Blenkinsop collaborated with the engineer Matthew Murray in designing a 2-2-2 locomotive whose central pair of driving wheels would be toothed. These engaged on the rack attached to the edge of the running rail.

On June 24 1812, the first run took place with a load of eight wagons containing 25 tons of coal and some 50 passengers. Following this train's successful initial run, a further three engines were built. Together, this quartet of locomotives contributed over 80 years' service.

THOMAS BRASSEY
1805–1870

During a career spanning 35 years, Thomas Brassey built railroads on every continent, and 6,500 miles (10,450 km) of route are attributable to him, including one-sixth of the rail network in Britain. Born into a farming family in Cheshire, in northwest England, he secured his first railroad contract in 1835 on the Grand Junction Railway. There he initiated a lifelong working relationship with British engineer Joseph Locke.

In 1841, they collaborated on the construction of the Paris-Le Havre Railway, and successful tenders followed for the Lancaster & Carlisle Railway, and the Caledonian Railway. Between 1852 and 1859 he worked on Canada's Grand Trunk Railway and then spent four years building railroads in Australia. Other commissions included the Crimean Railway in Russia, and lines in Moldavia (now Moldova), Argentina, and India. Between 1843 and 1848, Brassey was regularly employing over 75,000 workers worldwide, and in the period from 1848 to 1861 his contracts were worth £28 million. Brassey was a businessman of integrity who was renowned for his thoroughness and organizational skills. He was one of the first people to argue that a national rail network should be the responsibility of government.

THOMAS BRASSEY

ISAMBARD KINGDOM BRUNEL
1806–1859

This most celebrated of British engineers was the son of a refugee from the French Revolution, Marc Brunel, himself a notable engineer and inventor. Born in Portsmouth, Hampshire, in 1806, Isambard Kingdom Brunel assisted his father on projects such as the Thames Tunnel under London's river. In 1831, Isambard's design was accepted for a new suspension bridge over the River Avon at Clifton Gorge near Bristol. This connection with the west of England port was instrumental in Brunel's appointment in 1833 as chief engineer for the proposed Great Western Railway (GWR) between London and Bristol. With its bold engineering structures, designed to

ISAMBARD KINGDOM BRUNEL

minimize gradients, and its unprecedented track width of 7 ft (2 m 13 cm), known as the broadgauge, the line was built for high-speed running. For the visionary Brunel, the GWR, which opened in 1841, was only the first leg of a transatlantic journey. The second leg was the voyage from Bristol to New York that would be undertaken in steamships, which he also designed.

Brunel's genius can still be appreciated through his legacy of bridges, viaducts, tunnels, stations, docks, and the Great Western main line itself. Much of this remains as part of the transport system of western England. There were several instances where his ambition outstripped the limits of available technology, the most notorious example being the atmospheric propulsion system for the South Devon Railway. This system proved to be far too expensive and highly inefficient. Brunel undertook a huge workload throughout his 25-year career, and this finally took its toll. He died at the early age of 53 in 1859.

WILLIAM BUDDICOM
1816–1887

Though born in Britain, William Buddicom enjoyed most success in France. Initially a resident engineer on the Liverpool & Manchester Railway, he moved to the Grand Junction Railway (GJR) in 1840, where he was appointed locomotive superintendent. On his arrival, Buddicom discovered that GJR's inside-cylinder locomotives, built by Robert Stephenson, spent more time under repair than in service. In response, he designed a replacement with straight axles, inclined outside cylinders supported in outside framing, and a deep firebox located between the rear wheels. The key elements of this innovation were soon to be widely employed in Europe and around the world.

Joseph Locke recognized his engineering talent and recruited him to assist in the construction of the Paris & Rouen Railway in France. This led to Buddicom starting a locomotive-building enterprise at Sotteville, near Rouen, with a colleague from the GJR, William Allcard. It prospered, allowing Buddicom to retire to Wales at the age of 54.

OLIVER BULLEID
1882–1970

Born in New Zealand of English parents, Oliver Bulleid was the most unorthodox of locomotive designers. An apprentice at the Great Northern Railway (GNR), he was to remain with GNR and its successor, London & North Eastern Railway (LNER) for 36 years, over 20 of them as assistant to the LNER's chief mechanical engineer, Nigel Gresley. Gresley's more radical locomotive designs were undoubtedly influenced by Bulleid.

In 1937, Bulleid became the chief mechanical engineer of the Southern Railway at a time when they had been giving electrification precedence over the development of new steam engines. That approach changed with the appearance of Bulleid's first Pacific designs, the Merchant Navy class, and the Q1 class 0-6-0, the most powerful of its type built in Britain. In 1946, Bulleid began work on his most revolutionary concept, the Leader. He aimed to bring the flexibility of diesel and electric traction to a new breed of steam locomotive. It

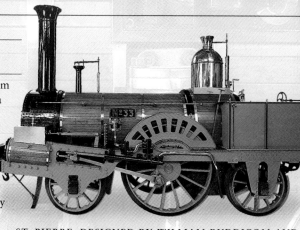

ST. PIERRE, DESIGNED BY WILLIAM BUDDICOM AND WILLIAM ALLCARD

was powered by two steam-driven trucks and had driving cabs at each end. However, the idea never moved beyond the prototype stage. Bulleid left the Southern in 1949 to become chief mechanical engineer of Irish Railways (CIE). Here, his major contribution was to design an ingenious steam locomotive that burned Irish peat rather than imported coal. He retired from CIE in 1958.

EDWARD BURY
1794–1858

Subsequently overshadowed by the Stephensons in Britain, Bury's locomotives sold well in the US, where some of his ideas, such as bar frames, became standard in locomotive construction. He owned a foundry in Liverpool where, in 1830, he assembled a locomotive incorporating a number of innovations. *Liverpool*, as it was named, was the first engine to combine horizontal inside cylinders with a horizontal tubular boiler. Equally significant was the frame, composed of bars rather than iron plates. Bury won the contract to supply locomotives for the London & Birmingham Railway (L&BR), but despite the reliability of the 58 2-2-0s he built for them, they proved underpowered.

From 1836 until 1847, Bury was employed as locomotive superintendent of the L&BR, and then as general manager of the Great Northern Railway. His locomotive-building company continued to flourish until he underpriced a contract and suffered chronic losses. The company closed in 1850 after building a total of 415 engines. In the same year he also left the Great Northern.

C

HENRY CAMPBELL
c.1810–1870

The archetypal American 4-4-0 was Henry Campbell's creation. Born around 1810, he became chief engineer of the Philadelphia, Germantown, & Norristown Railroad in Pennsylvania. In 1836 he patented a design that supplemented the usual

A BULLEID BATTLE OF BRITAIN PACIFIC

four-coupled driving wheels of the engine with a leading truck, also with four wheels. He realized that the truck's addition doubled the available weight of the engine upon the track, and would act as a guide for the engine on sharply curved or poorly laid track. The first 4-4-0 was constructed in Philadelphia, making its debut in May 1837. Although the design was primarily intended for coal traffic, it became one of the most common of all passenger-locomotive wheel arrangements. Between 1840 and 1890, 25,000 4-4-0s were manufactured in North American workshops. By the time of Campbell's death in 1870, over 80 percent of locomotives operating in North American were of this type.

ARTURO CAPROTTI
1881–1938

Italian engineer Arturo Caprotti began his career in the motor vehicle industry. In 1915, he used his experience there to devise a valve gear for steam engines that followed the principles of the valves in a petrol or diesel engine. Instead of horizontal piston valves, vertical poppet valves were operated by a rotating camshaft. The camshaft was driven from a gearbox mounted on the return crank located on the main driving wheel.

The Caprotti gear improved operative control of the poppet valves within the cylinder steamchest, leading to an increase in efficiency. A reduction in coal consumption resulted. However, the valve gear proved expensive to maintain. First fitted in 1921 to a 2-6-0 freight engine on Italian State Railways, the Caprotti valve gear was widely adopted in Italy and elsewhere. In Britain, the London, Midland & Scottish Railway (LM&SR) equipped a 4-6-0 with a Caprotti gear in 1926. Despite results showing a 20 percent fuel saving, no further Caprotti-fitted locomotives ran on Britain's railroads until a decade after the inventor's death in 1938. A quantity of LM&SR and British Railways-built 4-6-0s were later furnished with Caprotti gear, but the most famous recipient of the gear was British Railways' Class 8 Pacific No.71000 Duke of Gloucester.

ANDRÉ CHAPELON
1892–1978

Frenchman André Chapelon dominates the final chapter of steam locomotive history in the twentieth century. Following service in World War I, he joined the Paris, Lyons, Mediterranée Railway. In 1925 he became a research engineer on the Paris-Orléans Railway and the following year introduced an innovative double-chimney and blastpipe assembly. Deriving its name from Chapelon and his collaborator, Finnish engineer M.M. Kylala, the Kylchap exhaust significantly improved drafting and thus steam production.

This was Chapelon's first step in a quest to improve performance through scientific analysis. He examined the basic processes of converting heat into locomotive energy and noticed that

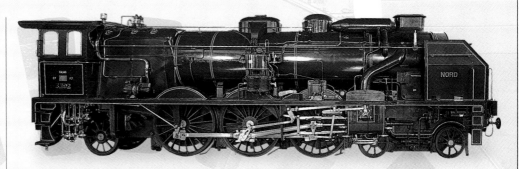

PACIFIC DESIGNED BY ANDRÉ CHAPELON FOR NORD RAILWAY OF FRANCE

substantial losses occurred as a result of poor steam circulation. From 1929 onward he utilized the results of his research and rebuilt the fleet of 4-6-2s and 4-8-0s on the Paris-Orléans Railway, and in so doing doubled their power output. In 1938, Chapelon joined the Department of Steam Locomotive Studies run by France's state railroad, SNCF, and remained there until his retirement in 1953. World War II and electrification diluted the impact of his later work, but his legacy shows he advanced the efficiency of the steam locomotive to a point where it is unlikely to be surpassed.

GEORGE JACKSON CHURCHWARD
1857–1933

George Jackson Churchward combined the best of North American and French practice with his ideas to equip the Great Western Railway (GWR) with a fleet of locomotives superior to those of other British railroads. His innovations influenced all later developments in British steam traction.

Initially employed at the locomotive department of the South Devon Railway (SDR), he transferred to the GWR works in Wiltshire when the SDR was absorbed into the GWR in 1876. By 1895 he was assistant works manager. In this role he developed his design skills and, by the time he was promoted to locomotive superintendent in 1902, he was more than ready to put his ideas into practice.

Churchward introduced several locomotive types, ranging from 2-6-2 passenger tanks to 2-8-0 heavy freight tender and tank engines. His parallel achievement, however, was to standardize the main components— such as boilers, cylinders, and wheels— used by each of the nine locomotives in the range. This level of standardization was unprecedented in Britain and greatly reduced the operating costs of the GWR.

By his retirement in 1921, Swindon Works had built 1,100 locomotives to Churchward's designs. He remained involved with activities at the works until his death, occasioned when struck by a train while crossing the London to Bristol main line.

PETER COOPER
1791–1883

The North American-born industrialist and inventor Peter Cooper is chiefly remembered for one engine, Tom Thumb. As the first section

of the Baltimore & Ohio Railroad (B&O) was approaching completion in 1830, he joined the debate on what was going to pull the trains. Many favored the use of horses, but Cooper believed in the potential of the steam engine. To demonstrate the feasibility of a steam locomotive, he decided to build Tom Thumb and to race it against a horse-drawn train. This locomotive was a lightweight, vertical-boilered engine that he built at the Canton Iron Works in Baltimore. It is widely rumored that the tubes he used inside the boiler of this peculiar-looking machine were fashioned from musket barrels!

The race took place between Baltimore and Ellicot's Mills near Washington, a distance of about 14 miles (23 km), on August 30 1830. Tom Thumb began well, hauling a carload of B&O directors, but its performance suffered because the ingenious belt-driven fan that Cooper had designed was not properly fitted. As a result, the belt repeatedly worked loose and then broke. This caused his locomotive to grind to a halt, so horsepower won the day. Nonetheless, Cooper's locomotive led the B&O to adopt steam traction. By the time of his death in 1888, the US was exporting locomotives all around the world.

PETER COOPER

THOMAS CRAMPTON
1816–1888

Thomas Crampton ranks among the most original locomotive designers to be born in Britain, where his work is largely unknown. From his time in the engine department of the Great Western Railway (GWR), Crampton was aware of the superior stability of the GWR's broad-gauge engines over their standard-gauge equivalents. This set him working toward a standard-gauge machine combining a boiler of broad-gauge dimensions and wheels large enough for high-speed running that would remain stable at speed because it had a low-slung boiler.

He faced a hurdle: with large driving wheels the underside of the boiler needed to be raised sufficiently to clear the revolving cranks. However, the stability would be improved if he used a low-pitched boiler. To resolve this dilemma, Crampton broke with convention and placed the driving axle behind the boiler, instead of under it. In 1843 he patented his design, building his first engines in 1845. They were delivered to the Namur-Liége railroad in Belgium, and led to the construction of around 300 Crampton engines for railroads in Belgium, France, and Germany. Strangely, they were not widely adopted in Britain which ordered only 25 Cramptons. Most of these went into service on the London & North Western Railway connecting London with the West Midlands and the industrial cities of the northwest. During trials on the Paris-Orléans Railway in 1890, a French Crampton set a world speed record of 89½ mph (144 kph).

Thomas Crampton also became a successful civil engineer, working on the London, Chatham & Dover Railway, and on projects in eastern Europe and the Middle East.

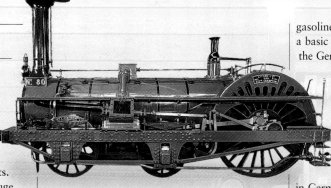

CRAMPTON-TYPE LOCOMOTIVE

D

ALFRED DE GLEHN
1848–1932

Born in England of French-German parentage, Alfred de Glehn worked in France throughout his career. As chief mechanical engineer of the Alsacian Engine Works at Mulhouse he achieved his greatest achievement by designing compound engines that utilized steam at high and low pressures.

In collaboration with Gaston du Bousquet, of France's Northern Railway (Nord), de Glehn improved the performance and efficiency of compounding. The partnership began in 1886 with a trial run on the Nord of an innovative 4-cylinder compound locomotive, the first of which emerged from the Mulhouse workshops in 1890. Their quality soon attracted attention from numerous railroads around the world. In this partnership they continued to develop ideas on compounding, and the Nord 4-4-2s, 32 of which were built from 1901, were the premier passenger engines of their era. As a result, orders came from four other French railroads, and from the Royal Prussian Union Railway which bought 79 engines. In recognition of his achievements, French railroads called all the compound engines they built after 1900 "de Glehn compounds."

RUDOLF DIESEL
1858–1913

The inventor who gave his name to the first practical compression-ignition engine, Rudolf Diesel, was born in Paris, France. However, he is best remembered for the development work he carried out in Germany on diesel traction.

After studying in Munich, he returned to Paris in 1880 to join a refrigeration company. In 1890 he moved to the company's Berlin branch and stepped up his quest for an internal combustion engine. He wanted his combustion engine to run on relatively crude oil and be less costly than comparable

ALFRED DE GLEHN

gasoline-driven engines. By 1892 he had patented a basic design and had begun to develop it with the German company Maschinenfabrik Augsburg, Nurnberg (MAN). The diesel engine, the first in which the heat of compression alone was enough to ignite the fuel, was demonstrated in 1893 and went into production in 1897. This engine was not installed in a working prototype until 1912, when trials were conducted on an experimental 1,000-hp locomotive in Germany. Following this, the first diesel railcar entered service in Sweden in 1913, and Sulzer of Switzerland began production of diesel locomotives in 1914 for the Prussian & Saxon State Railway.

Rudolf Diesel spent most of his later life at his factory in Augsburg until his tragic death in 1913. Diesel drowned after falling overboard from a steamship on his way to London. The exact circumstances of his death remain a mystery.

RUDOLF DIESEL

RICHARD DILWORTH
1885–1968

Richard M. Dilworth was an engineering genius with experience as a Navy electrician when he began servicing early "gas-electric" rail cars for General Electric (GE). In that capacity, he began GE's liaison with the Electro-Motive Corporation (EMC), a builder of self-powered rail cars.

In 1926 he joined the founder of EMC, Hal Hamilton, and other pioneers, in adapting the Kettering two-cycle diesel engine for mainline service. This resulted in the introduction of the first US-built diesel streamliners in the mid-1930s.

Dilworth followed this by developing a series of standardized diesel locomotives, including the highly successful F class freight diesel. The F series, introduced by General Motors in 1939, unleashed a diesel motive revolution. By the time Dilworth retired in 1952, General Motors' Electro Motive Division had sold over 75,000 diesel units in the US alone, and thousands more abroad.

M. DOLIVO-DOBROWOLSKI
1862–1919

Born in St. Petersburg, Russia, M. Dolivo-Dobrowolski was a pioneer in electric traction. After studying at Heidelberg, Germany's historic university, he joined the leading German electrical engineering company Allegemeine Elektrizitäts-Gesellschaft (AEG). He went on to become a leading technical director there, and gained widespread recognition for his pioneering research into multiphase AC systems for railroad electrification, which at the time was in its infancy. The basic principles of this emigré's three-phase AC electrification were put into practice in several of the most important early electrification projects, notably in Germany, Italy, and Switzerland.

ISAAC DRIPPS
1810–1892

Isaac Dripps introduced three of the distinguishing characteristics of North American locomotives: the headlight, bell, and pilot. He was apprenticed to a Philadelphia company, Thomas & Holloway, that built steamboat engines. It then moved into railroad construction, building the Camden & Amboy Railroad (an ancestor of the Pennsylvania Railroad) between 1830 and 1831. When the line's first locomotive arrived from Robert Stephenson & Co, Dripps was given the job of assembling the machine. Despite never having seen a steam locomotive before, Dripps accomplished this task, and then drove the engine named *John Bull* on its trial run. This earned him the title of "master mechanic." In 1832, Dripps equipped *John Bull* with a form of pilot and later perfected an oil-burning headlight that withstood both vibration and the elements. Another of his innovations was the eight-wheeled freight engine, which he developed between 1835 and 1838. The locomotive was dubbed *The Monster*.

Dripps left the Camden & Amboy in 1853. He became a partner in the Trenton Locomotive & Machine Works of New Jersey and, in 1859, was

**LOCOMOTIVE *JOHN BULL*
ASSEMBLED BY ISAAC DRIPPS**

placed in charge of motive power on the Pittsburgh, Fort Wayne & Chicago Railroad. In 1878, he retired from his final position as superintendent of the Altoona workshops of the Pennsylvania Railroad, then the biggest railroad works in the US.

DUGALD DRUMMOND
1840–1912

The Scottish engineer Dugald Drummond had railroad connections from birth. His father was an inspector on the Caledonian & Dumbartonshire Railway in western Scotland. Dugald trained on this railroad until he joined the Highland Railway as manager of its Inverness workshops. He then spent a short time in England with the London, Brighton & South Coast Railway, returning to Scotland in 1875. Back in Scotland, he greatly improved the locomotive fleets of two railroads – the North British Railway, where he worked as locomotive superintendent until 1882, and the Caledonian Railway, where he worked until 1890.

Drummond's finest achievements came late in his life following his move to the London & South Western Railway (L&SWR) in 1895. Here, as the chief mechanical engineer, Drummond replaced the L&SWR's outdated workshops at Nine Elms in London with a new, well-equipped facility at Eastleigh, in Hampshire. He went on to design and oversee the construction of a wide range of locomotives, including the highly successful T9 class 4-4-0. At L&SWR, where he worked until his death in 1912, Drummond sought to improve locomotive efficiency by introducing innovations such as smokebox steam driers, pre-heating for the boiler feedwater, and firebox watertubes.

GASTON DU BOUSQUET
1839–1910

French engineer Gaston du Bousquet is closely associated with the development of compound locomotives. Most successful in cooperation with the brilliant Alfred de Glehn, this relationship began in 1886 when they developed the first-ever 4-cylinder compound. In 1890, du Bousquet was appointed chief mechanical engineer of France's Northern Railway and over the next ten years he worked with de Glehn on compound

GASTON DU BOUSQUET

designs for the 4-4-0, 4-6-2, and 4-4-2 types. One of the 4-4-2s, *No.2.641*, was exhibited at the 1900 Paris Exhibition as an outstanding example of the class of 32 Northern Railway Atlantics. The following year, du Bousquet built several 4-6-0 compound tank engines for passenger service on the Ceinture Railway in Paris, but his most exotic design was a 0-6-2-2-6-0 tank locomotive that was used for freight work.

At his death in 1910, Gaston du Bousquet was engaged on a 4-6-4 compound express tender engine that, at the time, was the most advanced locomotive in the world. Only two prototypes were built, one of which survived and became a sectioned exhibit at the 1937 Paris Exhibition.

E

WILHELM ENGERTH
1814–1884

Along with Frenchman Anatole Mallet, German engineer Wilhelm Engerth was an originator of the articulated steam locomotive. He studied mechanical engineering in Vienna, then became professor of machinery at Graz. Between 1850 and 1852, he worked on an engine design capable of traversing the steeply graded, twisting route being built through the Semmering Pass. The result was the Engerth, which featured a two-part frame structure. The rear section enclosed the firebox and was pivoted immediately in front of it. The cylinders drove the coupled wheels of the leading chassis section, and these were linked to the rear axles through gearing. Similar machines were soon being built for railroads in France and Switzerland. Engerth later held the position of chief engineer at the Austrian Southern Railway. In 1851, in recognition of his achievements, he was invited to Britain to be a judge at the Great Exhibition held in London.

FAIRLIE-TYPE LOCOMOTIVE

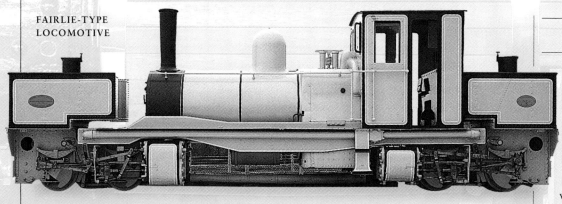

F

ROBERT FAIRLIE
1813–1885

The minimum standard of construction of a railroad line is determined by the weight and length of the locomotives that run on it, not by the length of trains they haul. The British engineer Robert Fairlie believed this discouraged railroad building, especially in under-developed areas of the world. He argued that locomotives should put no greater stress on the track than the wagons behind them.

After working in India, Fairlie set out to design an engine with low construction and operating costs. He patented the result in 1864, a double-ended articulated locomotive mounted on two steam-powered trucks that could be built with either one or two boilers.

The first Fairlie engine produced was a 0-4-4-0, built for the Neath & Brecon Railway in Wales. But it was the successful trial of his locomotive *Little Wonder* on the narrow-gauge Ffestiniog Railway in 1870 that brought his concept to the attention of the world. This, the first practical articulated locomotive, gained wide acceptance around the world, including North America.

Robert Fairlie died in 1885, but locomotives based on his patent were built up to 1914. The largest were 0-6-6-0s built for Mexico in 1911.

G

ROBERT GARBE
1847–1932

Chief engineer of the Berlin Division of Prussian State Railways, German-born Robert Garbe constantly sought to improve the performance of steam locomotives. He held the post from 1895 until 1917, during which time he introduced several forward-looking designs. Their success can be measured by the number of locomotives built according to these designs. They included: 3,850 P8 4-6-0 passenger engines; 3,000 Class G 0-10-0

heavy freight engines; and 5,260 G8 0-8-0 freight engines. Garbe's quest for improved efficiency made him a keen advocate of Wilhelm Schmidt's ideas on superheating. In 1898, Garbe experimented with Schmidt superheaters on two 4-4-0s, and he continued to develop superheated steam engines for the rest of his life. By the time of his death in 1932, the majority of Garbe's engines were still in service, and many outlived him by over four decades. The last German-based P8 4-6-0 was retired in 1975, while others of the class continued operating until 1979 in Poland and Romania, 73 years after the design had been introduced.

HERBERT GARRATT
1864–1913

The most famous British articulated locomotive, the Beyer-Garratt, derives its name from the inventors, Herbert Garratt, and Beyer Peacock, the firm that manufactured the type (*see Charles Beyer*). Born in England, Garratt was the British representative of the government of New South Wales, Australia, when he patented his concept for an articulated locomotive in 1907. His Australian employers encouraged Garratt to approach Beyer Peacock to develop the design. The first engines appeared in 1909 for the narrow-gauge Dundas Tramway in Tasmania. These engines were the forerunners of around 2,000 Garratts built for railroads the world over.

The layout of a Garratt consisted of two engine units made up of cylinders, wheels, and running gear at each end of a pivoted girder frame, and separated by the boiler and driving cab. The principal advantage over other articulated designs was that the boiler could be larger as there was no need for it to clear the driving wheels. This allowed the boiler a greater capacity within which more power could be generated. Herbert Garratt died in 1913, but engines bearing his name were built up to 1968.

HENRI GIFFARD
1825–1882

Frenchman Henri Giffard is most widely recognized as a pioneer of hot-air ballooning, but from the age of 16 he also worked on the Paris to St. Germain railroad. Giffard's enduring contribution to the development of the steam locomotive came in 1859 with his invention of the steam injector. He invented this device as a result of his fascination with air travel, since he envisaged the injector would be used on steam-powered dirigibles.

On a locomotive, the advantage of the Giffard injector over the axle-driven mechanical feed pump was that water could be fed into the boiler while the engine was stationary. The device quickly gained acceptance and its first application was in Britain, where it was fitted to locomotives built by Sharp Stewart in Manchester. The injector was introduced to the US in 1860 and was subsequently used on the majority of locomotives built around the world. The basic principle, using a jet of steam to force water into the boiler through a series of cones and non-return valves, remained unaltered.

The invention of the steam injector earned Henri Giffard the prize for mechanics from the Academie des Sciences in Paris.

KARL GÖLSDORF
1861–1916

Karl Gölsdorf was Austria's most successful locomotive engineer. During a 25-year career, he drew up a series of designs tailored to the particular demands of the railroad system of the Austro-Hungarian Empire; much of it lightly constructed and heavily graded. In the process, he introduced a number of new locomotive types into Europe.

Gölsdorf became the chief mechanical engineer of Austrian State Railways at the age of 30, in 1891, and proved to be an original thinker as well as a first-class engineer. In 1893 he unveiled the first 2-cylinder compound to work in Austria, and followed this in 1901 with a 4-cylinder version. Both types became standard classes throughout Austria and Hungary.

In 1900, Gölsdorf built the first ten-coupled engine in Europe, and he repeated the feat in 1904 with the first 2-6-2 tender design. His 2-12-0 of 1911, built specifically for the long 1-in-40 climb of the Arlberg line, was the first of its type in the world, as was an 0-12-0 tank locomotive he built in 1912 for the Abt rack railroad. Similarly unique in its day was Gölsdorf's masterpiece, the 310 class 2-6-4 compound express passenger design of 1908.

KARL GÖLSDORF

The four carrying wheels at the rear allowed a large firebox to be fitted without altering the low axle-loading demanded by Austria's lightly laid main lines. These well-executed, elegant machines continued to be used in front-line service until 1928, 12 years after Karl Gölsdorf's death.

DANIEL GOOCH
1816–1889

A native of Northumberland in England, Daniel Gooch designed the finest locomotives to operate on Isambard Kingdom Brunel's broad-gauge Great Western Railway (GWR). Brunel appointed Gooch superintendent of locomotive engines in 1837 at the age of 20. Throughout his long service, he committed much of his energy to establishing the GWR workshops at Swindon in Wiltshire. The first locomotive built there was his 2-2-2 *Great Western* in 1846, followed by the celebrated Iron Duke 4-2-2s. An internal disagreement led to Gooch's resignation in 1864. He then spent a year working on the project to lay the first transatlantic cable. The GWR

SIR DANIEL GOOCH

suffered acute financial problems during Gooch's absence and in 1865 he was recalled to head the GWR's board of directors. He solved its problems by imposing stringent economies, and remained chairman of the GWR until his death in 1889.

SIR NIGEL GRESLEY
1876–1941

The world's fastest steam engine, the *Mallard*, and Britain's most famous steam engine, the *Flying Scotsman*, were both the work of Herbert Nigel Gresley, son of a Derbyshire clergyman. Between 1893 and 1897, Gresley was an apprentice at the London & North Western Railway's works at Crewe; he then spent eight years with the Lancashire & Yorkshire Railway. In 1905 he joined the Great Northern Railway (GNR), and became its chief mechanical engineer in 1911. His appointment inaugurated three decades of unprecedented progress and innovation on the GNR. After the GNR became part of the London & North Eastern Railway (LNER) in 1923, Gresley began building

his range of famous Pacific-type locomotives. The third class of Pacifics were the Flying Scotsmans, and these locomotives ushered in a new era of high-speed travel. The streamlined A4 4-6-2s followed in 1935. These record-breakers made Gresley famous, but he had other successes, including one of the finest mixed-traffic engines ever built in Britain, the V2 2-6-2. Not all his ideas worked: the P1 and P2 2-8-2s were magnificent, but over-sized for the LNER's requirements; and the experimental 4-cylinder compound 4-6-4 built in 1929 was a valiant failure.

The Gresley era officially ended with his sudden death in 1941, but in reality the "golden age" he embodied ended abruptly two years earlier, with the outbreak of World War II in Europe.

H

TIMOTHY HACKWORTH
1786–1850

Coal mining gave birth to railroads, and from the colliery workshops of northeast England a group of engineers emerged at the beginning of the nineteenth century who made a significant contribution to the development of the steam engine. They included Timothy Hackworth, who joined Northumberland's Wylam Colliery as a foreman smith in 1807. In this role, he was closely involved in building the first locomotives to operate at Wylam, between 1813 and 1815.

George Stephenson noticed Hackworth, and appointed him resident engineer of the embryonic Stockton & Darlington Railway (S&DR). Stephenson asked him to set up an engine works at New Shildon, County Durham. Here, Hackworth constructed the first six-coupled locomotive, *Royal George*, and two years later he built *Sans Pareil*, which ran in the Rainhill trials in 1829.

In 1833, while contracted to the S&DR, Hackworth opened his own locomotive-building business. The engines Hackworth developed there were designed to improve reliability and efficiency. A notable innovation he incorporated into his engines was self-lubricating bearings. This development was to lead to the success of such types as his 0-6-0 goods engine of 1838 that allowed Hackworth to

SIR NIGEL GRESLEY WITH THE A4 PACIFIC NAMED AFTER HIM

relinquish his position with the S&DR in 1840. He then dedicated himself to his own company, delivering his final locomotive, a 2-2-2 for the York, Newcastle & Berwick Railway, in 1849.

WILLIAM HEDLEY
1779–1843

William Hedley's priority as a colliery manager was the efficiency of mining operations. He became interested in railroads when he perceived that the recently invented steam locomotive might enhance colliery efficiency. His name remains linked to one of the most famous early engines: *Puffing Billy*.

Hedley was born on the outskirts of Newcastle-upon-Tyne. Wylam Colliery in Northumberland, where he was employed from 1805, was 3 miles (5 km) from his birthplace. The colliery invested in two engines designed by Richard Trevithick, but the poor condition of the pit's wooden rails precluded the use of these heavy machines. After iron rails replaced wooden track, the colliery looked to Hedley to build new engines. With the aid of his foreman, Timothy Hackworth, Hedley built three four-wheeler engines, later fitted with eight wheels to reduce weight distribution over the still-fragile track. The engines reverted to four wheels after the relaying of the track in 1830.

Two engines, *Puffing Billy* and *Wylam Dilly*, remained in service until the 1860s.

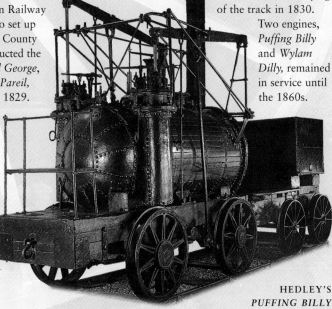

HEDLEY'S
PUFFING BILLY

SAMUEL JOHNSON'S CLASS 115 4-2-2 FOR THE MIDLAND RAILWAY

GEORGE HUDSON
1800–1871

George Hudson's rise from Yorkshire farmboy to powerful railroad entrepreneur was remarkable; as was his fall from grace. He was running a drapery business in York when, aged 27, he was left a bequest of £30,000. He used this money to buy shares in the embryonic North Midland Railway (NMR), and played a key role in its development. In 1837 he was appointed chairman, and sought parliamentary approval to unite the NMR with competing lines. As a result, the Midland Railway was formed in 1844, and at that time was the world's largest railroad company. As chairman, Hudson controlled over 1,000 miles (1,610 km) of Britain's railroad network.

GEORGE HUDSON

During the speculation frenzy between 1845 and 1847, Hudson's power grew. However, after some of his enterprises collapsed, his financial malpractices were exposed and he was forced into exile in France. Hudson was unscrupulous, but to his credit he was the first person to advocate the development of a unified national railroad.

J

SAMUEL JOHNSON
1831–1912

Samuel Johnson's single-wheelers were among the most elegant engines ever to be built in Britain. Born in Yorkshire, England, Johnson worked at several railroad companies before joining the Great Eastern Railway in 1866. After a successful tenure, he moved to Midland Railway in 1873 to become locomotive superintendent. Johnson's first Midland designs drew upon the 2-4-0 and 4-4-0 types that were displacing single-wheelers on express passenger trains. By their nature, single-wheelers (2-2-0s, 4-2-0s, 4-2-2s) lacked the adhesion of four- and six-coupled engines, and this became a problem as the trains they hauled became heavier. Johnson was able to revive the single-wheeler thanks to a device invented in his workshops at Derby: the steam-powered sander. This device fed sand on to the rail beneath the engine much more quickly than the existing gravity sanders could. This significantly assisted adhesion, and allowed single-wheeler engines to operate effectively once more.

In 1887, Samuel Johnson unveiled his first variety of sleek, fast-running 4-2-2s; they were nicknamed Spinners, from the whirling of their huge driving wheels at speed. By 1900, 95 Spinners had been built, many of which remained in service for over 40 years. Similarly celebrated and long-lived were Johnson's compound 4-4-0s, introduced in 1901, two years before he retired from the Midland Railway.

K

KALMAN KANDO
1869–1931

Hungarian-born Kalman Kando is remembered for his influence on railroad electrification. While working as an engineer, his employers, Ganz of Budapest, secured the contract to electrify the Simplon and Lötschberg lines in Switzerland and appointed him chief engineer for the project.

During the early 1920s, Kando began work on the use of single-phase alternating current (AC) in railroads. A key factor was the direct drawing of electric current from the national grid, at a frequency of 50 cycles (or hertz). This reduced the need for trackside installations, such as sub-stations. Under Kando's supervision, test tracks were built in Hungary (1923) and Germany (1936), the former being electrified at 16 kvAC, the latter at 20 kvAC. In 1939, Kando became responsible for the first high-voltage, 50 cycles AC mainline electrification. This joint venture between Ganz and Hungarian Railways (MAV) involved the 119-mile (192-km) line between Budapest and Hegyeshalom. The motive power was supplied by B-B electric engines, equipped with rotary converters to turn incoming 16 kv current into power for traction.

L

HUGO LENTZ
1859–1944

As the passage of steam through the cylinders of a locomotive is regulated by valves, engineers sought to improve the efficiency of these valves and valve gears. This improvement in efficiency was the quest that occupied the German inventor Hugo Lentz for much of his working life.

Lentz trained as an engineer in Hamburg and for a time served with the German navy. In 1887 he opened a works in Vienna, Austria, where he built a small stationary steam engines to his own specific designs. Lentz then moved to Brno, now in the Czech Republic, where he constructed the first locomotive to use poppet valves. This innovative engine was awarded a grand prize at the Paris Exhibition in 1900.

The first locomotive to use a version of the Lentz poppet valve gear was built in Hanover in 1902. In the ensuing years, Lentz refined the concept, replacing vertical valves with horizontal ones that utilized either oscillating or rotary camshaft drives. The oscillating cam-valve gear was introduced in 1907, and became a standard on the Austrian Federal Railway, while the rotary camshaft system was first used on a German industrial locomotive in 1921. By the time of Lentz's death in 1944, around 2,000 locomotives in various countries had been fitted with Lentz's oscillating cam-valve gear.

The rotary cam-type valve gear was used by Sir Nigel Gresley on several of his designs for the London & North Eastern Railway (LNER).

FRIEDRICH LIST
1789–1847

The father of German railroads, Friedrich List was born at Reutlingen, Württemburg. He emigrated to the US in 1825, where he became involved in railroad construction. The 21-mile (34-km) long, coal-carrying line he promoted between Tamaqua in Pennsylvania and Port Clinton in Ohio was the first German-built line in the world. The success of the project inspired List to draw up detailed plans for a complete railroad network in Germany. These were published in 1833, the year after he was appointed American consul in Leipzig.

List's plans did not earn wide approval, despite backing from the Crown Prince of Prussia (later King Friedrich Wilhelm IV). The major stumbling block he faced was the absence of unity among the German states. Undaunted, List built Germany's first railroad, the 4-mile (6.5-km) line between Nuremburg and Fürth that opened in 1835. He was also responsible for the lines between Leipzig and Alten (1837), Berlin and Potsdam (1838), and Leipzig and Dresden (1839).

JOSEPH LOCKE
1805–1860

Joseph Locke was a dominant figure among the group of British railroad engineers who pioneered steam traction at the beginning of the nineteenth century. His achievements match those of Brunel and the Stephensons. Born near Sheffield in Yorkshire, he was apprenticed at the age of 18 to George Stephenson and later worked on the construction of the world's first mainline railroad between Manchester and Liverpool. When Locke revealed errors in one of Stephenson's surveys, their relationship ended and the Yorkshireman set up his own civil engineering business. His company was responsible for the construction of several important routes in Britain, including those between Birmingham and Glasgow, and between London and Southampton. He also undertook similar construction projects in France, Spain, and the Netherlands.

By the time of his death in 1860, Locke had gained a reputation for completing all of his contracts on time and within budget. Wherever practical, his principal cost-saving tactic was to avoid building tunnels. The inevitable result of this policy was that the locomotives that operated on his lines had to travel up steep gradients, a task that used excessive amounts of fuel.

JOSEPH LOCKE

RAYMOND LOEWY ON THE RUNNING BOARD OF A STREAMLINED K4 CLASS PACIFIC

Consequently, a number of Locke's clients came to discover that the savings Locke had achieved in building his railroads left them with a legacy of relatively expensive operating costs.

RAYMOND LOEWY
1893–1986

The distinctive styling of some of North America's most famous streamlined trains is the work of French-born designer Raymond Loewy. At the age of 15, he designed a model aircraft, then patented the design, and formed a company to make and sell it. Following World War I, he emigrated to the US after acquiring a degree in engineering.

Loewy was fascinated by the design challenges posed by transport, and this led to an invitation from the Pennsylvania Railroad (PRR) to style its new GG1 electric locomotive. At first, the railroad's directors were shocked by his proposal for a streamlined casing for this locomotive that required a welding technique previously used only in the automobile industry. However, his ideas were adopted and his design won a gold medal at the International Exposition in Paris in 1937.

Loewy then went on to streamline the steam locomotives of the PRR. Beginning with the streamlining of the existing K4 Pacific, he then streamlined the S1 6-4-4-6 "Duplex" engine whose aerodynamic shape was the result of extensive wind-tunnel testing. Another Loewy design was the shark-nosed T1 4-4-4-4 "Duplex." During his long relationship with the PRR, Loewy undertook to restyle the railroad's prestigious express trains, the celebrated Fleet of Modernism. Diesel designs also benefited from Loewy's flair, including the Baldwin-built shark-nosed units and Fairbanks-Morse H-10-44 switchers.

Alongside his railroad work, Loewy was a consultant to organizations ranging from Coca-Cola and United Airlines to IBM and NASA. At his death in 1986, he was known as one of the most influential designers of the twentieth century.

GEORGE LOMONOSOFF
1876–1952

Born in Russia, George Lomonosoff was highly influential in the evolution of diesel locomotion. Appointed director general of Russian Railways, during World War I he headed a Russian mission to the US. The 2,000 engines he constructed on his return to Russia drew heavily on the designs of existing US locomotives.

In 1921, the Soviet government made Lomonosoff its high commissioner for railroad orders, which gave him the opportunity to experiment with high-power diesel traction. A diesel-electric prototype for Soviet Railways was completed to Lomonosoff's design at the Esslingen Maschinenfabrik works in Germany in 1922. It was a rigid-framed 1-Eo-1 weighing 122½ tons and powered by a 1,200 hp air-injection engine. Three years later, German State Railways ordered four locomotives based on Lomonosoff's prototype and these became the world's first mainline diesel-electric locomotives.

M

ANATOLE MALLET
1837–1919

The largest steam locomotives in the world were based on the work of Anatole Mallet. Born in France, Mallet set out to design a locomotive that could deliver high power as well as being light and flexible enough to operate on lightly laid track. In 1884 he patented a new 4-cylinder compound articulated design that consisted of a swiveling front engine, on which the low-pressure cylinders were mounted, and a fixed rear engine, on which the high-pressure cylinders were attached. The first locomotive to employ Mallet's principle was a narrow-gauge 0-4-4-0 tank built in Belgium in 1887. While Mallet's ideas did not find favor in Europe, where the development of superheating took precedence, they were widely adopted in the US. The first US railroad to run a Mallet-designed locomotive was the Baltimore & Ohio (B&O) railroad that introduced an 0-6-6-0 in 1903.

The culmination of Mallet's ideas came a long time after his death in 1919, when Union Pacific brought into service a fleet of 4-8-8-4 Mallet-type locomotives that became known as "Big Boys."

HENRY MEIGGS
1811–1877

The colorful life of American railroad contractor Henry Meiggs began in New York State. In 1849 he joined the Gold Rush migration to California, but was forced to flee the US state in 1854 after he was accused of embezzlement and warrants were issued for his arrest. He migrated to Chile, where his experience in construction work was put to good use. After successfully completing a bridge project that had run into difficulty, he received

HENRY MEIGGS

the contract to build a 90-mile (145-km) railroad line between Maiyo and San Fernando in southern Chile. Due to the success of this project other contracts followed and Meiggs went on to play an important role in developing Chile's rail network.

During the 1860s, Meiggs moved to Peru and encouraged its president, Jose Balta, to invest in major public works, principally railroads. The projects were financed by huge loans, negotiated by Balta, that left Peru with crippling debts. However, Meiggs prospered from completing contracts that included a generous bonus if work was completed ahead of schedule. Meiggs' successes in Peru included the construction of a 70-mile (113-km) line from Arequipa to the Pacific coast, and he also built much of the Central Railway that runs across the Andes, between Lima and Oroya.

Meiggs used part of the fortune he made in South America to repay all the debts he owed his Californian creditors. However, his attempts to make amends for his past misdemeanors failed and Meiggs was never allowed to return to the US.

EDMUND MOREL
1841–1871

British-born Edmund Morel was instrumental in the early development of New Zealand's railroads. He was then contracted to plan and construct the first Japanese railroad. He employed the same 3½-ft (1.6-m) gauge that he had used in New Zealand for the line connecting Tokyo with the port of Yokohama and historic Kyoto. As this gauge allowed trains to operate effectively on tight curves and steep gradients, it became the standard for all Japan's main lines, apart from the recently built Shinkansen routes, and it was also adopted as the standard gauge in New Zealand.

Morel contracted tuberculosis and died aged 30, a year prior to the opening of the first section of the Tokyo-Kyoto railroad. A bronze bust outside Sekuragicho Station in Yokohama commemorates his contribution to what has become one of the world's finest railroad systems. Significantly, this included teaching his Japanese staff the principles of surveying and constructing lines so they would not be dependent on imported knowledge.

MATTHEW MURRAY
1789–1826

The first commercially successful locomotives to operate in Britain were designed by Matthew Murray and built by a company of which he was the principal partner. His origins, like those of many early railroad engineers, were in northeast England. In 1789, Murray, then aged 24, moved to Leeds where his company, Fenton, Murray & Wood, gained a reputation for the high quality of its stationary steam engines. Later, in 1811, he was contracted to supply locomotives to replace

the 50 horses that until that time had been used to haul coal on the Middleton Colliery wagonway. A crucial advantage of Murray's designs was that, unlike his predecessors, his locomotives were light enough not to fracture the iron-plate rails.

Despite this, the engines were still capable of hauling heavy loads, as Murray proved in 1812 when he demonstrated four of these locomotives at Middleton. Thousands saw loads of up to 98½ tons hauled at 3 mph (5 kph). Murray died in

MATTHEW MURRAY'S RACK ENGINE USED ON THE MIDDLETON COLLIERY RAILWAY

1826, but the company he founded continued to build locomotives until 1843. The Great Western Railway was among the prestigious clients to buy engines from Murray's company after his death.

N

GEORGES NAGELMACKERS
1845–1905

That most romantic of trains, the Orient Express, was the brainchild of the Belgian entrepreneur Georges Nagelmackers. During a stay in the US, he was impressed by the luxurious dining and sleeping cars offered by the Pullman Company and became convinced that there was a market for similar services in Europe. On October 4 1872, he set up a carriage-building company in Belgium that he named Compagnie Internationale des Wagons-Lits et des Grands Express Europeéns (CIWL). Three weeks later he won a contract to supply luxury carriages for use on the Ostend to Cologne route, and this was followed by other prestigious contracts in France and Germany.

Despite this early success, financial difficulties forced Nagelmackers to go into partnership with ex-US colonel William d'Alton Mann, who was in England promoting his own luxury "boudoir sleeping cars." Operating under the name "Mann's Railway Sleeping Carriage Co.," Nagelmackers sold enough carriages to raise the money to reestablish CIWL in 1876. After buying a fleet of

53 boudoir cars from Mann along with 22 railroad contracts, Nagelmackers wasted no time in establishing CIWL as continental Europe's leading supplier of luxury carriages. His crowning achievement, however, was the setting up of the *Orient Express* that first ran between Paris and Istanbul in 1896.

By the turn of the century, CIWL was conveying two million passengers per year in its fleet of 550 dining, saloon, and sleeping cars. In 1912 it went on to operate a luxury train service on the Trans-Siberian Railway across Russia.

THOMAS NEWCOMEN
1663–1729

The first practical static engine to use the power of expanding steam to move a piston back-and-forth within a cylinder was unveiled by Thomas Newcomen in 1712. Newcomen, born in Devon, was a blacksmith. The engines he built with Thomas Savery were used to pump water from flooded tin mines located in Cornwall.

In his engines, steam was condensed into water beneath a piston. This created a vacuum under the piston that was pushed down by external atmospheric pressure. This in turn pulled down on one end of a pivoted beam, attached to the opposite end of which was a pump rod. As the piston descended, the pump rod rose, bringing with it water from the mineshaft.

Thomas Newcomen died in 1729 having laid down the principles upon which later pioneers, such as James Watt and Richard Trevithick, would build.

WILLIAM NORRIS
1802–1867

One of the most successful early American engine builders, William Norris turned to engineering in the 1820s. In 1832 he set up a workshop in Philadelphia that, by 1836, had assembled the modest total of seven engines. Crucial to the company's subsequent success was that Norris came up with a winning design, and that year he built the first 2-cylinder 4-2-0. It so impressed its buyer, the Philadelphia & Columbia Railroad, that a further eight engines were ordered. The first of these economical and reliable machines, *Lafayette*, was delivered in 1837. In 1839 Norris went on to build other similar engines for the

4-2-0 EXPORTED BY THE WILLIAM NORRIS COMPANY TO AUSTRIA

Champlain & St. Lawrence Railroad of Canada that were the first locomotives to be exported from the US. Orders followed from Austria, Britain, and Germany: between 1837 and 1847, around 100 Norris 4-2-0s and 4-4-0s were the first US engines to be sold to European railroads. In 1847 he added the world's first 4-6-0 to the list of types available. The popularity of these engines led Norris and his brother, Octavius, to set up a locomotive building factory in Vienna.

During the 1830s, Norris supplied 27 American railroads with locomotives from his range of four types. For a time, his company was the largest engine manufacturer in the US: by 1860, over 1,000 of the 9,000 locomotives working in the US came from the Norris factory.

P

GEORGE MORTIMER PULLMAN
1831–1897

The name Pullman remains synonymous with luxury train travel. Before founding his company, George Mortimer Pullman was a cabinetmaker. Through the practice of this craft, applied to trains, he went on to develop a company that, at its peak, enjoyed a near-monopoly in sleeping car services throughout the US.

In 1859 Pullman ran his first sleeping car, a converted passenger coach, on the Chicago & Alton Railroad. The first custom-made Pullman car entered service six years later, and rapidly became a familiar feature of North American trains. The year 1867 saw the foundation of the Pullman Palace Car Company and the birth of the "Hotel Car." This originally ran on the Great Western route of the Canada Railroad and was equipped with a kitchen and dining facilities.

Pullman's arrangement with the railroads was simple: he would provide the cars and staff them, they would heat, light, and supply the locomotive to haul his cars. His income was derived from a supplement charged on top of the normal fare. He went on to open the largest coach-building plant in the world, near Chicago, and was among the first manufacturers to replace wooden coach bodies with

GEORGE MORTIMER PULLMAN

steel cars. Pullman was not the only sleeping car operator in the US. During the 1870s, Pullman had around 40 competitors, but by the time of his death in 1897, they had all either been absorbed into the Pullman empire or gone out of business. Pullman also supplied rail coaches to Britain.

R

JOHN RAMSBOTTOM
1814–1897

The ideas and innovations of British engineer John Ramsbottom resulted in significant advances to the evolution of the steam engine during the nineteenth century. In 1842, Ramsbottom became locomotive superintendent of the Manchester & Birmingham Railway (M&BR), which was absorbed into the London & North Western Railway (L&NWR) in 1846. He rose through the ranks to become head of their locomotive department in 1862.

During this period, he introduced piston rings in 1852, the displacement lubricator and tamper-proof safety valves in 1856, and the screw reverse in 1858. He also introduced the water trough and water pickup apparatus in 1860, allowing an engine to replenish its water supply from trackbed reservoirs while running at speed. He was also one of the first engineers in the UK to fit injectors to his locomotives.

Ramsbottom advocated standardization, and his DX class 0-6-0, 943 of which were built between 1858 and 1872, remains the most numerous locomotive class ever developed in Britain. He also began a full modernization of the L&NWR's works at Crewe, introducing steel as a component in the manufacturing process, and built a foundry to produce it. He left the L&NWR in 1871 and became a consultant for the Lancashire & Yorkshire Railway.

CECIL RHODES
1853–1902

The British colonial statesman and industrialist Cecil Rhodes first saw railroads as a way to open up the undeveloped territories of southern Africa. He expanded this vision into a railroad covering 6,100 miles (9,817 km) from Cape Town, in South Africa, to the Egyptian capital Cairo, in the north of the continent. "The object," Rhodes asserted, "is to cut Africa through the center and the railroad will pick up trade along the route."

Rhodes arrived in Africa in 1870, and made a fortune from mining and selling diamonds found near Kimberley. A Royal Charter gave his British South Africa Company half a million square miles (1.3 million sq. km) of largely unexplored territory, subsequently named Rhodesia. Rhodes knew that efficient transport links were needed if this region was to be successfully exploited and settled.

A railroad running between Cape Town and Bulawayo was Rhodes's first ambition – this was completed in 1897. The venture was jointly financed by Rhodes's company and the British government. He continued to build a line that ran northward, across the Zambesi River at Victoria Falls. Keeping alive his vision for a Cape to Cairo railroad, Rhodes then ordered the construction workers to build a line that ran northeast toward Lusaka and the northern Rhodesian (now Zambian) copper belt. The railroad crossed into the Belgian Congo (now the Democratic Republic of Congo) at Ndola and reached north to Bukama, 2,600 miles (4,190 km) from Cape Town.

CECIL RHODES

The impetus to continue building the Cape to Cairo railroad was lost following Rhodes' death in 1902 at Muizenberg, in the Cape Colony.

After World War I, all the remaining territory along the route fell under British control. However, the depleted British economy was in no state to underwrite further building, and Rhodes' visionary project was never completed.

ROBERT RIDDLES
1893–1983

Robert Riddles was the last in a line of brilliant British steam locomotive designers that began with Richard Trevithick in the early nineteenth century. Riddles was apprenticed at the Crewe Works of the London & North Western Railway (L&NWR), where he gained his basic engineering skills. On the outbreak of World War I, he left to serve in the army. After the war, Riddles returned

to the railroads to reorganize the locomotive workshops at Crewe and Derby for the newly named London, Midland & Scottish Railway (LMS). In 1933, he was promoted to the post of principal assistant to William Stanier, the new chief mechanical engineer of the LMS.

During World War II, Riddles was allotted the task of providing locomotives and rolling stock to supply the Allied forces after the Normandy invasion of 1944. The 2-8-0 and 2-10-0 designs he came up with were simple and rugged machines, ideal for their purpose. They proved much more durable than Riddles had expected, and some of these engines remained in service until the 1980s.

After the nationalization of Britain's railroads in 1948, Riddles joined the Railway Executive, and was entrusted with the construction of a range of standard engine types. Twelve of his designs were produced, most of which were updates of his LMS designs, with the exception of the 9F 2-10-0, which was the last, and probably the very best, heavy-freight steam locomotive to be built in Britain.

Robert Riddles resigned from British Railways in 1953, provoked by the government's reluctance to sanction a widespread electrification of the railroad network. He firmly believed that electric traction would prove to be a better alternative than diesel after the demise of steam power. By the time of his death in 1983 that viewpoint had been wholly vindicated. Around 50 locomotives designed by Riddles have been preserved.

NIKOLAUS RIGGENBACH
1817–1899

Nikolaus Riggenbach gave his name to a rack adhesion system suited to the mountain railroads of his native Switzerland. In 1847, Riggenbach imported the first steam railroad locomotive into Switzerland, and by 1862 was building his own rack railroad locomotives. One year later, he patented the Riggenbach rack system. This employed a channel

SWITZERLAND'S RIGI-BAHN NO.7 WITH RIGGENBACH RACK SYSTEM

ROBERT RIDDLES' STANDARD CLASS 4MT 2-6-0

laid centrally in the track, with upwards facing flanges supporting a series of pins that produced a "ladder" for the train to climb. Riggenbach's rack system was first used around 1872 on the 4½-mile (7.2-km) standard-gauge Rigi-Bahn line that runs from Vitznau to the summit of the Rigi. The final 2 miles (3 km) of line, which rises to an altitude of 5,741 ft (1,750 m), opened on June 27 1873.

The Riggenbach principle can also be found in use on other Swiss mountain lines, in particular the Brunig and Bernese Oberland railroads. This pioneer of rack railroads died in 1899.

THOMAS ROGERS
1792–1856

Thomas Rogers is credited with introducing many of the characteristics that made the American 4-4-0 one of the most numerous and successful of all locomotive types. He was responsible for using the Stephenson link valve gear, balance weights on the coupled wheels, and "I" section coupling rods. In 1837, Rogers founded his engine works in Peterson, New Jersey, the same year as the world's first 4-4-0 was built in Philadelphia to a patent by Henry Campbell. Rogers adopted and refined the design into a multipurpose machine that was relatively cheap to construct, uncomplicated to service and repair, and powerful enough to haul most train services at that time. A large percentage of the 6,300 locomotives built at Rogers' works prior to 1905,

when it became part of the American Locomotive Company (ALCO), were 4-4-0s. In 1863, seven years after Rogers' death, his workshops built the forerunner of another American classic, the 2-6-0. It was the first of 11,000 similar locomotives built by North American workshops for domestic use.

S

WILHELM SCHMIDT
1859–1924

Locomotive engineers understood from the outset that power output could be increased, and fuel consumption reduced, if steam produced by the boiler could be heated to a higher temperature before it reached the cylinders. By superheating the steam, the energy lost through condensation would be lessened appreciably.

The most successful superheater type was the work of the German Wilhelm Schmidt. Born in Saxony in 1859, Schmidt spent 20 years as a locksmith's assistant in Braunschweig, now Brunswick, prior to setting up his own workshop in the city. He built his first steam engine here, and then moved to Kassel in 1891, where he built the first engine to employ superheated steam.

Schmidt's first superheater design was tried on 4-4-0s of the Prussian State Railway in 1898. By 1901, he had evolved the firetube superheater that was first fitted on to a Belgian Railways' 4-6-0. Within ten years, the device had been fitted to the majority of the larger types of locomotive in use around the world, bringing savings of up to 20 percent in the coal and water they consumed.

In the firetube superheater, steam was passed through a series of small tubes threaded into the main boiler tubes. Here, the steam's temperature was raised by 250°F (121°C) before the steam was admitted to the cylinder. Wilhelm Schmidt died in 1924, but with his innovative superheater he could justifiably claim to have been responsible for the greatest advance in steam locomotive design in the twentieth century.

MARC SÉGUIN
1786–1875

A native of Annonay, in the Ardéche département of southern France, engineer Marc Séguin's major contribution to locomotive development was in the field of boiler design. Like George Stephenson in England, Séguin realized that to improve boiler efficiency, multiple firetubes needed to be fitted in order to increase the heating area in the boiler. Séguin patented his multi-tube boiler in 1827: its design featured the use of two rotary fans on the tender that supplied a draft for the fire and were driven by belt drives attached to the tender wheels. Séguin's ingenious multi-tubular boiler was incorporated in 1828 into the first locomotive to

be built in France. This engine was first tested on November 7, 1829, on the Lyons & St. Etienne Railway. At these trials, Séguin's 0-4-0 locomotive, weighing around six tons, proved itself capable of hauling a 30-ton train at a top speed of 5 mph

MARC SÉGUIN

(7 kph). However, when it entered regular service on the Lyons & St. Etienne Railway in 1930, the belt drive proved problematic, causing the engine to run short of steam. After correcting this fault, Séguin built 12 more of his 0-4-0s. He also wrote the first French study of railroad engineering prior to his death on February 24, 1875, aged 88.

HIDEO SHIMA
1901–1998

Born in Osaka, Japan, in 1901, Dr. Hideo Shima is known as the "Father of the Shinkansen" – the high-speed line that pioneered the Bullet Train. After graduating from Tokyo University in 1925, he joined the Ministry of Railways (later Japanese National Railways). By 1948 he had become director of rolling stock for the JNR, and was later promoted to the post of vice-president for engineering in 1955, a post he held until 1963.

As far back as 1948, Dr. Shima had presided over a study group concerned with the development of coach trucks for high-speed running. In 1958 he was placed in charge of the planning of the first Shinkansen (New Railway), the Tokaido line between Tokyo and Osaka. Dr. Shima believed that this project would achieve standards no other railroad, or

HIDEO SHIMA

rival transport system, could match. His aim to have the line operational for the Tokyo Olympiad of 1964 was an ambitious one, since it involved constructing a new rail network independent of existing Japanese main lines. He also decided to use a wider gauge than the Japanese standard of 3½ ft (1.6 m) to give his trains more stability so that they could operate at higher speeds.

The Tokaido line opened on time but, at a cost of 380 billion Yen (US$3.65 billion), the project was overbudget. As a result, Hideo Shima and his chief backer, JNR president Shinji Sogo, both felt obliged to resign, and neither attended the opening ceremony. However, Dr. Shima's ground-breaking achievement was soon recognized, and he was appointed president of the Japan Railway Engineers' Association and became a member of the Science Council of Japan. In the US, he was honored as a fellow of the American Society of Engineers, receiving its Elmer A. Sperry Award. The British Institution of Mechanical Engineers also presented him with its prestigious James Watt International Medal in 1969.

FRANK SPRAGUE
1857–1934

Born in 1857, Frank Sprague became a highly regarded electrical engineer and inventor, and was one of the pioneers of electric traction in the US. Sprague began working on the development of electrically powered tramcars in 1887. The following year he constructed a tramway on which, for the first time, the cars used a trolley-pole for collecting electric current from an overhead wire. A roller fixed to the top of a wooden, spring-loaded rod maintained constant contact with the overhead power cable.

Another of Sprague's far-reaching innovations came in 1897, when he devised a method of operating electrically powered railroad vehicles in multiple. Sprague's multiple-unit trains allowed an unlimited number of rail vehicles to be controlled by a single driver. Electric multiple-unit trains became by far the most common type of train to operate on urban and suburban railroads around the world.

By the time of his death in 1934, Sprague's work on developing electric traction was internationally recognized and many of his ideas provided the foundations for the development of high-speed electric traction after World War II. The revolutionary new generation of high-speed electric trains that transformed mainline express services were all multiple units.

SIR WILLIAM STANIER
1875–1965

Britain's most powerful class of express passenger locomotive, the Coronation Pacific, was designed by Sir William Stanier. Of the eight types of engine he designed, a total of 2,000 were built, including 38 Coronation Pacifics. These designs transformed the efficiency of the trains working on Britain's largest railroad system, the London Midland & Scottish Railway (LMS).

Stanier was linked with railroads from birth: his father worked for the Great Western Railway (GWR) at its Swindon Works and William joined as an apprentice there in 1892. He remained at the Swindon works under George Jackson Churchward, whose revolutionary redesigning of the GWR's locomotives inspired Stainer's later work. The experience was put to good use when he took on a similar task as chief mechanical engineer of the LMS in 1932. He combined the best features of GWR and LMS practice in his engine designs to produce notable locomotives such as the Class 5 4-6-0, of which a total of 842 were built, making it Britain's most numerous mixed traffic engine. Stainer's 8F 2-8-0 was another successful design with over 650 built, many for military use during World War II. Stanier also began equipping the LMS with diesel-electric shunting engines, descendants of which are still Britain's standard class of diesel switcher.

GEORGE STEPHENSON
1781–1848

Universally acknowledged as "The Father of the Railways," George Stephenson was born into a mining family in Northumberland, England. He worked as a farmhand and a pitboy before finding employment as an engineman at Killingworth High Pit in 1812. Two years later he designed and built his first locomotive, *Blucher*, and then patented an engine that used the blast of the exhaust steam to create a draft for the fire. This innovation, a primitive form of the blastpipe, and his tubular boiler, constitute Stephenson's most important contributions to the early development of steam traction. Stephenson's main strengths were his leadership and organizational ability. These were tested to the full when he undertook the contract that earned him his place in history: building the world's first public railroad between the English towns of Stockton-on-Tees and Darlington.

By the time the Stockton and Darlington Railway (S&DR) opened in 1825, Stephenson had won a bigger prize, the contract to build a railroad from Liverpool to Manchester. In 1829 the locomotive trials held at Rainhill prior to the opening of the London & Manchester Railway (L&MR) earned Stephenson and his son, Robert, the contract to

MIXED TRAFFIC 4-6-0 DESIGNED BY WILLIAM STANIER

supply engines for the L&MR when it opened in 1930. *Rocket*, the engine they entered for the trials, won first prize. Through subsequent railroad contracts, colliery ownership, and stockdealings, this one-time uneducated pitboy earned himself a sizeable fortune and was appointed as president of the Institution of Mechanical Engineers.

ROBERT STEPHENSON
1803–1859

Like his father George, Robert Stephenson made an enormous contribution to the development of railroads in Britain and beyond. He was also a much greater engineer than his father.

The only son of George Stephenson, Robert was born in Northumberland and received a good education, first in Newcastle-upon-Tyne and then at Edinburgh University. In 1823 the Stephensons

GEORGE STEPHENSON

set up the world's first purpose-built locomotive factory in Newcastle. Within 12 months, the relationship between father and son was under strain, so Robert left to work in South America. Here he found work as the chief mechanical engineer of the Colombian Mining Company.

Robert's father requested he return to Britain in 1827 and, following his reappointment to the family firm, he devoted his energy to locomotive design. Most of the credit for the design of *Rocket* belongs to Robert, who remained in the forefront of steam locomotive development for the ensuing 15 years. Robert also undertook major civil engineering projects, among them building the 112-mile (180-km) long London & Birmingham Railway that opened in 1838. Several famous bridges were also built to his design, including: the Britannia tubular bridge across the Menai Strait, linking north Wales with the Isle of Anglesey; the High Level Bridge at Newcastle-upon-Tyne; and the Royal Border Bridge at Berwick.

Alongside Isambard Brunel, Joseph Locke, and George Stephenson – Robert Stephenson ranks as one of Britain's railroad engineering giants.

JOHN STEVENS
1749–1838

Colonel John Stevens was one of the first North Americans to appreciate the potential of railroads. Born in Hoboken, New Jersey, he was granted the first American railroad charter in February 1815. His proposal was for a railroad connecting the Delaware and Raritan rivers between Trenton and New Brunswick in New Jersey. However, he failed to raise the capital for this venture.

Stevens developed an interest in motive power for railroads and built the first American steam engine in 1821. He demonstrated this four-wheel machine on a small circular track at his home in Hoboken. It was propelled along a toothed rack, sited between the rails and was guided by vertical rollers running against the inside of the rail.

In 1823 Stevens obtained his second railroad charter. This authorized him to construct a line from Philadelphia to Columbia in Pennsylvania, and was the first railroad to be incorporated in the US when a section of it opened in 1829. The 81-mile (51-km) line was completed in 1834.

WILLIAM STROUDLEY
1833–1889

Working with two of the more impoverished railroad companies in Victorian Britain, William Stroudley had to design locomotives that were economical and reliable. Despite these restrictions, Stroudley's locomotives displayed award-winning grace and proportion. After gaining experience with marine and stationary steam engines on the Great Western Railway and the Great Northern Railway, he was appointed works manager on the Edinburgh & Glasgow Railway in 1861. He went on to become locomotive superintendent of the Highland Railway (HR), where his achievements in improving their fleet of locomotives on a tight budget was noted by another underfunded line, the London, Brighton & South Coast Railway (LB&SCR). Stroudly was persuaded to relocate to LB&SCR in 1870 to sort out their chaotic motive power structure. This he achieved by introducing a program of standardization based on just five classes of locomotives. These engines included the diminutive yet powerful and long-lived "Terrier" passenger tanks, and his most celebrated engines, the Gladstone 0-4-2s, 36 of which he introduced in 1882. These handsome machines proved their worth on the London to Brighton route, where their fastest running times match those of the present electric trains that run on this line.

One of Stroudley's 0-4-2 locomotives, *No.189 Edward Blount*, was awarded a gold medal at the 1889 Paris Exhibition. While he was in France to receive this accolade, William Stroudley suffered an asthma attack and died.

T

RENÉ THURY
1860–1938

The Swiss-born engineer René Thury made an important contribution to the development of electrically powered railroad traction. At 24, he successfully built an experimental rack railroad in Territet, a suburb of Montreux, in Switzerland. The railroad climbed around 1,000 ft (300 m) up to a mountain-side hotel at a gradient of 1 in 33, and employed a two-axle electric car that took up to four people. On the descent, the car's motor was used to generate braking force.

Thury left Switzerland and moved to the US to work for Thomas Edison, the famous inventor of, among other things, the electric phonograph and the light bulb. In the US, Thury made a number of important innovations in electrical engineering, many of which had railroad applications. These included a means of coupling electric motors in series, a principal that was widely adopted.

Thury later returned to Europe, and worked for the British electrical machinery manufacturer Dick, Kerr & Company of Preston, in Lancashire. His efforts made the company, later part of the English Electric group, a leader in its field.

CHAN TIEN-YU
1861–1919

Chan Tien-Yu was the first notable Chinese locomotive engineer. He was born in Guangdong (Kwantung), a province in the far south of the country. Educated in the US, he spent seven years in the Chinese navy before embarking on a career in railroad engineering in 1888. In 1902, Tien-Yu was appointed chief engineer in charge of the construction of the Peking (Beijing) to Hsiling railroad. From 1905 until 1909 he was responsible for building the Peking to Kalgan railroad that ran northward to the Mongolian border. The project presented Tien-Yu with numerous engineering challenges, as did his final project, the building of the Hankow to Szechuan railroad. He remained working on the construction of this line until his death in 1919 at the age of 58.

RICHARD TREVITHICK
1771–1833

Born in Cornwall, England, Richard Trevithick was the first visionary among British locomotive pioneers. He brought about several fundamental advances in steam traction, as well as being the first person to harness the power of high-pressure steam in an engine. Prior to this, steam had been used at atmospheric pressure: this was ineffective because it did not produce enough power to drive a heavy vehicle nor lift heavy weights.

Trevithick first constructed stationary pumping engines for mines, but soon began experimenting with steam-driven road carriages. In 1803 he built the first locomotive designed to run on rails. The next year, its successor was used at the Penydarren ironworks in South Wales, where it hauled an unprecedented ten tons of iron and 70 men. Trevithick's next innovation was to fit flanged wheels to a locomotive to improve stability.

Wanting a wider audience to witness the great potential of rail-borne transport, Trevithick set up a circular track in London's Euston Square in 1808, around which his *Catch Me Who Can* locomotive hauled passenger wagons. Unfortunately, the track broke, causing his locomotive to topple over. As a consequence of this accident, steam traction was not used for

RICHARD TREVITHICK

passenger transport for another 17 years as the idea was judged to be little more than a novelty. Disillusioned, Trevithick returned to designing mine engines until the lure of steam locomotion took him to South America where, in 1833, he died destitute following an ill-starred attempt to build a line across the Andes.

V

SAMUEL VAUCLAIN
1856–1940

Son of Andrew Vauclain, an associate of the great North American locomotive builder Matthias Baldwin, Samuel Vauclain was born in Philadelphia, Pennsylvania. He followed his father into railroad engineering, training at the Altoona workshops of the Pennsylvania Railroad.

In 1887, Vauclain joined Baldwin's company as superintendent of one of the workshops. Three years later, he was charge of the entire plant. He now had the chance to pursue his own locomotive designs that developed the effectiveness of compound cylinders. In 1889 he built his first four-cylinder compound engine, and by 1907 more than 2,000 engines were using his compound designs. Vauclain was responsible for many other innovations. In 1886 he built the world's first ten-coupled heavy goods engine; and in 1897, he built the first 2-8-2 for a Japanese client. Consequently, 2-8-2s were nicknamed "Mikados."

VAUCLAIN COMPOUND
TANK LOCOMOTIVE

AUGUST VON BORRIES
1852–1906

August von Borries was one of Germany's most influential railroad engineers. At the age of 23, he became the locomotive superintendent of the Hanover Division of Prussian State Railways. After studying new developments in Britain and the US, he returned to Germany and became a leading proponent of the compound steam engine.

Von Borries introduced his first two-cylinder compound locomotive in 1880, which he upgraded to a four-cylinder version by 1899. Among the most famous of his designs was the S3 class compound 4-4-0, of which 1,027 were built for the Prussian State Railways between 1892 and 1904. A further 424 smaller compound engines of similar design were also produced. Von Borries shared his ideas on compounding with other railroads, most notably Britain's North Eastern Railway which built 270 locomotives employing his principles.

In Germany, von Borries was responsible for a number of other key innovations including, in 1891, replacing wrought iron with nickel steel in the fabrication of boilers. His inventiveness was recognized with a professorship at the Berlin Technical School in 1902.

ERNST WERNER VON SIEMENS
1816–1892

Rail traction was one of several areas in which the German engineer Ernst Werner von Siemens pioneered the use of electricity. At the age of 18, Siemens joined the Prussian Artillery, where he was employed on the army's technical staff. By 1844, he was head of the artillery workshops in

ERNST WERNER VON SIEMENS

Berlin. Returning to civilian life, he set about developing an electric telegraph system. In order to develop and manufacture this product he co-founded the firm Siemens & Halske in 1847.

In the summer of 1879, Siemens demonstrated the first practical application of electric traction at the Berlin Trades Exhibition. Here he built a narrow-gauge oval track, around 909 ft (277 m) in length, and installed a third conductor rail to supply current (at 150 volts DC) to the locomotive. This was a small, four-wheeled machine with geared transmission, and a modest output of three horsepower. It proved capable of pulling three carriages containing 30 passengers at a top speed of 4 mph (6.5 kph).

Siemens died at Charlottenberg in 1892, but his company grew to become one of the largest in Germany and a major supplier of electrical equipment to railroads the world over. In 1901, an electric locomotive developed by Siemens & Halske became the first engine to reach 100 mph (160 kph).

W

EGIDE WALSCHAERTS
1820–1901

Egide Walschaerts worked as a mechanic for the Belgian State Railways. In 1844 he was appointed foreman of its Brussels locomotive depot, and that year patented the valve gear that bears his name.

The valve gear on a steam engine operates the valves that control the admission and expulsion of steam into and out of the cylinders. Walschaerts' patent offered good control over steam distribution, with the bonus of simplicity and easy maintenance.

The first practical use of Walschaerts' gear came in 1848 when it was fitted to an inside-cylinder 2-2-2. The gear was subsequently installed on all outside-cylinder engines built in Belgium. In 1859, four Crampton-type engines in France were fitted with Walschaerts, but the gear did not appear in the US until 1874, and in Britain two years later. The universal application of this valve gear came in the twentieth century, when new locomotive construction began to consist almost exclusively of outside-cylinder designs. Egide Walschaerts died in 1901, but his valve gear was still being fitted to engines built in China during the 1980s.

SIR EDWARD WATKIN
1819–1901

Born in Manchester, England, Edward Watkin's dream was to travel by train from his home city to Paris using a tunnel built beneath the English

Channel. Watkin entered the railroad business in 1845, and in 1854 became general manager of the Manchester, Sheffield & Lincolnshire Railway (MS&LR). This trans-Pennine line was at the time primarily used for transporting coal. However, Watkin extended it westward to Liverpool and North Wales, and eastward to the fishing port of Grimsby, creating in the process a viable passenger railroad. His ambition did not end there; during the 1860s, Watkin began implementing his plan for a railroad to France. He gained control of two railroads that would connect him to the English Channel: the Metropolitan Railway, which ran through London; and South Eastern Railway, which

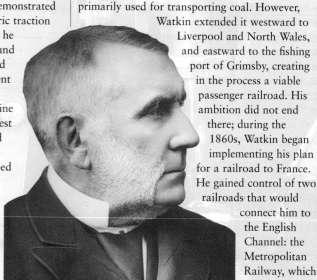

SIR EDWARD WATKIN

linked the capital with the coast of Kent. Watkin then pushed ahead with the 92-mile (148-km) link between the MS&LR near Nottingham, and his railroads in southern England. The entire MS&LR system was renamed the Great Central Railway, and the London Extension of Watkin's rail network opened in 1899, five years after ill-health forced him to relinquish all his railroad posts.

Despite Watkin's ambition and competitiveness, his railroads achieved only moderate financial success. His vision of cross-channel rail travel remained unfulfilled for a further 90 years.

JAMES WATT
1736–1819

Scottish engineer James Watt made two vital contributions to the development of the steam engine. The first was to significantly improve its efficiency by separating the heating and cooling stages of its operation; and the second was to reveal how steam power could turn wheels.

Born at Greenock on the River Clyde, Watt started out as a surveyor and instrument maker. In 1796, while working at Glasgow University, he was asked to repair a working model of Thomas Newcomen's steam engine. The inefficiency of the Newcomen system was apparent: 80 percent of the energy in each charge of steam was wasted heating cold metal. Watt transformed the engine's performance by fitting a separate steam condenser and by insulating the cylinder to maintain it at a higher temperature. He also employed expanding steam to move the piston, another advance on the Newcomen process, which relied entirely upon atmospheric pressure. Boulton & Watt, formed by Watt and Matthew Boulton, began manufacturing static locomotives to Watt's design in Birmingham, England, in 1774. At the same time, Watt began work on a double-acting steam engine in which steam pushes on one side of a piston then the other. He also focused on the movement of the engine that, until then, was limited to moving up and down. He extended the movement by developing a set of gears which, when powered by a piston, could turn a wheel. The requirements for a mobile steam engine were now in place and, before his death in 1819, Watt would witness their first practical applications in the shape of early railroad locomotives.

JAMES WATT'S ROTATIVE STEAM ENGINE

FRANCIS WEBB
1836–1906

Francis Webb was one of the most controversial and brilliant British locomotive engineers. Even as a child, he displayed a remarkable aptitude for mathematics and mechanics. Apprenticed at the London & North Western Railway's (L&NWR) Crewe Works in 1851, by 1866 he had risen to the post of assistant to the chief mechanical engineer, John Ramsbottom. He then left the L&NWR to manage a steelworks.

In 1871, Webb rejoined the L&NWR to replace Ramsbottom as chief mechanical engineer. The L&NWR was one of the busiest railroads in the world, and had a huge need for locomotives and rolling stock. During his 32-year term as chief mechanical engineer, Webb met this need. By 1882, 256 passenger coaches had been built and between 1881 and 1887, 300 0-6-2 passenger tank engines and 500 "coal engines" were constructed.

As well as excelling in performance, his 0-6-0 design became one of the simplest locomotives to build. He also pioneered the use of steel in engine frames and boilers, and was far-sighted enough to propose the electrification of the main line between London and Glasgow prior to 1900.

Unfortunately, Webb was a remote autocrat who would not tolerate criticism. From 1878 he began to experiment with compound engines and, given a free hand by L&NWR, pursued his ideas unchecked. He produced ten compound designs contrasting in performance. The unreliability of these designs overshadowed his earlier achievements and, with support ebbing away, Webb retired in 1903. By his death in 1906, many of the compound engines that he had designed were being revamped.

GEORGE WESTINGHOUSE
1846–1914

North American engineer George Westinghouse played a central role in developing signalling systems and electric traction in both the US and Europe. However, his most important invention was the compressed-air brake. He produced a non-automatic air brake in 1869 that was demonstrated on the Panhandle Railroad in 1870. The performance of his brake at this trial encouraged him to set up the Westinghouse Air Brake Company in Pittsburgh, Pennsylvania. A more sophisticated braking system that would be applied automatically if a train split apart was introduced in 1873. Significantly, Westinghouse insisted that the braking systems used on all US railroads were standardized.

During 1875, successful braking trials in Britain encouraged him to set up the Westinghouse Continuous Brake Company in London. Further companies were set up in Europe and Australia. Westinghouse went on to improve signalling, and in 1880 founded a subsidiary: the Union Switch & Signaling Company. The Westinghouse Electric Company was founded in 1886, and by the 1900s it began to play a major role in the evolution of electrified railroads. Westinghouse died in 1914, but companies bearing his name continue to supply railroads around the world with a wide range of equipment.

GEORGE WESTINGHOUSE

GEORGE WASHINGTON WHISTLER
1800–1849

Born in Indiana, in the southern US, George Washington Whistler became a pioneer of engineering in North America. He was also one of the first North Americans to cross the Atlantic to study the growing British railroad system. This learning proved invaluable when he returned home to build the Baltimore & Ohio, the first railroad in the US to have two sets of tracks

running in parallel. Whistler contributed many other railroad projects in the US before he was contracted in 1842 to build the first main line in Russia. When the Tsar Nicholas I was asked to select the route for this line linking St. Petersburg to Moscow, he simply drew a straight line on the map between the two cities! Fortunately, the flat landscape made it possible for Whistler to follow his decree and the railroad was built in a straight line for most of its 402-mile (644-km) length. He also used a wide 5-ft (1.5-m) gauge that was adopted as the standard track gauge for Russia's railroads. The line was completed in 1851, but Whistler was not alive to witness it as he died from cholera in 1849.

ROSS WINANS
1796–1877

When Ross Winans first approached the Baltimore & Ohio railroad (B&O) to sell them horses, he noted that they had moved on from horse-drawn wagons and decided that "iron-horse" construction was the business to be in. He promptly set about educating himself to become an engineer and set off across the Atlantic to study the railroads in Britain, where he saw *Rocket* winning the Rainhill trials of 1829. Two years later he became the assistant head of machinery for the B&O and, in 1835, he and his partners leased the B&O Mount Clare workshops to set up a locomotive-building business.

Winan's designs were always innovative. In 1841, he built the first eight-coupled locomotive. The following year he unveiled the Camel, so-called because its driving cab was located on top of the boiler rather than behind it. These distinctive locomotives were the first successful burners of anthracite coal, which was mined extensively in the eastern US. Winans was quick to realize that bigger engines would be needed, and built the *Centipede* in 1854. For its time, this 4-8-0 was a giant locomotive.

CAMEL-TYPE DESIGNED BY ROSS WINANS

GLOSSARY

ALTERNATING CURRENT (AC)
An electric current that reverses its direction of flow rapidly at regular intervals. The rate at which it reverses per second is the frequency, and is calculated in cycles, or Hertz (Hz).

ARTICULATED LOCOMOTIVE
A locomotive (often steam) with two or more engine units that can move independently of each other. This gives it greater flexibility.

ARTICULATED TRAIN
Interconnected train set that has cars that are each linked together by a single, pivoting truck.

ASHPAN
Located beneath the firebox of a steam locomotive, this pan collects the ash and cinders that fall through the grate of the firebox.

AXLELOADING
The weight imposed on the track by a locomotive's heaviest pair of wheels.

B-B
Diesel and electric locomotives and powered cars are categorized by the number of powered and unpowered axles that they have. The unpowered axles, which often carry the leading and the trailing wheels, are listed numerically, while the powered axles supporting the driving wheels are designated an alphabetical description. A common axle configuration is 1-B-B-1, which describes an engine that has one leading axle, two groups of twin-set powered axles, and one unpowered rear axle.

BLASTPIPE
A pipe that conveys exhaust steam from the cylinders up the smokestack of a steam locomotive. This creates a partial vacuum, increasing the flow of air passing through the firebox.

BOILER
The part of a steam engine in which steam is produced and circulates.

BRAKES
A locomotive has a set of brakes to slow itself down. It is often fitted with an additional control that engages

brakes along the length of the train. These brakes are activated by either air, steam, or a vacuum.

C-C
Refers to any diesel or electric engine that has two triple-sets of powered axles. (*See also* **B-B**).

CAR, CARRIAGE, COACH
Various terms employed to describe either a powered or an unpowered passenger-carrying rail vehicle.

CATENARY
Cables supporting the conductor wire of an overhead electrification system.

COMPOUNDING
A method of obtaining more work from each charge of steam. Steam first powers one or more high-pressure cylinder(s) and is then exhausted into one or more low-pressure cylinder(s), where it is reused.

CONNECTING ROD
On a steam engine, a connecting rod links the piston rods to the crankpins of the driving wheels. In some early electric locomotives, the connecting rods linked the crankshaft with the driving wheels.

CRANKPIN
A large steel pin that is pressed into the wheel center. On steam engines, the driving wheels are driven by rods that transmit rotary force to the wheels through the crankpins.

CRANKSHAFT
A shaft that acts upon cranks in order to convert the linear motion of the piston into rotary motion. This rotary motion drives the wheels.

CROSSHEAD
The point of connection between the piston and the connecting rod that, along with the slidebars, keeps the piston rod in line as it moves in and out of the cylinder.

CYLINDER
An enclosed chamber in which a piston moves to produce power that is transmitted to the wheels.

DIESEL-ELECTRICS
Any locomotive or car powered by a diesel-electric engine. Unlike gasoline engines, diesel engines use compressed air, rather than a spark, to ignite the oil that fuels them. The mechanical power generated by combustion is then converted into an electric charge in a generator, and this electricity powers motors that drive the axles.

DOUBLE-HEADING
The use of two locomotives, with separate crews, at the head of a train.

DRIVING WHEELS
The powered or driven wheels of a locomotive that, in rotating, provide traction. They are sometimes known as coupled wheels.

ECCENTRIC
The eccentric is a rod attached to the gear of a steam locomotive to impart movement to the valve gears.

ELECTRICS
Refers to all locomotives, multiple-unit trains, and railcars that draw the electric power for traction from an external source. The electric supply is either drawn from a conductor rail placed beside the track, or from overhead cables.

EXHAUST
The used steam and combusted gases produced by either a steam or a diesel locomotive.

EXHAUST PIPE
A vertical pipe inside the smokebox of a steam locomotive that lines up with the smokestack and draws exhaust away from the cylinders.

FIREBOX
The section of a steam locomotive boiler in which combustion occurs.

FIREHOLE DOOR
The aperture in the firebox of a steam locomotive through which coal or wood is shoveled.

FIRETUBES
Tubes running between a steam engine's firebox and smokebox. Hot gases drawn through the firetubes heat the water surrounding the tubes.

FLANGE
The projecting lip on a wheel that guides the wheel along a rail.

FOOTPLATE
The floor of a locomotive driving cab where the crew stands. Footplate can also refer to the entire cab.

GAUGE
The distance between the inside running edges of the rails of a track. Also a visual display of, for example, steam- or brake-pressure readings.

GENERATOR
A device for turning mechanical energy into electrical energy in a diesel locomotive.

HORSEPOWER (hp)
A unit of power equal to 745.7 watts or 550 foot-pounds per second. Used to express the power produced by steam, diesel, or electric locomotives.

INJECTOR
A device that feeds water into the boiler of a steam locomotive against the pressure of steam in that boiler.

JOURNALBOX
A metal casing housing the bearing in which the end of an axle rotates.

LOCOMOTIVE
A detachable, wheeled engine used for pulling trains. Steam and diesel engines generate their own power, while electric locomotives collect electricity from an external source.

MULTIPLE UNIT
A term used in diesel and electric traction terminology that refers to the semipermanent coupling of several powered and unpowered vehicles to form a single train.

PANTOGRAPH
An assembly on the roof of an electric locomotive or electric multiple-unit power car that draws current from an overhead wire. Many pantographs are diamond shaped. Also known as a current collector.

PILOT
A sloping plate or grid fitted to the front of an engine; it is designed to push obstructions off the track.

PISTON
The cylindrical assembly that moves back-and-forth inside the cylinder of a steam or diesel engine.

PISTON ROD

The rod linking the piston in a steam-engine cylinder with the crosshead.

RAILCAR

A self-propelled diesel- or electric-powered passenger rail vehicle.

REGULATOR

A lever used by the driver of a steam locomotive to control the supply of steam to the cylinders.

REVERSER

A wheel or lever situated in the cab of a steam locomotive that controls the forward and reverse motion.

RUNNING BOARD/PLATE

The footway around a locomotive's engine compartment or boiler.

RUNNING GEAR

The parts involved in the movement of an engine. Includes wheels, axles, axleboxes, bearings, and springs.

SAFETY VALVES

Valves set to lift automatically to allow steam to escape if the boiler pressure exceeds its safe limit.

SANDING

The application of sand between the wheel tires and the rails to increase grip and prevent wheelslip. The sand is piped from a sandbox, which is often situated on top of the boiler.

SIDE RODS

The driving wheels along both sides of a locomotive are linked together by coupling rods. Coupling the wheels spreads the power and reduces the possibility of wheel slippage.

SLIDEBARS

On a steam locomotive, slidebars combine with the crosshead to guide the movement of piston rods.

SMOKE DEFLECTORS

Metal sheets attached to the smokebox to funnel air upward, forcing smoke and steam emitted from the smokestack away from the cab. Their main purpose is to improve visibility.

COMMON STEAM LOCOMOTIVE TYPES		
WHEEL	TYPE	NAME
	4-4-0	American
	4-4-2	Atlantic
	2-6-0	Mogul
	2-6-2	Prairie
	4-6-0	Ten Wheeler
	4-6-2	Pacific
	4-6-4	Hudson
	2-8-0	Consolidation
	2-8-2	Mikado
	2-8-4	Berkshire
	4-8-2	Mountain
	2-10-0	Decapod
	4-6-6-4	Challenger
	2-8-8-4	Yellowstone
	4-8-8-4	Big Boy

SMOKEBOX

The leading section of a steam locomotive boiler that houses the main steampipes to the cylinders, the blastpipe, the smokestack, and the ends of the firetubes. Ash drawn through the firetubes collects here.

SPLASHER

Semicircular guard used to enclose the top section of a large-diameter driving wheel. They are often fitted when the wheel protrudes above the running board of a locomotive.

STEAM DOME

A chamber on top of the barrel of a steam locomotive's boiler where the steam collects and is directed to the cylinders in a steam engine.

STEAM LOCOMOTION

Steam locomotion is founded on the principle that when water is heated above its boiling point, it turns to steam and its volume becomes 1,700 times greater. If this expansion takes place within a sealed vessel such as a boiler, the pressure of the steam will become a source of energy.

SUPERHEATING

Raising the temperature and volume of steam by adding extra heat as it passes between the boiler and the cylinders. This dries the steam by turning the remaining water droplets into gas, thus delivering more power.

TANK ENGINE

A steam locomotive that carries its fuel and water on its own chassis rather than in a separate tender. The water is often held in side tanks or in saddletanks that encase the boiler.

TENDER

A vehicle, attached to a steam engine, that carries the fuel and water.

TRACTION MOTOR

Converts incoming electrical energy into mechanical energy at the shafts that drive on to the axles. Used in both diesel and electric traction.

TRACTIVE EFFORT

A measure of a locomotive's pulling power; the effort that it can exert in moving a train from standstill. This force is calculated by measuring the energy the locomotive exerts on the treads of its driving wheels.

TRAIN

Passenger or freight vehicles coupled together and traveling as one unit along a railroad line. Trains can be self-propelled or locomotive-hauled.

TRUCK

A swiveling set of wheels positioned under or at the bottom of a car, either end of a locomotive to spread the load on the axles.

TURBOCHARGING

A method of introducing more air into the cylinders of a diesel engine, through the use of a turbocharger to force air through the inlet valves at higher than atmospheric pressure.

VALVE GEAR

Linkages that connect the valves of a steam locomotive and control the movement of the valves.

VALVES

In a steam engine, valves coordinate the movement of steam into and out of the cylinders. In a diesel engine, valves control the intake of fuel and the expulsion of exhaust gases.

VERTICAL CYLINDER

Vertically mounted cylinders used in early locomotives such as George Stephenson's *Locomotion No.1* and, later, in specialized forms of shunting engine or narrow-gauge locomotive.

VOLT (v)

The unit of electromotive force or pressure that carries one ampere of current against one ohm resistance.

WATER GLASS

A vertical glass tube in a steam locomotive cab that indicates the water level in the boiler and firebox.

STEAM LOCOMOTIVE TYPES

In the Whyte system, used in this book, steam locomotives are defined by the total number of leading, driving, and trailing wheels they have. This chart shows the most common steam locomotive types and identifies them both by their wheel arrangement and by their generic name.

INDEX

In this index, page numbers refer to main entries only. *Italic* numbers indicate illustrations. Steam engines are listed by type; numerical types are listed at the end of the index.

ACKNOWLEDGEMENTS

I WOULD LIKE TO THANK the following for their advice, help, and encouragement during the production of *Ultimate Train*: all my colleagues at Dorling Kindersley, especially Peter Adams, Sean Hunter, Phil Ormerod, Amir Reuveni, and Nichola Thomasson; Colin Garratt and Colin Nash of Milepost 92½; Keith Lawrence; Jim Winkley; Detlef Gerth; Hans-Dieter Berns; and John Dittrich of Sony UK.

Photography by: Gary Ombler
Additional photography by: Dave King, Akhil Bakhshi, Mike Dunning
Map artworks: by Anderson Peters

Dorling Kindersley would like to thank:
Chris Walker for design assistance; Jane Bolton, Michael Downey, and Sean O'Connor for editorial assistance; Tyrone O'Dea and Andy Komorowski for photography assistance; Joe Cunningham for technical advice on trains in the United States; Alpana Khare and Radhika Singh at DK India for help in India.

The publishers would also like to thank the following individuals and their colleagues for their help with photography: Courtney B. Wilson at the **B&O Railroad Museum**; Rainer Mertens at the **DB Museum**; Jean-Marc Combe at the **Museé du Chemin de Fer**; Molly Carsten, Ron Goldfeder at the **Museum of Transportation**; Detlev Schubsky at **Transrapid**; Shri Agarwal at the **National Railway Museum, New Delhi**; Richard Gibbon at the **National Railway Museum, York**; Angela Murphy at the **Science and Society Picture Library**; Kilian Elsasser at the **Verkehrshaus der Schweiz**.

Dorling Kindersley would also like to thank the following for their kind permission to reproduce their photographs:

a=above; b=below; c=centre; l=left; r=right; t=top

Alvey & Towers: 47cla; **Amtrak:** 135tl; **The Blue Train:** 113tl, 113cl; **Bridgeman Art Library, London / New York:** Museo Nazionale di San Martino, Naples 14-15t; **Ian Britton:** 54cla; **Ian D. C. Button:** 76tr, 76cla, 77crb; **California State Railroad Museum:** 6-7, 20tl, 66-67b; **Canadian Pacific Archives:** 60-61b, 60cl, 60tl; **Chicago Transit Authority:** 58-59b; **Colour-Rail:** 19cr, 51cr; **Corbis UK Ltd:** 34-35c, 153tr; Bettmann 83tr, 142-143; Wolfgang Kaehler 77c; **Culver Pictures Inc:** 39tl, 39tr, 46tr, 46clb, 56br, 161br; **DB Museum, Nürnberg, Germany:** 21bc, 94c; **Deutsche Bahn AG:** 135cl; **East Japan Railway Company:** 122tl, 122c, 122cl, 123tr; **Editorial El Ateneo S.A.:** 115tr; **Mary Evans Picture Library:** 30tl,

144c, 145cl, 151cl, 154bl, 159tr, 160tr; **Institution of Civil Engineers** 146cl; **Ferrovie Dello Stato:** 78cr, 100cla; **©Flohic Éditions:** 59tr; **Glasgow Museums:** 161tl; **Alfred Gottwaldt:** 96cl; **Great Southern Railway, Australia:** 128tl, 128tr, 128cla, 128clb, 129tl; **HSST Development Corporation:** 139tc; **Robert Harding Picture Library:** Hungarian War Museum copyright Rainbird 82tr; Schuster 77tl; **Peter Hautzinger:** 24tl, 101cra, 120-121b, 121cr, 130bl, 131cr; **Rob Heron:** The Wagon Lits Society 42-43c, 54tr, 66tr, 70cr, 92-93b, 92cr; ©Wagons-Lits Diffusion 1999, Paris, France 83cr; **Peter Herring:** 20br, 35br, 36cla, 36clb, 36tl, 37cla, 54br, 70tr, 74cla, 82bl, 88tl, 144bl, 146bc, 156tl, 158tc; **Frank Hornby:** A.J. Pike 67c; **Hulton Getty:** 122tr, 148cr, 153bl; **Image Bank:** Archive photos 50cl, 56-57t, 79tl, 95tr, 106tr, 106cla, 147br, 155tr, 158bc, 161cr; LASS 22; **Images Colour Library:** 122-123b; **Images Of India:** Dinodia 126bl; Dinodia – J.R. Paul 100tr; **Impact Photos:** Philip Gordon 123cr; **Imperial War Museum:** 82-83b, 82cl, 83tl, 104-105b, 105tr, 105clb; **Institution Of Mechanical Engineers:** I MECH E © 1999 11tc, 149tr, 152cl, 157bc; **J.M. Jackson:** 114cla; **Japan National Tourist Organisation:** 134-135b; **Brian Jennison:** 61crb, 115bc; **Kobal Collection:** Canal + 93ac; **K. P. Lawrence:** 12tl, 46bl, 89crb, 119tr; **Thierry Leleu:** 89tr; **Raymond J. Marsh:** 112-113; **Milepost 92½:** 16tc, 24-25b, 30-31c, 31bl, 36tr, 38-39b, 38bl, 42cla, 42clb, 42bl, 43tr, 43br, 47t, 54clb, 62cla, 62br, 63tl, 63tr, 66bl, 74-75b, 74tr, 75t, 84-85t, 85cl, 85crb, 95bl, 106-107c, 106cb, 113cb, 115cra, 118-119c, 118cla, 119tl, 121bc, 131b, 135tr, 137cra, 138-139c, 138-139b, 139br, 145t; Howard Ande 127tl, 127cra, 130cl, 131tr; Dr. Finch 121tr, 139c; Colin Garratt 16clb, 23tc, 118bl, 126-127c; John P. Hankey Collection 38-39c; National Tramway Museum 62-63c; A.J. Pike 29bc, 35cr, 35tl; Brian Solomon 38tr, 56tr, 94tr, 95crb; Neil Wheelwright 138bc; Ron Ziel 50-51b, 50tr, 51cl, 54-55t, 56clb, 70-71b, 74-75c, 76cr, 84bl, 88-89b, 88cl, 89tl, 96-97b, 96cr, 97tr, 104cla, 104tr, 118tr, 119crb, 159bc; **G. W. Morrison:** 17tr, 75cr, 114-115t; **National Archives of Canada:** 60ac; **National Motor Museum, Beaulieu:** 8-9b; **National Railway Museum, York:** 1, 6c, 8-9b, 8cl, 9tc, 10-11b, 10tl, 28, 30bl, 31tr, 31ac, 31br, 32-33b, 32tr, 33tl, 33tc, 34cl, 39br, 42-43b, 55b, 67tl, 74clb, 79c, 87b, 89cra, 97tl, 98-99b, 98tr, 98cla, 99tc, 99tr, 102, 115crb, 116-117b, 116cla, 117tl, 117tr, 117cr, 119b, 150tl, 151br, 154cra, 155b, 161tl; **Peter Newark's American Pictures:** 13tr, 46-47b, 51tr, 149bl; **New York Transit Museum:** New York Transit Museum Archives, Brooklyn 58clb; **Dr L. A. Nixon:** 16-17c, 43cr, 114-115b; **Nostalgie**

Orient-Express: 93cr; **Novosti:** 105br; **David Othen:** 61cl, 61cra; **J. H. Price Collection:** 54cr, 62bl, 66cla, 70cl, 76-77b, 84cl; **© QA Photos Ltd.:** Eurotunnel 136-137, 136tr, 137tc, 137cl; **Rail Europe Limited:** 125bc, 134cl, 135cr, 135tl; **Science & Society Picture Library:** 34bl; National Railway Museum 9cra, 30bl, 31tr, 36-37b, 79br, 84cr, 105tl; 151tr, 152tr, 154tr; Science Museum 10tl, 37tc; **Science Museum:** 31tl, 39br, 67t; **SiemensForum, Munich:** 18tl, 21tr, 58tr, 58cla, 59tl, 78-79b, 78tc, 121cl, 160bl; **South China Morning Post:** Dickson Lee 126tr; **Tony Stone Images:** 26-27; Pete Seaward 123cl; **John Stretton:** 130tr; **Edward Talbot:** 63bl; **Topham Picturepoint:** 12-13b, 105ac, 144tr, 145b, 148bl, 150b, 156c, 157tc; **Transnet Heritage Foundation:** 112ac; 18569 112tr; **Union Pacific Railroad Museum Collection:** 13bl, 50tl, 110tr; **Verkehrshaus der Schweiz, Luzern, Switzerland:** 67tr, 100-101b; **La Vie du Rail:** 79tr, 120tr; ©Wagons-Lits Diffusion 1999, Paris, France 93tl; **Virginia Museum of Transportation Inc., Resource Library & Archives, Roanoke, Virginia:** A.A.R. Collection 12tc, 56cla, 94-95; A.A.R. Collection / Le High Valley Railroad 46cla; **Archives Compagnie des Wagons-Lits:** ©Wagons-Lits Diffusion 1999, Paris, France 76tl, 92tr, 92cla; **Richard Wainscott:** 101t; **Jim Winkley:** 57bl, 57br, 60tr, 85bl, 97ac, 106bl, 107t, 121tl, 126cla, 126br, 128-129b, 130-131c, 139cr

Jacket: Peter Herring: inside front t; Impact Photos: Philip Gordon back b; Milepost 92½: inside front t; Brian Solomon front; Ron Ziel back tcr; Jim Winkley: back tl, cr.

The trains featured on pp.2-3, 15br, 23br, 44-45, 44tc, 45tl, 45tr, 52, 72-73, 72ca, 73tl, 73tr, 86, 90-91, 91tr, 92tr, 92ca, 100bl; are from the **Collection du Museé du Chemin de Fer, Mulhouse / SNCF, France**; the trains featured on pp.5tl, 14b, 41b, 67br, 68, 69b, 80-81, 81tl, 82tl, 82tr, 101ca are from the collection of the **Verkehrshaus der Schweiz, Luzern, Switzerland**; the trains featured on pp.5b, 48-49, 48tl, 49tl 49tr, 96 are from the Collections of the **B&O Railroad Museum, Baltimore, Maryland, US**; the trains featured on pp.17br, 96ca, 103b; are from **DB Museum, Nürnberg, Germany**; the trains featured on pp.5ra, 26ca, 108-111, 109t, 110tl, 111tr, 124, 132-3, 132lc, 133t, 133r are Copyright of the **Museum of Transportation, St. Louis, Missouri, US**; the trains featured on pp.64-65, 64tl, 65tl, 65tr, 100tr are from the **National Railway Museum, New Delhi, India**; the trains featured on pp.140-141, 140la, 40tr, 41tl, 41ca, 41r; are courtesy of **MVP-Besucherservice, Transrapid Versuchsanlage, Emsland (TVE), Germany**.